Mathew Analogbei

Retail Entry Strategies for emerging markets

Mathew Analogbei

Retail Entry Strategies for emerging markets

Cost & Institutional dynamics

Scholar's Press

Impressum / Imprint

Bibliografische Information der Deutschen Nationalbibliothek: Die Deutsche Nationalbibliothek verzeichnet diese Publikation in der Deutschen Nationalbibliografie; detaillierte bibliografische Daten sind im Internet über http://dnb.d-nb.de abrufbar.

Alle in diesem Buch genannten Marken und Produktnamen unterliegen warenzeichen-, marken- oder patentrechtlichem Schutz bzw. sind Warenzeichen oder eingetragene Warenzeichen der jeweiligen Inhaber. Die Wiedergabe von Marken, Produktnamen, Gebrauchsnamen, Handelsnamen, Warenbezeichnungen u.s.w. in diesem Werk berechtigt auch ohne besondere Kennzeichnung nicht zu der Annahme, dass solche Namen im Sinne der Warenzeichen- und Markenschutzgesetzgebung als frei zu betrachten wären und daher von jedermann benutzt werden dürften.

Bibliographic information published by the Deutsche Nationalbibliothek: The Deutsche Nationalbibliothek lists this publication in the Deutsche Nationalbibliografie; detailed bibliographic data are available in the Internet at http://dnb.d-nb.de.

Any brand names and product names mentioned in this book are subject to trademark, brand or patent protection and are trademarks or registered trademarks of their respective holders. The use of brand names, product names, common names, trade names, product descriptions etc. even without a particular marking in this work is in no way to be construed to mean that such names may be regarded as unrestricted in respect of trademark and brand protection legislation and could thus be used by anyone.

Coverbild / Cover image: www.ingimage.com

Verlag / Publisher:
Scholar's Press
ist ein Imprint der / is a trademark of
OmniScriptum GmbH & Co. KG
Heinrich-Böcking-Str. 6-8, 66121 Saarbrücken, Deutschland / Germany
Email: info@scholars-press.com

Herstellung: siehe letzte Seite /
Printed at: see last page
ISBN: 978-3-639-66987-9

Zugl. / Approved by: Glasgow, University of Strathclyde, Thesis 2012

Retail Entry strategies for emerging markets: Cost and Institutional dynamics

By

Mathew A. ANALOGBEI

Dedication

This book is dedicated to my lovely wife (Meg) and children Brenda Esuabom; Valentine Ekenemchukwu; and Ella Dumebi for their patience, love and support.

Acknowledgements

I have very many persons and institutions to thank for all the help, support and encouragement I received over the course of this project. Let me start by acknowledging the immense help, guidance, and encouragement of very senior and experienced academics like: Prof. Kevin Ibeh whose expertise and knowledge of Marketing and International Business shaped this entire research project. Despite his very busy schedule, he always made out time to read drafts of this book and to meet with me to provide the much needed direction. THANK YOU SO MUCH Prof. IBEH. So also is Prof John Finch whose assistance and comments were immensely useful to me in the course of undertaking this project.

I will equally like to thank staff of the firms I researched during the empirical stage of this work. The managers and executives of these firms were immensely helpful: Anton Wegner, GM Shoprite, Game's Director for Africa, Ms Tanya Williams, Mr J.D. Wiese, Mr P.C. Engelbrecht, and so many more top executives I cannot remember at the moment. Also, I acknowledge the assistance of some key staff of the National Agency for Food & Drug Administration and Control (NAFDAC) in Nigeria, staff of Nigeria Investment Promotion Council (NIPC), Management of TINAPA project, Nigeria Export Processing Zone Authority (NEPZA), and the Ministry of Commerce and Industry. Their assistance was very useful and particularly note worthy.

I will equally like to thank members of my family for their love, encouragement, and support, particularly my dear mum, wife and my other siblings: Grant, Caroline, and Mariam, as well as the love and support from all members of the Ogosi family. My sincere gratitude goes out to you all.

TABLE OF CONTENTS

CHAPTER SIX: DATA PRESENTATION AND FINDINGS 146

CHAPTER SEVEN: DISCUSSION OF RESEARCH FINDINGS 203

List of Figures

List of Tables

Abstract

Chief executives and management teams of large retail organisations and other type of firms acknowledge that globalization is the most critical challenge they face today. They are also keenly aware that it has become tougher now to identify internationalization strategies and to choose which countries to do business with. While some have stuck to the strategies they have traditionally deployed, which emphasize standardized approaches to new markets, others have operated with a few local twists. As a result, many multinational corporations are struggling to develop successful strategies especially in emerging markets.

Retail entry into the developing Nigerian market has been seen to be particularly challenging as a result of the absence of specialized intermediaries, regulatory systems, and contract-enforcing mechanisms - "institutional voids," which hamper the implementation of company strategies. Using a multiple case study of twelve retail firms in the Nigerian market, this study assesses the entry mode strategies used by foreign retail firms in Nigeria. It draws on both the Institutional theory and the Transaction cost theory.

The present study reveals that both internal and external factors (firm specific and host market environmental factors) influence the entry strategies adopted by foreign firms in the Nigerian market. These include unique brand concept, international experience, product/company reputation, firm size/ market resource commitment, cost of operation, network relationships in the market, as well as company habits, market population and wealth, close retail market distance, regulatory, legal, political and economic systems in the host Nigerian market, etc.

The cost of operation and network relationships in the market directly relate to the transaction cost perspective while the formal and informal classifications of the institutional theory cover such other areas as: regulatory, legal, political and economic systems in the host Nigerian market, unique brand concept, international experience, product/company reputation, firm size/ market resource commitment, as well as company habits, market population and wealth, and close retail market distance.

This study is one of the foremost to consider these two important perspectives in the context of a developing market like Nigeria. Several recommendations are provided some of which are that: international retail firms should consider granting greater autonomy in decision making and use of networks to the subsidiaries in Nigeria because this increases their ability to learn from the foreign market and to realise innovation advantages associated with linkages to valuable sources of information and knowledge. The firms should better understand the characteristics of the various entry modes open to them and align these with their company strategies. The host Nigeria government is also called upon to improve the various institutional frameworks to boost FDI into the retail sector of the economy.

CHAPTER ONE   INTRODUCTION

In this section, the focus and context of this research is set out highlighting the very important issues that are of interest to this study. The need for retail internationalisation is considered and the reason for the choice of the developing Nigerian market is equally provided. The inadequacy of extant empirical literature on retail internationalisation in markets in Africa is a key justification for the present study. So also is the absence of an empirical study that jointly considers the effect of the external institutional variables and the transaction cost economics of foreign retail firms in their quest to serve foreign markets; especially those looking to go into developing markets like the Nigerian market. The remaining part of this section provides a brief outline of the research approach, intended contributions, as well as a guide on the structure of the entire thesis.

1.0   Research Background & Objectives

Despite the large size of Nigeria in terms of land mass and population and the position the country occupies in Africa and the world at large, there is still a very limited number of foreign retail firms operating in the country. On a broader scale, there are many attempts by the Government since about the last two decades to attract foreign direct investment into the country[1].

A close look at the few existing retail firms operating in the country shows that they have come in using different entry mode choices. For firms doing business outside of their home market, their method of entry into the Nigerian market has been identified as a determining factor of their success in such a foreign market therefore entry mode decision choices become a "frontier issue" for their management Wind and Perlmutter (1977). The choice of the correct entry mode for a particular foreign market is "one of the most critical decisions in international marketing" (Alexander and Doherty 2009). The chosen mode determines the extent to which the firm gets involved in developing and implementing marketing programs in the foreign market, the amount of control the firm enjoys over its marketing activities, and the degree to which it succeeds in foreign markets (Anderson and Gatignon 1986; Root 1987; Hill *et al.* 1990). Very many factors have been

---

[1] There have been very many policies of government directed at this some of which include: Establishment of the free trade zones with very many concessions, one day incorporation of businesses, establishment of Nigeria Investment Promotion Council, etc.

1

suggested as influencing the choice of entry mode used by foreign retail firms in operating outside the home market. These range from individual company characteristics- size and resources, international experience, image and reputation, as well as product adaptability (Burt 1997). Others include factors in the external environment in the host market such as – cost of entry and research, infrastructural inadequacy, low domestic capacity, unstable political climate, policy inconsistencies etc Wright *et al.* (2005). Strong indications, however, exist to bring to question the choice of entry mode used by international retail firms in entering the Nigerian market particularly in the light of the existing institutional frameworks in the Nigerian market. This makes up a major part of the external environment of the international retail firms each of which have a specific nature and possess some resource advantages operating in the market.

This study is therefore aimed at exploring the entry mode decision choices of the foreign retail firms operating in the Nigerian market. In order to achieve this, the following **objectives** are set for the study:

- *To understand the entry mode approaches used by the foreign retail firms operating in the Nigerian market, including how these might have been affected by transaction cost considerations and institutional factors.*

- *To explore how the characteristics of the various entry mode options (independent and collaborative) might have influenced their adoption by the foreign retail firms operating in Nigeria.*

- *To examine the influence of company-specific and host country environmental factors on the entry mode choices made by the foreign retail firms operating in Nigeria.*

- *To make appropriate managerial and policy recommendations as well as extend the existing literature on retail firm internationalisation with a focus on market entry strategies and effect of host market institutional factors and the transaction costs faced by the firms in an emerging market like Nigeria.*

The foregoing therefore provides the background for the following research questions:

Research Question 1 Which entry modes do international retail firms use to internationalize into the developing Nigerian market and what institutional and transaction cost variables influence their choice of entry mode?

Research Question 2 What characteristics of the available entry modes (independent and collaborative) affect the retailers' entry mode choice?

Research Question 3 What major company and environmental factors influence the entry mode choices of the foreign retail firms operating in the developing Nigerian market?

1.1 Research justification

The need for this research derives from the fact that the world is fast turning into one global market, especially with the level of saturation of major markets across the world. The survival of most firms is therefore hinged on their ability to find markets outside of their present area of operation (which means looking beyond their domestic boundaries). The selection of overseas markets and entry modes lies at the very heart of any international strategy (Paliwoda 1993). It becomes imperative for these firms to fully understand the various options open to them as they seek entry into foreign markets (Pehrsson 2008). So as many international retailers are seeking to expand their operations beyond national boundaries, they need to understand the entry mode options available to them as well as the required criteria. This study aims to consider the entry mode choices of these retail firms in Nigeria, as suggested by Whitehead (1992) who wrote on the nature of the decision-making process and the relationship between company behaviour and entry strategies. Also, the effect of the host country environment will be considered in the assessment of the entry mode choice of these retail firms in Nigeria in addition to their various internal company assets and other characteristics.

Available studies on retail internationalisation recognize the effect of the internal and external environmental factors in company decision making (Park and Sternquist 2008; Alexander and Doherty 2009). Given the peculiarities of international retailing[2], there is the need to identify which

---

[2] Unlike export, retailing requires the presence of the international retailer in dealing with the various stakeholders: customers, agents, government regulatory agencies, employees, etc.

specific factors influence the entry mode choices of the firms especially for a developing market like Nigeria.

International retailing activities started in Nigeria even before the turn of the 19th century[3]. With the size, resources (both human and material) and position of the country in the world, one would imagine there would be a very large number of foreign retail firms operating in the country but the reverse is the case. There are a limited number of international retail firms operating in the Nigerian market at present. This study will aim to ascertain the reasons for the limited presence of foreign retail firms in the Nigerian market.

This study will also attempt to add to the literature on retail internationalisation from the developing markets of Africa, particularly Nigeria. This is because current studies are mainly western based with only a handful of studies from other developing markets around the world like those from Asia and South America. As noted by Porter *et al.* (2007) writing about retailing in Nigeria stating that:

> 'There are no detailed official government statistics pertaining to retailing...only surveys of rural periodic markets conducted over time, supplemented by archival material from colonial records, trading company records, and interviews with senior management in the larger European-style retailing companies are available from which only general impression of current trends in retailing can be gained therefore, the need for more detailed field research'.

There is so much saturation in the developed markets such that firms in these markets now are looking to move into emerging markets. The markets in Africa have been identified as fertile gold mines waiting to be explored by international firms (Wrigley 2007) with the large Nigerian market being one of such. The need has arisen to investigate the usefulness and relevance of some models/theories used by these international retail firms in their entry into developed markets and its applicability to emerging markets like Nigeria.

---

[3] Available records show that international retail activities started in Nigeria as far back as 1852 well before the establishment of colonial rule see Mabogunje, 1964; Lovejoy, 1980.

1.1.1. Why study retail Internationalisation?

The world over, commerce (exchange) is known to be a major driving force in the business sector that contributes to the economic growth of a country (Schumann *et al. 2010*). Retailing is an important aspect of this process. Over the last two to three decades, international retailing has attracted the interest of very many practitioners and scholars because of its very many contributions to the survival of nations and businesses. In one of these many studies, Akehurst and Alexander (1996), while concluding their edited collection on 'The Internationalisation of Retailing', suggested a research agenda based, amongst others, on the need to ascertain why retailers are internationalising as well as how transnational retailers are internationalising. Also Wrigley (1992) called for a study on the globalisation of retailing; which should consider every part of the world rather than specific areas like: Europe, North and South America, and Asia, but other parts of the globe, including Africa.

Therefore, knowing why retailers internationalise into foreign markets and how they do this in terms of the various entry modes open to them are of crucial importance especially in the context of a developing market like Nigeria. The developing markets of Africa have been seen to operate huge and unregulated markets; the size of these markets makes them potential goldmines waiting to be explored by innovative foreign retailers (Wrigley 2007; Coe and Wrigley 2009). The saturation of most developed markets around the world and the need for some retailers in these markets to increase their growth and profitability have led them into looking at entry into some developing markets like the markets in Africa.

With a realisation that retail internationalisation can contribute immensely to the growth of not only the firms but also the country, increased attention has been paid to this practice by both the governments of developing and developed countries and management of international retail firms.

Scholars believe the nature of most developing markets make entry into such markets particularly difficult with very high risks (Humphrey 2007; Coe and Wrigley 2009).

The fundamental question is why do retailers internationalise? This has been a key question in the effective conceptualisation of the retail internationalisation processes. As such the literature has considered very many reasons for this. A wide variety of theoretical and analytical approaches have been applied to the issue. However, Davies and Ferguson (1996) provide a useful categorisation of these approaches. Firstly, they draw attention to a wide variety of studies delimiting the broad range of 'push' and 'pull' factors, both company-specific and environmental, as well as those identified as 'facilitating factors' that may be involved in the decision of retailers to internationalise or not. The table below offers a summary of the key factors.

Table 1.0 **Factors traditionally cited as influencing retail internationalisation**

'Push factors'	'Facilitating factors'	'Pull factors'
- Perceived/imminent saturation in domestic markets - Spreading of risk - Consolidation of buying power - Public policy constraints - Economic conditions - Maturity of format	- Use of surplus capital/access to cheaper sources of capital - Entrepreneurial vision - Inducements from suppliers to enter new markets - Removal of barriers to entry - ICT's	- Unexploited markets - Pre-emption of rivals - Higher profit potential - Consumer market segments not yet exploited - Access to new management - Reaction to manufacturer internationalisation - Following existing customers abroad

Source: Wrigley and Lowe,2002

Viewed from another angle, retail internationalisation has also been considered from studies that identify the range of factors that firms will consider when evaluating the relative merits of overseas markets. For example, Chain Store Age (2000) identifies the following: macro-economics, country background (e.g. political stability), distribution structures, competitive nature of market, sophistication of customer base, technical feasibility, supplier base, retail market size and growth, additional growth drivers such as lifestyle and pricing trends, real estate issues, market forecasts, relevant regulation, and taxation.

On the aspect of how they do it, the literature on retail internationalisation contains much discussion of the various market entry mechanisms that can be employed. The range of potential options, offering varying degrees of cost and control, have been summarised by Dawson (1993) and McGoldrick (1995) as shown below:

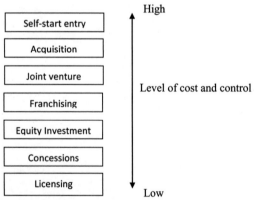

Figure 1.0: Mechanisms of market entry.
Source: adapted from McGoldrick, 1995.

Following from the above, one is tempted to ask: which of these mechanisms might account for the expansion of international retail firms into developing markets like the Nigerian market? Does the method of market entry differ between developed and developing economies? Is the distinction between these mechanisms clear-cut for the developing markets? Available records show international retail firms go into foreign markets using different entry modes ranging from one of complete ownership (integrated/independent) mode, to one of partnership with other firms in the foreign market (cooperative/collaborative) mode. Some foreign retail firms have also been seen to operate in different foreign markets each with different entry mode choices. Therefore, realising the importance of the entry mode choice of foreign retailers to their survival, growth, and success, and recognising the benefits derivable from internationalisation/globalisation, it becomes imperative to consider the approaches and practices that yield maximum returns.

In an attempt, therefore, to find answers to the above questions, this present study is designed to explore retail internationalisation in terms of the entry mode strategies for the retail firms in the Nigerian market. In doing this, the view of experts (Burt 1991; Alexander and Myers 2000; Peng 2003) that firms differ along several lines and that different environments have peculiar characteristics is acknowledged as part of the scope of the research. So along with changes to the living standard of the people, increased socio economic welfare, wider market utilisation of resources, economies of scale reduction, removal of major trade restrictions, saturation of home markets, and many other factors mentioned by these scholars as possible reasons why retail firms are looking at operating outside of their domestic boundaries, this present research aims at trying to ascertain the entry mode decision choice of the retail firms in Nigeria based on the influencing environmental factors from the market and the various company characteristics inherent in each of the internationalising retail firms.

1.1.2. Why focus on a developing market like Nigeria?

Activities of organisations show companies from all sectors are engaging in internationalization as an opportunity to achieve further growth; and a growing number of international retailers have shifted their attention to developing economies (Alexander 1997; Wrigley 2007). These companies are driven by the opportunities and characteristics of these markets, such as high growth rates, growing middle class, absence of fierce competition, etc. These conditions hold true for the

Nigerian market and could account for the presence of some foreign retail firms in the market. However, it is possible that these foreign retail firms will face a very different institutional framework as: a new supply base, unknown consumer demands with little market research, an under-developed logistics system, different government regulations, store requirements, amongst others, all of which will make their operations more challenging.

As contained in section (3.1), Nigeria is the second largest economy in Africa after South Africa. It has a huge potential as a market for international retailers with a population of over 150 million inhabitants (National Population Commission 2007). The market is one of the foremost economies in Africa to attract International retail activities, but at present have such a small number of international retail firms. In the past years, the government have come up with policies directed at regulating the economy that have negatively impacted on retailing[4]. Since about the last decade, however, so many changes have also taken place in both the political, economic, and developmental landscape in the country[5] that either directly or indirectly affects the retail sub-sector of the economy. The recent efforts of the government are to try to attract foreign direct investment (FDI) into the country with the formulation of some major regulations, establishment of some institutions, and provision of certain incentives. Understanding the influence and impact of all of these on the international retail practice in the country is one basis for this present study. It is hoped that this study will provide some important insight into all of these dimensions in trying to ascertain the entry modes choices of the retail firms in the Nigerian market. All of these would provide a better understanding as to why the developing Nigerian market has been used for this research study.

This developing Nigerian market has also been used for this present study in response to the argument by Nwankwo (2000:144) that:

> "the available literature has not been altogether helpful in providing frameworks useful for objectively assessing the relative attractiveness of many alternative country-markets in Africa. The conventional models for foreign market evaluation which are often

---

[4] A good example is the Indigenisation Decree of 1972 & 1977
[5] See section on: Post-Independence Retailing in Nigeria and Retailing and government policies

applied have proven to yield unsatisfactory outcomes…thereby, calling for much more understanding of the embedding institutional factors- and how they interact to create new conditions. These new conditions directly or indirectly represent the threats and opportunities to business which must be taken into account in formulating marketing strategies".

As noted by Hartland-Peel (1996), Africa's business environment is rapidly changing and businesses willing to make serious, long-term commitments are likely to reap attractive rewards. Also as observed by Kibazo (1995), a "new scramble for Africa" is ensuing, driven by perceptive investors who are beginning to look for ways to diversify their portfolio as they face up to the prospect of lower returns in more mature markets.

It is important to note that while there has been no consensus on the definition of the term "developing/emerging market," Czinkota and Ronkainen (1997) identified three characteristics associated with a developing/emerging economy namely: level of economic development, economic growth and market governance. The economic development level is typically measured in terms of GDP per capita. This is a useful measure of economic development because it is related to the population's wealth, extent of middle class, and level of industrial and service sector development (Alon and McKee 1999). The usage of the level of economic development as a demarcation criterion for distinguishing developing/emerging markets equates with the classifications of the World Bank and the United Nations, which include terms such as Less Developed Countries (LDC's), and Third World Countries. The World Bank divides countries on the basis of GDP per capita into four classes namely: high income, upper middle income, middle income and low income countries. The developing/emerging countries have been seen to enjoy a surge of growth in recent years in different aspects of its economy. According to the United Nations, only about 15 percent of the world's population reside in developed market economy countries (United Nations Report 2009) meaning the bulk of the world markets is in the developing/emerging markets.

The second characteristic is economic growth measured in terms of the country's GDP growth rate. The usage of economic growth is consistent with the concept of "developing/emerging markets". Most of the countries referred to as developing markets have enjoyed growth rates with some markets, particularly in East Asia, displaying double-digit growth rates (United Nations Report 2009). The level of economic growth is among the most important considerations for international retail expansion (Alon and McKee 1999). When examining a developing/emerging market's GDP growth, these scholars advise that one must contrast it to the growth in the population. If population growth rates exceed GDP growth rates, then the standard of living in those countries will actually drop over time. The most useful measure that captures both growth rates is GDP per capita growth rate.

The third criterion for judging emerging markets is the country's market governance. Market governance includes the level of free market activity, government control of key resources, stability of the market system and the regulatory environment (Sauvant 2008). Market governance influences a wide range of country risk elements such as government regulation and red tape, political stability, bribery, ownership restrictions, controls of capital flows and import restrictions. All of these factors are important to international retailers in their evaluation of foreign market potential and essential to determination of expansion method to use in the international retail arena (Alon and McKee 1999; Sauvant 2008).

The above conditions describe the case of the Nigerian economy. This present research is therefore aimed at ascertaining the influencing factors (both from within the organisations, and those from the host Nigerian market) helping to shape the entry mode choices of the foreign retail firms internationalising into the developing Nigerian market.

1.2 Research Approach

This research study has adopted phenomenology as its philosophical position given the relevance of this approach which realises that reality is socially constructed and not objectively or externally determined. Therefore, based on the premise that human actions arise out of the meanings people attach to their experience, the focus here is on understanding why people or organisations have different experiences. The key to explaining organisational behaviour in this case, lies both within the individual firm and some external sources. The fundamental task is therefore to uncover meanings, not gathering facts and measuring how often certain patterns occur (Denzin & Lincoln 2005). Golafshani (2003) added the following other essential characteristics: this approach allows the researcher's involvement in what is being observed, aids the development of ideas and theories based on post hoc analysis of collected data (induction), helps in the examination of the full complexity of the data (systems view), utilises multiple methods to establish different views of the phenomena; and it is an intensive investigation of small samples, over time (longitudinal analysis). Also, the fact that the phenomenon being studied has not been researched sufficiently to attempt generalisation (especially as in the context of this study), and the existence of this single reality with multiple perspectives (Tsoukas 1989; Perry *et al.* 1999) have all justified the use of this approach.

So this research study has been designed as a qualitative multiple case study of twelve international retail firms operating in the Nigerian market. The qualitative research method therefore appears suitable to meet the research need to explore and find meaning to the events occurring from multiple perspectives with the possibility of theory building (Patton, 2003). According to Eisenhardt (1989) and Miles and Huberman (1994) qualitative research enhances theory and improves understanding of business processes and structures through contextual analyses that connect processes and strategies to developments in the business environment. The case based research method facilitated an in-depth inquiry of the phenomenon, enabling the researcher to study in a natural setting, provide a holistic picture, study context specific influences and processes, isolate and define categories as precisely as possible and then determine the relationship between them (Stake 1995; Yin 2003)[6].

The various retail firms in this study are the *unit of analysis*. The data collection process used multiple sources of evidence – in-depth interviews, documentation, archival records, observation, published reports, etc. Data was gathered from a number of key employees of these retail firms (top level executives in charge of strategic decision making) as well as staff of some of the regulatory agencies in Nigeria. The data management and analysis approach of this study considered the multiple sources of evidence and adopted appropriate measures for data management in using the NVIVO data management software which allowed for indexing, retrieval, coding and sorting procedures of the data. At an overall level, the thesis followed the inductive analysis framework proposed by Shaw (1999). Furthermore, the quality of this study's case research in terms of validity and methodological reliability was critiqued against the 12 themes of qualitative inquiry suggested by Patton (2003).

1.3 Intended Research contributions and Potential Impact

1.3.1 Theoretical Contribution

This present study greatly contributes to the theoretical developments in the area of International business strategy and particularly retail internationalisation into developing markets. The combined consideration of both the transaction cost theory and the new institutional theory in this study under the context of a developing market is a notable contribution to the existing theoretical frameworks. Previous studies on retail internationalisation have looked at the effect of either of these theoretical frameworks with some considering just certain aspects of these theories; none has looked at the effect of both theories on the entry mode strategies of international retail firms into developing markets especially those in Africa.

---

[6] Section 5.1 provides further justification on this methodology

Another interesting theoretical contribution is the dimension to which the transaction cost theory has been applied in this present research. Coase's (1937) original proposition is that firms and markets are alternative governance structures that differ in their transaction costs. In his view, transaction costs are the "costs of running the system". Going by this proposition, the unit of analysis was the individual transactions the firms engaged in. Williamson (1975, 1985, and 1996) added to Coase's contribution by augmenting the initial framework to suggest that transactions include both the direct costs of managing relationships and the possible opportunity costs of making inferior governance decisions basing this on the interplay of two main assumptions of human behaviour (bounded rationality and opportunism) and two dimensions of transactions (asset specificity and uncertainty). The firm level in this case, became the unit of analysis rather than using the individual transactions; this present study is based on this latter view which also considers non-transaction cost benefits flowing from increased control or integration, such as co-ordination of strategies in multinational corporations (Kobrin 1988; Hill *et al.* 1990), to extend market power (Teece 1981), and to obtain a larger share of the foreign enterprise's profit (Anderson and Gatignon 1986).

Also, this present study further extends Williamson's (1985) contribution by considering not only the micro-level effect of institutions, but also the country level (macro-level) influence of institutions on entry mode strategies of international retail firms (Meyer *et al.* 2009). Again, it enriches the institution-based view of business strategy by providing a fine-grained conceptual analysis of the relationship between institutional framework and entry strategies. It is argued here that institutions moderate firm based characteristics when crafting entry strategies.

Furthermore, this present study again goes on to highlight Hoskisson et al.'s (2000) view of the institutional theory as one of the three most significant theories when probing into emerging economies (the other two are transaction cost economics/agency theory and the resource-based view). A hallmark of emerging economies is that they tend to have more "fundamental and comprehensive changes introduced to the formal and informal rules of the game that affect firms and players" labelled "institutional transitions" (Peng 2003: 275). The key question for foreign firms in such economies is: how to play the game, when the rules of the game are changing and not completely known. This present study intends to look into some of these. Equally important is the design of this present study to help find strong empirical support for several dimensions of the transaction cost theory, particularly those regarding asset specificity and vertical integration decisions as well as observation of present areas of considerable disagreement, especially those surrounding the operationalization of some of TCE's central constructs and the unpacking of hybrid forms of governance.

Again, according to (Nwankwo 2000; Hoskisson *et al.* 2000; Burgess and Steenkamp 2006) contextual international business studies have concentrated on studies of developed markets and the extant theories are not necessarily applicable to emerging and developing markets. These scholars call for more studies of business in Africa. The existing studies on foreign firms in Africa are mainly cross-sectional surveys or FDI studies based on macroeconomic data (see, e.g., Asiedu 2005; Malgwi, Owhoso, Gleason, & Mathur 2006; Bartels *et al.* 2009). This present research therefore responds to the above call and tries to provide some added theoretical understanding to firm internationalisation into the developing African market.

1.3.2 Empirical Contribution

The use of the developing Nigerian market (second largest economy in Africa with a huge growth potential and an experience of international retail practice that dates back to 1852) for this present study represents an appropriate and under-studied setting. Much of the studies in retail internationalisation have been done in the developed economies of the west (Europe and America) and in other developing markets in Asia and some in Latin America. Only a handful of studies have looked at international retail practice generally in the developing African market.

This present study is about the first to consider entry mode entry choices of international retail firms into the developing African market and that of the Nigeria market particularly. This present study will therefore add to the understanding on retail internationalisation from this developing African market context thereby improving on the existing literature on this subject. Scholars and practitioners generally believe that developing markets have their peculiarities and difficulties in international retail practice, but no study has been directed at identifying the specific factors needed to be considered in entry mode decision choices of international retail firms going into a developing market like the Nigerian market.

Therefore, given that this study is one of the first systematic attempts to empirically investigate retail internationalisation into the developing African market, the study is aimed at empirically exploring some of the conceptual discussions in the extant literature. This research aims to contribute conceptually towards theory building by gathering empirical support for concepts so far not sufficiently researched in a context like that used in this study thus adding to the extant literature on retail internationalisation.

Also, this present study contributes to the research on international expansion moves of retail firms by combining the firms' economic rationale for entry into distant markets with influencing factors in the social context to show that these perspectives point to different characteristics of the same decision. While the former looks at economic rationale of risky foreign market entry, the latter refers to ways of reducing this risk. A detailed discussion of the research contribution of the findings of this study in light of the research gaps identified during the literature review as presented in Chapter 2 of this thesis can be found in sections 8.2 under Chapter 8.

1.3.3 Potential Impact

Based on the aforementioned contributions, it is expected that this present research will have an influential impact on the international business and strategy fields especially from the context of developing markets as used in this study. It is expected that this research will provide much more understanding and answers to the very many questions asked in conducting international business (particularly retailing) in developing countries. Its focus on internal and external variables that either directly or indirectly affect this process will be particularly useful.

First, the combined use of the transaction cost theory and the institutional theory has broadened the framework used for the evaluation of entry mode decision choices of international retail firms into foreign market especially the developing/emerging markets. Critical influencing variables important for such strategic decisions are identified from this study. Future research can equally test these frameworks in other developing markets of the world in advancing the contributions of these frameworks. Also, these theoretical foundations can equally be considered in other developed markets around the world in a bid to determine any significant variations and effect of the context in which the frameworks can be applied. Findings from such studies will go a long way to better enlighten the management of these firms on this all important decision area.

Secondly, this present study sets out the foundation for an understanding of the entry mode choices used by international retail firms in entering the Nigerian market. The findings of this study will greatly assist the government and its various regulatory agencies in the formulation of policies and directives geared towards growth of the economy. Operating in a way that enables them to gain legitimacy and acceptance in the host market is an objective international retail firms aim to have; how and why this is important is an added dimension this study provides. Hopefully also, this research may also not only help in strategy formulation for international retail firms, but also shed significant light on the most fundamental questions confronting international retailers mostly those operating in developing markets such as "what drives the firms' strategy in deciding on the entry mode to use in such developing markets?".

1.4 Overview of structure of the research project

This thesis is structured in eight chapters. The content of each of these chapters is briefly set out in the section below. The final bits are made up of a written and diagrammatic guide to the entire thesis.

Chapter 1 sets out the context and focus of the research. It highlights the key issues of interest to this study, underlining the inadequacy of extant empirical literature. It thus justifies the need for this research based on these perceived gaps, in addition to the potential contributions of the findings of this study to help the management of international retail firms in deciding their choice of entry modes as well as helping the government and its agencies coordinate and regulate the practice of retailing in the country. The research problem for this study is set out in this chapter also and the remaining part of the chapter provides a summary account of this study's design and methodology including the data analysis procedures.

Chapter 2 reviews the literature on firm internationalisation generally, as well as retail internationalisation including the various theoretical perspectives developed for its study. Thereafter, the chapter reviews the underpinning models/theories for this study specifically institutional and transaction cost perspectives to determine the research gaps and situate this research study.

Chapter 3 this chapter contains an in-depth review of the context of this study: Nigeria. It traces the development of modern retailing in the country and also contains a review of the economic, political, and regulatory dimensions in the country. This contextual background provides the foundation for an understanding of the link between the literature and the empirical design for this study to allow for a meaningful contribution.

Chapter 4 captures the conceptual background for this present research. In this section, the identified frameworks from the extant literature on retail internationalisation – entry mode strategies is used to build a conceptual picture that explains the situation. This chapter draws from the literature on institutional theory; transaction cost analysis and international retailing, and proposes a conceptual framework for examining the entry mode choices of international retail firms. This framework addresses the effect of company characteristics and the host institutional environment on the firm's choice of market entry. A detailed explanation to enable an understanding of the conceptual framework is also provided in this section of the thesis.

Chapter 5 contains the research philosophy and methodology used for this study. The basis for use of the qualitative research method is explained, so also the case study methodology, after which a detailed account of the research procedure is given highlighting the procedure used for the case selection, unit of analysis, and the case design. The final part of this chapter explains the data collection procedures: Documents, observation, and in-depth interviews.

Chapter 6 is made up of the data presentation and statement of research findings. It starts with profiling of the retail firms investigated, then goes on to do a cross-case analysis based on the underlining models on which this research is hinged: The Institutional theory and the Transaction cost analysis. The important dimensions of these models were used to report the findings from the study.

Chapter 7 discusses the research findings from the present research in the light of the institutional and transaction cost theories. This chapter shows areas of support as well as areas of non-support to the research findings from the extant literature; discussed under firm characteristics, institutional environmental factors, regulatory forces in the Nigerian market, as well as the effect of collaborative/hierarchical network relationships in the market.

Chapter 8, the last chapter, follows up on the previous chapter to draw conclusions in respect of the key questions and objectives of this present research, notably the entry mode decision choices used by the international retail firms operating in the Nigerian market, the characteristics of these modes that have influenced the choice of the firms, as well as the major company and environmental factors that are critical in the decision making process of the retail firms as they consider the appropriate mode of entry to use to better serve the market profitably. The last section of the chapter discusses the research implications, makes appropriate recommendations and proposes areas for further research.

Figure 1.2 Structure of research project

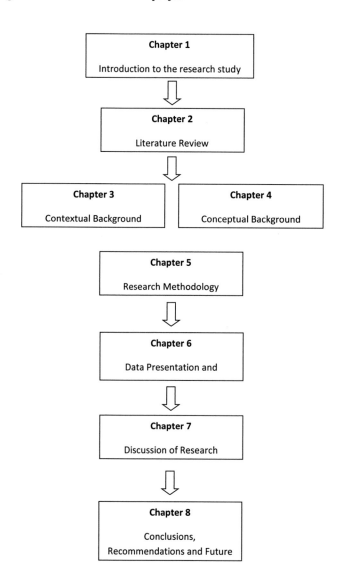

Source: Researcher

CHAPTER TWO: INTERNATIONALISATION THEORIES: A REVIEW

The main purpose of this chapter is to explore the very large and relevant literature on different aspects of the internationalisation of the firm (and retail internationalisation particularly) in a bid to gain a very good understanding of this subject area under investigation, especially with respect to the entry mode choices used by international retailers in entering emerging markets like the Nigerian market. Different sections make up this chapter; the first part reviews the literature on the general internationalisation of firms, service firm's internationalisation, and the internationalisation of retail organisations and highlights the main theoretical frameworks developed to explain this phenomenon. An area worth emphasizing is the effect of foreign environmental factors on firm internationalisation hence models for foreign market selection and the entry modes are looked into. The second part of this chapter looks at the institutional economics view and the transaction cost theory as frameworks to address the internationalisation of retailing. Within this framework, the main focus is on describing the elements of both theories as they affect the entry mode choice particularly of international retail firms.

2.0   Introduction: General theories

As mentioned above, this chapter considers important theories of international trade and theoretical developments that underpin an understanding of the internationalisation process. International retailing is part of a wider process of internationalisation and globalisation of trade. By exploring this theoretical material from outside of the direct remit of international retailing, this chapter establishes the foundations on which specific theories of retail internationalisation are built.

Alexander and Doherty (2009) noted that the internationalisation of retailing must be considered in the context of theories of international trade, foreign direct investment, and the internationalisation process of the firm. International retailing does not exist in an academic vacuum: therefore, it is essential that those theoretical developments that are firmly established in the wider international business literature should contribute to the development of a framework within which international retailing may be analysed. They added that without an appreciation of the development of this theoretical material, it is difficult to understand some of the assumptions that economists and managers make when analysing world trade. From a retailer's perspective, unless there is an understanding of the foundations of theory there is a danger that false assumptions will be made when considering retail-specific theory.

From the early twenty-first century, free trade appeared to be the norm with the institutions set up after the world wars to encourage economic and trade development. The foundation for this was laid very many years ago in what experts now classify as **classical theory** (absolute advantage, comparative advantage), and **neoclassical theory** (Hecksher-Ohlin principle). The classical theories of international trade provided an understanding of the merits of the international exchange of goods and how such exchange creates greater wealth. Along this line, Adam Smith described the conditions necessary for free trade and the reason why countries should specialise in the production of certain products for export. He suggested that specialisation should occur where a country enjoyed absolute advantage in the production of a particular product. David Ricardo while recognising that absolute advantage provided an understanding of international trade added that there are advantages in specialisation even when absolute advantage did not exist: that there were opportunity costs associated with production that enabled production to occur on the basis of relative advantage.

The economic theory in its simplest form suggests that opportunity costs are constant such that a country achieves complete specialisation in those products in which it has comparative advantage and will stop production of those in which it does not have such an advantage; but in reality it is recognised that opportunity costs will increase as production of a product falls. Dissatisfaction with Ricardo's lack of explanation for the reasons underlying how comparative advantages occurs led Bertil Ohlin (1933) to develop an explanation of market difference. He sought to explain why trade occurred and not to identify its benefits. He suggested that different relative factor endowments give rise to observable and measurable advantages. Therefore, where a country has an abundance of a factor, it would be reasonable to expect that the country in question would produce goods that utilise that factor intensively. So, in terms of international trade, a country will export those products that demand the intensive use of those factors of which the country has abundance. This has become known as the Hecksher-Ohlin principle.

Samuelson (1953) developed the factor price equalization theorem to address the relationship between factor prices and factor endowments essentially completing the Hecksher-Ohlin-Samuelson paradigm. This considers the proposition that free trade substitutes for the free mobility of factors of production – free trade reduces the differences in commodity prices and thus equalizes the prices of factors of production. Despite its contribution, this theory failed to fully account for the fact that technology is not the same in all countries and that non-price competition plays an important role. Therefore, Leontief's (1953) analysis seriously undermined this theory when he showed that countries do not necessarily export products that demand intensive inputs of the factors of which they are well endowed and import products that demand the intensive use of factors of which they do not have abundance.

All of these theories attempted to describe economic conditions that are different from what obtains in the present time; while David Ricardo looked at an agriculturally based economy, Hecksher, Ohlin, Samuelson, and Leontief considered production of primary products and not industrial or service economies. A consideration of other theories of international trade therefore becomes important.

Factor Endowments & International Product Life Theories are some other aspects of the theories of international trade worth mentioning. Linder (1961) identified a fundamental difference in the trade of primary and manufactured products. In his analysis, he noted that for primary products, factor endowments played a very important role in marketing the products internationally, while, in the case of manufactured products, it was not factor intensities but demand factors that lay behind patterns of international trade.

Linder suggested that international trade was effectively an extension of domestic trade, not only in that products are initially launched in the domestic environment, but that domestic production subsequently limits international production. Here, Linder (1961) recognized the importance of international markets that have reached similar levels of GDP per capita and other factors that facilitate the ready adoption of the exported product.

International Product Life Cycle on the other hand, addresses the issues of foreign direct investment (FDI) and international trade (Vernon, 1966). Just like Linder (1961) Vernon began by looking at the development of a product in the market of origin identifying the importance of the market of origin in determining the characteristics of the product. In this case, products newly introduced onto the market are seen to follow an S-shaped curve, which passes through an initial phase of adaptation and hence through other stages of maturity and senility. Research and development occur in more sophisticated markets, and the product is, in time, transferred to markets that are also economically advanced.

The demand in the market of origin is usually small, until the product is developed to meet the needs of the home market. At the mature stage, the product's uniformity and standardization facilitate manufacture of the product in markets that do not have the same research and development conditions in markets with lower costs. As the product enters a phase of standardization, then the product will demand less research and development. It will spread further into markets around the world that do not show the same level of development as the market of origin. Production costs will determine the location and this will increasingly be newly industrialising countries.

2.1   The Internationalisation Process of firms – Extant Theoretical Streams

Several studies of international business have indicated that internationalisation of the firm is a process in which the firm gradually increases their international involvement. It seems reasonable to assume that, within the frame of economic and business factors, the characteristics of this process influence the pattern and pace of internationalisation of firms. Paliwoda and Slater (2009: 374) noted that

> 'internationalisation/globalisation has been accelerated by falling trade barriers, the spread of free trade and trade harmonisation in an electronic age, bringing a reduction in the bureaucracy surrounding international trade and increased speed to the way in which communications relay changes anywhere in the world. Following this idea of internal institutional change in the corporate context, we, as a society have lived through what may be seen as the different ages of the multinational corporation and how we have also come to perceive it'.

Over the years, the process of firm internationalisation has been the subject of widespread theoretical and empirical research within the field of Management, International business, and Marketing (e.g. Johanson and Vahlne 1977; Cavusgil 1980, Alexander and Myers 2000). The internationalisation of firms has been studied from very many perspectives: From all of these dimensions, five theoretical approaches can be identified namely: (1) Economics-oriented perspective, (2) stage of development models, (3) Network approaches, (4) Business strategy framework, and (5) Resource-based theory.

2.1.1 Economics-oriented perspectives

International business economists like: Hymer (1960), Kindleberger (1970), Caves (1971), Hirsch (1974), Dunning (1977), Helpman (1984), Markusen and Venables (2000), Markusen (2002) and many others like them have tried to explain the conditions under which Multinational Enterprises (MNE) extend their activities beyond national boundaries and establish their operations overseas. Various frameworks have been developed by these experts such as: internalisation (or transaction cost) theory, and the eclectic paradigm.

2.1.1.1. Internalisation (or transaction cost) theory

This theory of internationalisation and the transaction cost associated with it, has its origin in the seminal work of Coase (1937) with later significant contributions by Williamson (1975, 1981). This theory was originally devised to explain why firms exist in domestic markets. Coase (1937) believed that firms were faced with transaction costs such that 'a firm would continue to expand until the cost of organising an extra transaction within the firm will become equal to the cost of carrying out the same transaction by means of an exchange on the open market' (Coase 1937:395). This was subsequently developed to explain why MNE arises and FDI takes place (Buckley and Casson 1976; Hennart 1977, 1982). The major problem is in how technology, knowledge, and goodwill are embedded and how good the legal system is at protecting the firm's intangible assets that which Doherty (1999) referred to as the problem of information asymmetry.

The idea remains therefore, that the greater the risk of opportunism and dissemination of this knowledge on the open market, the more likely it is that a firm will want to protect this knowledge and invest in its own facilities outside the domestic market. Therefore, a firm will opt to internalise its assets in international markets when intermediate markets are subject to high transaction costs.

This transaction cost influence of the internalisation theory has a direct relevance to the expansion of international retailers and the entry methods they employ in international markets which is the focus of this thesis. In her work, Doherty (1999) reviewed the development of the internationalisation theory and within that framework, explained how international retailers choose entry methods. A point that is made clear is that it is the transaction cost market imperfections, as opposed to the structural market imperfections emphasized by Hymer (1960) that form the basic foundations of internalisation theory. So, in assessing the cost of running the system, firms decide the most appropriate governance mechanism to use along with a consideration of other influencing external variables. This thesis will focus on this.

2.1.1.2.   Eclectic paradigm

This was an attempt by Dunning (1977, 1979, 1983, 1988, 1989) drawing on various approaches to international production to provide a holistic framework to explain the extent and pattern of international production. The eclectic paradigm proposes that international production is contingent on three sets of advantages: Ownership advantages, Location advantages, and Internalisation advantages. These three advantages at its core is the reason why this paradigm is sometimes called the OLI framework. These advantages are to be exploited in a foreign market in a timely way.

The eclectic paradigm refers to these advantages as competitive advantages or ownership-specific advantages rather than firm-specific advantages, attributing the productivity differences to the factors associated with the country of ownership of the firm rather than the firm itself. The types of advantages initially identified include:

- Advantages gained over other firms from other countries large enough to cover additional costs and risks of producing abroad;
- Those associated with the use of a firm's internal markets rather than external alternatives;
- Those that arise as a consequence of geographical diversification (trade incentives, lower labour costs, raw materials, etc.) which makes foreign production preferable to exporting/licensing.

This paradigm therefore postulates that if an MNE possesses ownership-specific advantages, it will benefit most by internalising those assets within the firm through hierarchy – that is, FDI rather than selling them to a foreign based firm. According to Dunning (1988:4), 'enterprises will engage in foreign production when they perceive it is in their best interests to combine spatially transferable intermediate products produced in the home country, with at least some immobile factor endowments or other intermediate products in another country'. Both structural and market imperfections can influence the location decision. The former includes some of those distortions

27

arising from government interventions that have an impact on the costs and/or revenues of producing in certain locations; the latter can result in costs and/or revenues arising from varying exchange rates, multiple sourcing policy, and variations in payment periods (Alexander and Doherty 2009).

A cursory look at this paradigm would reveal some aspects of its limited relevance to this present research. Different entry modes such as: licensing, joint ventures, and wholly-owned subsidiaries are used by International retail firms in international markets. This paradigm is focused on international production- mainly FDI. Its attempt is to explain why international production takes place; which is not what this thesis aims to do. Also, this theory does not account for pressures and difficulties that affect ownership, location, and internalisation advantage in a new environment.

Some other aspects of this paradigm have direct implications for international retailing and are indirectly linked to the main objectives of this thesis. Foreign Direct Investment (FDI) describes many different types of investment such as: ownership of sources of raw materials, or ownership of service-based operations which may take the form of marketing subsidiaries. So, companies desiring to protect market share, learn from innovative markets, acquire intangible assets like trademarks or desiring to spread risks may use this as possible motives for their foreign operations, some of which international retail firms do. This present research, however, is focused more on the factors that affect the entry mode decision choices of international retailers in entering foreign markets attributing the productivity differences to the factors associated with the firm itself rather than the country of ownership of the firm as this paradigm explains. Besides, this theory does not account for pressures and difficulties that affect ownership, location, and internalisation advantage in a new environment.

2.1.2 Stage of development models

Unlike the above theories of FDI firmly rooted in international economics, the stages theory and the related psychic distance argument have a more behavioural underpinning. The 1970s witnessed the development of theory on the internationalisation of the firm particularly from academics from the University of Uppsala in Sweden (Johanson and Vahle 1977; Johanson and Weidersheim-Paul 1975) on the internationalisation of the firm, which has its basis in the behavioural theory of the firm (Cyert and March 1963; Aharoni 1971) that sees internationalisation as a process whereby the firm gradually increases its international involvement. According to Johanson and Vahlne (1990) 'this process evolves in interplay between the development of knowledge about foreign markets and operations on one hand, and an increasing commitment of resources on the other'.

The stages model (Cavusgil 1980; Johanson and Vahlne 1977, 1990) holds that firms internationalise through a process of incremental stages. This model suggests that the internationalisation of a firm is an incremental process where firms initially enter markets that are psychically similar and successively expand into more distant foreign markets. This assumption that the psychological proximity of foreign markets to the domestic market dictates expansion decisions has, however, been challenged by the work of Evans et al. (2000) and Evans and Mavondo (2002). Based on the initial work of Johanson and Vahlne (1977) other academics (Bilkey and Tesar 1977; Cavusgil 1980; Czinkota 1982) have contributed to this debate on the stages of internationalisation by developing frameworks suggesting that companies pass through stages of increasing commitment to, and involvement with, the international market place. So firms are said to initially target neighbouring, 'psychically close' countries, and subsequently enter foreign markets with successively larger 'psychic distance' – 'defined in terms of such elements as language, culture, political systems etc., which disturb the flow of information between the firm and the market' (Johanson and Vahlne, 1990).

While these models offer an interesting understanding of the process of internationalisation, they have not been without their critics. *Reid (1981) and Turnbull (1987) have criticized the model for being too deterministic. They argue that, in reality, firms do not necessarily move smoothly along the stages continuum. It has also been argued that the process model says something important only about the early stages of internationalisation when the lacks of market knowledge and market forces are still constraining factors. The stages model does not address the role of time or firm-specific competitive advantages, but instead describes a sequential process of internationalisation. This model, for example, assumes that international expansion is gradual, in stages, and influenced mainly by managerial learning and commitment. It acknowledges that firms gradually learn from new environments, but does not address the specific potential barriers that firms may encounter in different environments (Forsgren, 1989). Also, studies by Sharma and Johanson (1987) and Engwall and Wallenstal (1988) on banks and technical consultancy firms show that this internationalisation model is not valid for service industries – sector to which retailing belongs. Lastly, not only has the stages theories been subject to question, but the relevance of the psychic distance argument for the future of international business has also been called into doubt. Nordstrom (1990) has stated that as world markets become more homogenous, firms will be able to internationalise initially into large markets, as psychic distance will decrease.*

2.1.3 Network theories

Developments from international industrial marketing produced another significant strand of internationalisation research like the Network theories. This theory emerged from the Industrial Marketing and Purchasing group's research on buyer – supplier relationships (Ford, 2002). In this case, internationalisation is described as proceeding through an interplay between increasing commitment to, and evolving knowledge about foreign markets, gained mainly from interaction in the foreign markets; these interconnected exchange relationships evolve in a dynamic, less structured manner, with greater internationalisation commitment arising out of increased mutual knowledge and trust between international market actors (Johanson and Mattson 1988; Johanson and Vahlne 1992; Kogut and Zander 1990). It focuses on business level contacts with other firms and actors.

Coviello and Munro (1997), observed that 'the network perspective goes beyond the models of incremental internationalisation by suggesting that firm's strategy emerges as a pattern of behaviour influenced by a variety of network relationships'. In the network theory, markets are seen as a system of relationships among a number of players including customers, suppliers, competitors, family, friends, and private and public support agencies. Strategic action therefore, is rarely limited to a single firm, and the nature of relationships established with others in the market influences and often dictates future strategic options (Sharma, 1993; Coviello and Munro 1995).

The central focus of the network approach is in bringing the involved parties closer by using the information that is acquired to establish close relationships with customers, suppliers, the industry, distributors, regulatory and public agencies, and other market actors; the relationships will be based on mutual trust, knowledge and commitment towards each other. So firms going abroad are engaged in a domestic network with the main goal of developing business relationships in the foreign country. The firm's position in the local network determines its process of internationalization since that position determines their ability to mobilize their resources within the network. This theory is another approach to internationalisation which draws on the theories of social exchange and resource dependency and focuses on firm behaviour in the context of inter-organisational and interpersonal relationships (Bianchi 2006). This approach accounts for the role and influence of social relationships and argues that the internationalisation process is influenced by networks of both formal and informal relationships (Johanson and Mattsson 1988).

The network approach which is widely applied may have relevance to the study of retail alliances, and, in some cases, of joint ventures, but, in general, the network approach is directed towards the understanding of vertical international relationships rather than the horizontal ones which occur in retailing. As such, the approach is of more use in exploring the international sourcing activities of retailers rather than the internationalisation of operations. Along this line, (Williams, McDonald, Tuselmann, and Turner 2008) noted that the general development of local-network connections is important for the growth of domestic sourcing. The view here is that local networks increase the ability to benefit from collective learning and to realise innovation advantages that is associated with linkages to valuable sources of information and knowledge.

The network perspective has brought immense value to the understanding of the internationalisation process and has stimulated the search for a more holistic view of firm internationalisation. According to Burt (1997) network relationships result in ties that are hard to imitate with consequences in very many dimensions, one important area being that information about what is going on in the market is open to the network itself. Information that is not available to everyone in the market. The ties are expected to be strong. Granovetter (1973:1361) defines the strength of ties as 'a combination of time, emotional intensity, intimacy and the reciprocal services of the ties'; meaning some tight interactions. No tie is static; as time passes by firms can make the ties stronger or weaker depending on the relation between them.

The effect of building ties- establishing network relationships is one important area that international retailers are engaged in which is relevant to this present study. This will only be taken a step further in trying to see how the type of networks available in the foreign market in addition to their number and quality would go to influence the entry mode decision choice of the international retailer.

2.1.4 Business Strategy/Contingency theories

Reid (1983) wrote that foreign expansion is contingency based and "results from a choice among competing expansion strategies that are guided by the nature of the market opportunity, firm resources, and managerial philosophy". The business strategy viewpoint proposes a strategically-planned and organised system to internationalisation, where the major company decisions are made in the context of the firm's overall strategic development, and supported by rigorous analysis of relevant internal and external environmental factors (Young *et al.* 1989). Root (1987) and Turnbull and Ellwood (1986) discuss the factors which should be evaluated using this approach, which for market selection include: market attractiveness, psychic distance and accessibility and informal barriers, while the choice of organisational structure to serve the market will be dependent on these market characteristics "as well as company specific factors such as international trading history, size, export orientation and commitment" Turnbull and Ellwood (1986). Competition in the market is another important factor added by Porter (1985).

Contingency theory on the other hand, originated with the seminal works of Burns and Stalker (1961) and has been associated with Reid (1983) as well as Kumar and Subramaiam (1997). The main emphasis of the theory is that the best way a firm can organize its operations depends on the nature of the environment to which the organization relates. According to Reid (1983) firms' responses to international opportunities are determined by current circumstances and availability of resources such that decision makers strive to align their organization goals with the conditions in their external environments in a bid to achieve strategic fit.

Some of the criticism of this theory is that it focuses unduly on the manager as the decision maker and ignores other important performance antecedents such as class domination or attitudes of stakeholders that can also shape organizational behaviour, requires each firm to possess a unique "bundle" of resources, somewhat dependent on managers' perceptions of opportunity and risk, insensitive to the fact that firm's international trajectory will be highly situation specific and hard to draw general implications for public policy support[7].

---

[7] See Robertson and Chetty, (2000); Harzing and Sorge (2003)

2.1.5 Resource-based theory

Wernerfelt' (1984) and Barney's (1991) Resource-Based View has been described as a more grounded restatement of the business strategy and contingency theories. This theory has become one of the major building blocks in strategic management research. According to RBV, there exist firm heterogeneities that allow some firms to develop stronger and sustained competitive advantages and, consequently, earn higher economic rents than others. Hence, unlike the external environment models, which focus on the opportunities and threats to firms' performance, RBV theory is concerned with the internal resources in terms of strengths and weaknesses of firms (Wernerfelt, 1984; Barney, 1991). RBV posits that some firms are more profitable than others, not because they invest resources to deter entry, but because they possess advantages that allow them to maintain lower costs and/or higher quality of product differentiation (Teece, Pisano, and Shuen 1997: 513).

Resources are perceived as costly-to-replicate firm-specific assets, capabilities, technological know-how, information, competent human capital, brand name and brand equity in the minds of consumers, organization design, and many others (Wernerfelt 1984). The role of these "core competencies" is to improve firms' efficiency and effectiveness and lead to sustainable competitive advantage over time. Barney (1991) argued that resources have to be valuable, rare, inimitable, and non-substitutable in order for firms to earn abnormal returns on the market. Bell et al. (1998) noted that in the RBV of firms, major strategic decisions are made not on stand-alone basis, but within a well-coordinated framework of resources and capabilities as well as environmental realities. The RBV therefore, just like the Business strategy and Contingency theories, recognises that internationalisation is affected by multiple influences, and that a range of the firms' internationalisation decisions are made in a holistic way (Bell *et al.,* 1998; Luostarinen 1979).

The resource-based view has been criticized for its "little effort to establish appropriate context" (Priem and Butler 2001:32). Valuable, rare, and hard-to-imitate resources and capabilities in one

34

context may become nonvaluable, plentiful, and easy to imitate in other contexts (Brouthers, Brouthers, and Werner 2008). Barney (2001:52) himself acknowledged the validity of this criticism, noting that "the value of a firm's resources must be understood in the specific market context within which a firm is operating".

2.2   Internationalisation of Retailing

As noted above, while conceptualization and theoretical development of the internationalisation of the firm have been widespread in the international business and international marketing literatures, the focus has been predominantly on the internationalization of the manufacturing sector and, to a much lesser extent, service sectors other than retailing (Buckley and Ghauri 1999). Bianchi and Arnold (2004) write that although several topics have been investigated for manufacturing multinational forms, there has not been much research within the retailing and service fields. So far, there remains much debate about the generalizability of these analyses from the manufacturing firms to service firms (Erramilli 1990; Agarwal and Ramaswami 1992; Erramilli and Rao 1993; Ekeledo and Sivakumar 1998). Some recent empirical results have found support for only a limited application of the determinants of manufacturers' entry mode decision to service firms (Ramon-Rodriquez 2002; Ekeledo and Sivakumar 2004) thus questioning the extent to which existing theories and frameworks can apply to services and calling for additional studies.

Retailing has been neglected in the wider literature because historically, internationalisation within the manufacturing sector has been prevalent in a way that it has not been in the retail sector. Therefore, as noted by (Alexander and Doherty 2009) research into and conceptual development of activity within the manufacturing sector have reflected commercial activity and tended to ignore a retail sector that has previously been largely based within domestic markets. Consequently, the study of international retailing has had to develop its own theoretical structures in order to explain the process of internationalisation. Nevertheless, the development of international retailing theory has been influenced by or attempted to adopt concepts from the wider literature. This present research follows this path. So, in trying to understand the process of retail internationalisation, the literature on international business has contributed to the development of several theoretical frameworks. These models have mainly been tested within the context of manufacturing firms but are recently being applied to explaining the internationalisation process of retailing (e.g. Sternquist 1997; Vida and Fairhurst 1988). Some of the relevant models are: the stages model, the eclectic paradigm, and the network perspective.

Internationalisation of Retailing has been defined as "the transfer of retail management technology or the establishment of international trading relationships that bring to a retail organisation a level of international integration that establishes the retailer within the international environment in such a way as to transcend regulatory, economic, cultural, social, and retail structural boundaries" Alexander (1997:37). Available records have shown that overall; retailers started their internationalisation process later than manufacturing firms. Bianchi (2002) noted that Hollander's (1970) "Multinational Retailing" is regarded as the seminal work on retail internationalisation and a starting point for increasing exploratory research that addresses different aspects of the internationalisation process.

Alexander and Doherty (2009) noted that while development of international retail theory may be traced to Hollander's seminal thesis (1970), attempts to provide a structure for international retailing research did not begin until the late 1980s (Treadgold 1988, 1990; Salmon and Tordjman 1989) and even then it was observational rather than theoretical. Alexander and Myers (2000) wrote that the study of international retailing developed from a position of observation, through one of analysis, to one of conceptual development. Quite a number of conceptual frameworks have been developed in this field of international retailing, some of which are now considered in the following section.

2.2.1 Theoretical models for retail Internationalisation

Very many theoretical frameworks have attempted to assess the retail internationalisation process (e.g. Salmon and Tordjman 1989; Dawson 1994; Sternquist 1997; Vida and Fairhurst 1998; Doherty 1999; Alexander and Myers 2000 and Picot-Coupey 2006). These studies draw from the broader literature on international business, and also incorporate specific elements of retailing found in the literature. In general, these studies attempt to understand the drivers of retail international expansion. They are as discussed below:

2.2.1.1.   Hollander's contribution (1970)

This work offered five categories of international retail operations namely:
- Dealers in luxury goods
- General merchandise dealers
- Trading companies
- Specialised chains
-Direct selling and automatic vending

This classification provided a very valuable basis for future classifications and provided an insight into the fundamentals of internationalisation. These categories, derived from the environment and using the vocabulary of the late 1960s, require reconstruction in the contemporary landscape. However, in great part, Hollander's broad classifications (1970) are still relevant today. This original attempt to classify and understand the fundamentals of international retailing have provided academics with a valuable starting point for further theoretical developments.

2.2.1.2.   Salmon and Tordjman's Classification (1989)

Salmon and Tordjman's (1989) analysis focused on the problem of reconciling the need to adapt to local conditions and the operational advantages of maintaining a common approach in all markets. While they noted that there are three fundamental retail strategies- global, multinational, and investment- they were primarily concerned with the global and multinational approach. The

37

fundamental value of this classification is that it tacitly draws attention to the ability, or lack of ability, of a retail organisation to transfer its operation to another market. A valuable aspect of their findings relates to the transfer of retail knowledge across national boundaries. For them, the multinational strategy recognizes the fact that some retailers, while maintaining distinct operations, operate in similar markets, and this encourages the transfer of information across national boundaries. Therefore, it is the difference within an organisation that will facilitate innovation and cross-organisational learning.

2.2.1.3.   Dawson's Assessment (1994)

Dawson's article (1994) was a recapitulation of knowledge in the area of international retailing. It revisited the antecedents of contemporary international activity highlighted by Hollander (1970) and considered the state of understanding in the areas of the motivations behind internationalisation, the entry methods used in international activity, and the direction of international development. However, what Dawson more importantly provided was a warning against the misplaced introduction of theories devised in other contexts to explain processes in international retailing with fundamentally different characteristics.

Dawson (1994:270) identified eight differences 'in organisation and management' between the retailing and manufacturing sectors:

- the balance between centralized and decentralized decision making;
- the relative importance of organizational and establishment scale economies;
- the degree of spatial dispersion in the multi-establishment enterprise;
- the relative size of establishment to the size of the firm;
- the relative exit costs if decisions are reversed;
- the speed with which an income stream can be generated after an investment decision is made;
- different cash flow characteristics;
- the relative value of stock and hence importance of sourcing.'

Dawson's assessment (1994) provided a timely warning against the wholesale and ill digested use of concepts and theories designed to serve very different conditions.

2.2.1.4.   Sternquist's (SIRE) Model (1997)

The strategic international retail expansion (SIRE) model attempts to combine theories and concepts from various sources- that is, the OLI framework from Dunning (1988), the global and multinational strategic approaches to retail internationalisation from Salmon and Tordjman (1989) as well as stages theory and risk theory. The SIRE model considers ownership advantages to comprise company assets such as 'unique products or superior company reputation' and 'transaction based advantages' that 'come about because of the way things are done' (Sternquist 1997:264). Location advantages she describes as the 'pull factors... that make a foreign market attractive' such as: cultural proximity, market size, competitors' moves, geographical proximity, low cost of land/labour, and so on.

Sternquist (1997:265) moves on to describe her interpretation of internationalisation advantages in the retail context by discussing entry methods: 'internationalisation brings to the forefront the issue of how company secrets are handled. The greater the company's ownership assets, the more important it is to protect these assets by guarding company secrets.' Therefore, for Sternquist (1997:266), 'franchising is a particularly dangerous idea for retailers with a strong asset or transaction-based ownership advantages'.

Salmon and Tordjman's division of retailers (1989) into global and multinational is adopted here and the SIRE models goes further to consider entry modes in the light of the stages theory logic. Thus, retailers using the franchising or licensing method are said to 'obtain little information that will help them in new foreign markets' 'when they expand internationally'. Conversely, 'multinational retailers expand into locations that they perceive to have greater location advantages'.

The SIRE model also briefly introduces risk theory, which facilitates the inclusion in the model of organisational characteristics: firm size, operating experience, top management's perception of firm's competitive advantage suggesting that these characteristics will decide the retailer's choice between internalizing or externalizing international activities.

This work is criticized as being directly concerned only with the internationalisation process of a franchise system. This present research has a much broader scope as such the direct relevance of this SIRE model to the internationalisation process of retail firms is questionable. Also, there is a big unanswered question when these four concepts and theories are combined together without any discussion of the completely differing perspectives from which they originate, the assumption being that there are no methodological issues that should be addressed before applying the theories and concepts to international retailing.

This model is a good example of why Dawson called for caution in applying international manufacturing-based research directly to that on international retailing. While there are elements of worth in the model, the lack of justification of how they can be combined into one model ultimately limits its use and application.

2.2.1.5.   Doherty's contribution (1999)

Doherty (1999) on her path uses theory from the literature on the economics of international production and corporate governance to explain how international retailers choose entry methods in international markets. Her work explored some of the salient issues from internationalisation and agency theories as a basis for a theoretical discussion on how a retail firm entering into an international market would choose between, for example, an owned store operation and franchising.

40

By combining market transaction costs associated with internalisation theory with information and monitoring costs associated with agency theory and therefore highlighting issues of information asymmetry, she establishes a more coherent basis for exploring the entry mode decision process of international retail firms.

Mindful of the warning of Dawson (1994) against the wholesale introduction of non-retail-specific theory to the international retailing debate, Doherty (1999) explains the bases of both internationalisation theory and agency theory before she applies them to the international retailing context. She also compares the behavioural assumptions on which both theories are predicated as a means of justifying their use in the international retailing literature and emphasizing the importance of information asymmetry in the entry mode decision process. Doherty then employs examples on secondary sources, of retailers' entry mode choices and explains them through internationalisation and agency theory perspectives.

This theory has some relevance to this present research. Importantly, this theory is one of the first to consider the unexplored area of entry mode strategies of retail firms an area that is the focus of this present research. However, one of its major criticisms has been that it is not predicated on primary research. The theory makes its arguments effectively through secondary data mode providing explanation for both theoretical perspectives by returning to the original literature from which the theories have emerged. Though this present study is not based on Doherty's model, the findings from this study will make an interesting contribution to this model in that most of its postulations would have been tested empirically either directly or indirectly in the course of this research that which has been given as its major drawback. The context of this present study (a developing market setting) has called for a consideration of many more variables that were not contained in Doherty's contribution.

2.2.1.6. Vida, Reardon, and Fairhurst's IRI Model (2000)

The International Retail Involvement (IRI) model by Vida, Reardon, and Fairhurst (2000) borrowed from the behaviourist international marketing and business literature to focus on the stages approach to internationalisation as a basis for its development; discussing the antecedents, the process, and the outcomes of international involvement of retail firms.

Their model suggests that there are five factors that act as determinants of international retail involvement:

- Competitive advantages: retail image/brand, merchandise, logistics, etc.
- international knowledge: information-seeking behaviour;
- international experience: international expertise of the management, foreign direct sourcing;
- management attitudes: complexity, cost, risk, returns, etc.;
- Retailer size.

Aware of Dawson's concerns (1994), Vida, Reardon and Fairhurst (2000) borrowing from the manufacturing literature, provide a comprehensive review of the relevant literature, exhibiting a thorough knowledge of the subject area by providing a rigorous conceptualisation in terms of both the review of the literature and methodological underpinnings. Overall, their findings show that strategic management characteristics and retail specific competitive advantages have the most significant impact on retailers' decisions to engage in international activity. Notably, they found that size did not have a strong effect on retailers' decisions to operate internationally.

This model has some limitations in the sense that it is developed from an empirical study of US retailers, which is not directly relevant to this present study. The findings from this present study will to a large extent provide the much needed explanation as to the general applicability of most of these theories and models of retail internationalisation.

2.2.1.7. Picot-Coupey's Framework (2006)

Picot-Coupey's (2006) study seeking to explore which determinants influence a retailer's operation mode choice, found that marketing, internal, and environmental variables moderated by relational and motivational factors were key to retailers' operation mode decisions. In this framework, a distinction was made between explanatory (motives for internationalisation, and relationship networks) and moderating variables in a bid to help clarify the impact of these variables and proposed a meta-theoretical model combining the Nordic, network, and born-global approaches. The argument here is that conclusions about elements considered as idiosyncratic to the international retail sector could find echoes in problems developed recently in the international management literature; suggesting turning towards the new theories of the internationalisation process.

2.2.2   Institutional and Transaction cost influences on firm   internationalisation

What drives the strategies of international firms? This is an important question the management of international firms must answer. Peng *et al.* (2008:920) noted that "traditionally, there are two perspectives to address this question. An industry-based view, represented by Porter (1980) argues that conditions within an industry, to a large extent, determine firm strategy and performance. A resource-based view, exemplified by Barney (1991) suggests that it is firm-specific differences that drive strategy and performance... insightful as the industry- and resource-based views are, they can be criticised for largely ignoring the formal and informal institutional underpinning that provides the context of competition among industries and firms studied with these lenses (Kogut and Zander 2003). Peng *et al.* (2008) add that this is not surprising since both perspectives were developed from research on competition in the United States, in which it may seem reasonable to assume a relatively stable, market-based institutional framework.

A study of competition around the world, and especially in emerging economies whose institutions differ significantly from those in developed economies, bring in the increasing appreciation that formal and informal institutions significantly shape the strategy and performance of firms – both domestic and foreign in emerging economies (Wright *et al.* 2005).

That multinational enterprises entering a new market must adapt their strategies to the host country environment has been a hallmark finding in the international business literature. In recent years, increasing attention has been paid to the adaptation of these strategies to the demands of the various institutions that exist in the host economies (Oxley 1999; Peng 2000). Institutions play a key role in any economy as they constrain or facilitate business transactions. Understanding business strategies in emerging markets therefore calls for analysing the role and effect of institutions in reducing transaction costs (Hoskisson *et al.* 2000). This requires the investigation of different institutional contexts and their effects on entry strategies.

Organisations are known to use either independent or collaborative modes in entering into foreign markets. These entry modes which come with different degrees of control over local operations, have been analysed with the transaction costs approach (e.g. Anderson and Gatignon 1986; Hennart 1991). As noted by Meyer *et al.* (2009) the various modes of entry allow firms to overcome different kinds of market inefficiencies related to both characteristics of the resources and the institutional context. Supporting Institutions help to reduce transaction costs by reducing uncertainty and establishing a stable structure to facilitate interactions. In emerging and transitional economies, organisations need to identify not only potential types of business and the preferences of these potential business partners; but must also learn to assess the demand and supply composition to set the right prices (Meyer 2000). This increases the search, negotiation and contracting costs of new business relationships. The lack of knowledge of a market economy thus magnifies transaction costs in the market (Meyer 2001). Rapidly changing institutions at any point in time create call for changes in business practices. Businesses have reacted by relying on inherited systems of personal networks serving as a coordination mechanism under these uncertain situations. Networks are extensively used when formal institutions are weak (Peng 2000).

As correctly noted by Bockem and Tuschke (2008),

> 'So far, traditional FDI theory and the more recently emerging institutional perspective have been explored almost independently. We believe, however, that both perspectives

provide valuable insights into different characteristics of the same decision problem. In order to get a more fine-grained picture of market entry decisions, a joint treatment of both perspectives is needed'.

Also, while acknowledging that resources and capabilities are important (Peng, 2001; Meyer, 2006, 2007) suggest that strategies are moderated by the characteristics of the particular context in which firms operate. In particular, institutions- the 'rules of the game' – in the host economy also significantly shape firm strategies such as foreign entry mode (Wright *et al.* 2005). It is therefore in response to calls like these that both perspectives have been chosen to investigate the entry mode decision choices of international retail firms operating in emerging markets like Nigeria. The arguments of both perspectives are to be compared and contrasted both theoretically and empirically so as to improve our understanding and to see if both approaches provide complementary explanations for foreign market entry for retail firms. Bockem and Tuschke (2008) further stress that it is not a straight forward exercise to draw the border line between these two perspectives for real world decisions but nevertheless, the interplay between them can be studied if we take a common baseline setting which we can then supplement by assumptions such that one or the other kind of mechanism drops out as the result of the model.

Interestingly, the transaction cost analysis of entry strategy essentially argues that a decision over governance mechanisms, such as entry mode choice, requires a rational trade-off between the transaction costs associated with market and with hierarchy modes (Anderson and Gatignon 1986; Hennert 1988). So as transaction costs are moderated by the peculiarities of the institutional environment, scholars applying transaction cost theory to explain the choice of organisational forms especially in transitional and emerging context often integrate institutions in their transaction costs theory reasoning (Meyer and Peng 2005). They also added that transaction costs theory-based research in transition and emerging economies has redirected its focus from firm specific variables indicating sensitivity to transaction costs to contextual variables that moderate transaction costs in specific markets. Meyer (2001) follows North (1990) in arguing that institutions shape transaction costs, which in turn determine investors' internationalisation decisions. Both theories are now considered in greater detail.

2.2.2.1.   Institutional Economics Perspective

It is important to note that the notion of the institutional environment varies across disciplines. For example, economic theorists view the institutional environment as the exchange environment in which economic transactions are conducted by rationally-bounded individuals (Williamson 1985). For economic historians, the institutional environment is the set of political, social and legal rules such as government norms (North 1990). Both disciplines emphasise the regulative structures as constraints for social actors within the institutional environment.

For sociologists and organisational behaviourist, the institutional environment is viewed as socially constructed and characterised by a variety of norms that serve to legitimate organisational actions (Zucker 1987; Scott 2001). These disciplines emphasise the cognitive and normative structures of institutions that provide social meaning and prescribe appropriate behaviour for social actors, in addition to the regulatory environment.

Peng, Sun, Pinkham, and Chen (2009: 74) in trying to explain their use of the term "institution-based" label coined by Peng (2002) stated that this was done because of the confusion in the literature and the decision to avoid an interdisciplinary turf battle. In their words:

> "First, the proliferation of "institutional" research has produced some confusion. In our (impartial scholarly) view, broadly speaking, any theory that invokes a new institutionalism framing can be legitimately labelled the term "institutional theory". However, in the literature the term "institutional theory" increasingly refers to the *sociological* version of the institutional literature (DiMaggio and Powell 1983). The economic version, represented by North (1990), is often labelled simply "institutional economics". Because of the interdisciplinary nature of strategy, using either label ("institutional theory" or "institutional economics") would cause confusion".

Hence, they used the term "institutional-based view" in strategy. Following from this analogy, and the focus of this present study on the transaction cost theory (which is economics based) and its

46

direct links in building on, modifying and extending the neo-classical theory in economics, the "institutional economics" label is used. As noted by Peng *et al.* (2009) regardless of disciplinary roots, there is a remarkable consensus on a core proposition: '*Institutions matter'*. This brief review of institutional theory, suggest that the environment for organisations can be conceptualised by two separate environments, the technical (or competitive), and the institutional. According to these scholars, organisations need to deal with both environments, and in some cases the institutional environment may be even more important than the technical. It is important to state that from an institutional perspective, this thesis adopts the economic theorists' view of the institutional environment as the exchange environment in which economic transactions are conducted by rationally-bounded individuals (Williamson 1985). It contends that all economic action (technical environment) as well as non-economic action (social environment) is socially constructed and embedded in an institutional environment. Thus, organisational action is seen as shaped by economic-based and societal-based institutional norms, which are the rules and beliefs of society. The present view of economic theorists on institutions is summed up by the new institutional economics.

2.2.2.2.   Main concepts of the New Institutional Economics Perspective

According to Klein (1999) and Demirbag *et al.* (2010) the new institutional economics builds on, modifies, and extends neo-classical theory to permit it to come to grips and deal with an entire range of issues heretofore beyond its ken. What it retains and builds on is the fundamental assumption of scarcity and hence competition the basis of the choice theoretic approach that underlies micro-economics. What it abandons is instrumental rationality the assumption of neo-classical economics that has made it an institution-free theory. He further added that:

> "In a world of instrumental rationality, institutions are unnecessary; ideas and ideologies don't matter; and efficient markets- both economic and political- characterize economies. In fact, we have incomplete information and limited mental capacity by which to process information. Human beings, in consequence, impose constraints on human interaction in order to structure exchange. There is no implication that the

consequent institutions are efficient. In such a world, ideas and ideologies play a major role in choices and transaction costs result in imperfect markets".

The view expressed here is that individuals possess mental models to interpret the world around them that is culturally derived by the intergenerational transfer of knowledge, values, norms which vary radically among different ethnic groups and societies as earlier noted by Simon (1986). In part, these mental models are acquired through experience which is "local" to the particular environment and therefore also varies widely with different environments. The incomplete information and limited mental capacity by which to process information determines the cost of transacting, which underlies the formation of institutions (Williamson 2000). The cost of transacting arises because information is costly and asymmetrically held by the parties to exchange. The cost of measuring the multiple valuable dimensions of the goods or services exchanged, or the performances of agents, as well as the costs of enforcing agreements all determine transaction costs (Nicita and Vatiero 2007).

The neo-classical result of efficient markets only obtains when it is costless to transact. When it is costly to transact, institutions matter and are crucial determinants of the efficiency of markets. Therefore, in addition to modifying the rationality postulate, the new institutional economics adds institutions as a critical constraint and analyses the role of transaction costs as the connection between ideas and ideologies into the analysis, modelling the political process as a critical factor in the performance of economies, as the source of the diverse performance of economies, and as the explanation for "inefficient" markets. Modern economic problems are then to be studied precisely in the economic and social context (Meyer *et al.* 2009).

As earlier mentioned, according to Klein (1999), Development economists have typically treated the state as either exogenous or as a benign actor in the development process. Neo-classical economists have implicitly assumed that institutions (economic as well as political) don't matter and that the static analysis embodied in allocative-efficiency models should be the guide to policy; that is "getting the price right" by eliminating exchange and price controls. In fact, the state can never be treated as an exogenous actor in development policy and getting the prices right only has the desired consequences when you already have in place a set of property rights and enforcement that will then produce the competitive market conditions. Institutions in this case are the rules of the game of a society or more formally are the humanly-devised constraints that structure human interaction. They are composed of formal rules (statute law, common law and regulations), informal constraints (conventions, norms of behaviour, and self imposed codes of conduct), and the enforcement characteristics of both (Meyer and Peng 2005).

2.2.2.3.   Institutions and Entry Strategies

The fact was earlier mentioned that in as much as most literature has focused on the characteristics of the entering firm, in particular, its resources and capabilities (Barney 1991; Anand and Delios 2002) and its need to minimise transaction costs (Anderson and Gatignon 1986; Hill et al 1990) recent work has suggested that strategies are moderated by the characteristics of the particular context in which firms operate (Hoskisson *et al.* 2000; Meyer and Peng 2005) to determine their foreign market entry strategies. The institutions in this case, significantly shape firm strategies such as foreign market entry (Wright *et al.* 2005).

In a broad sense, macro-level institutions affect transaction costs (North 1990). However, traditional transaction cost research (exemplified by Williamson 1985) has focused on micro-level analytical aspects such as opportunism and bounded rationality. As a result, questions of how macro-level legal and regulatory frameworks influence transaction costs have been relatively unexplored, remaining in the 'background' (Meyer *et al.* 2009). The emphasis now is that institutions directly determine what arrows a firm has in its quiver as it struggles to formulate and implement strategy and to create competitive advantage (Ingram and Silverman, 2002). Nowhere is this point more clearly borne out than in emerging economies where institutional frameworks differ greatly in developed economies (Gelbuda, Meyer and Delios 2008).

International firms have been known to decide between using either the independent mode of entry or the collaborative modes (Franchising, joint ventures, etc.). Each of these modes has different risks, control, ownership structures, and satisfies different objectives (Elango and Sambharya 2004). Collaborative entry modes are used to access resources previously embedded in another organisation (Meyer and Peng 2005). The question therefore is: why wouldn't the international firm just buy the specific resources they need using standard market transactions? (Haspeslagh and Jemison 1991; Capron, Mitchell, and Swaminathan 2001) noted that a firm that buys another is exposed to major challenges of managing the purchased business creating substantial coordination challenges (Buckley and Casson 1998). Thus, if the local markets for the necessary resources are efficient, foreign entrants may buy the required resources using market transactions and thus establish an independent operation. However, efficiency of local markets is not always the norm (Estrin 2002). Markets for buying and selling companies may be especially problematic in emerging economies (Peng and Heath 1996). More generally, markets for acquiring local resources may be suboptimal because of the institutional environment governing the transaction (North 1990; Peng 2006). They may also be suboptimal because of the sought resources (Williamson 1985).

Institutions have an essential role in a market economy to support the effective functioning of the market mechanism, such that firms and individuals can engage in market transactions without incurring undue costs or risks (North 1990; Peng 2008). These institutions include, for example, the legal framework and its enforcement, property rights, information systems, and regulatory regimes. Institutional arrangements are considered to be 'strong' if they support the voluntary exchange underpinning an effective market mechanism. Conversely, the institutions are 'weak' if they fail to ensure effective markets or even undermine markets (as in the case of corrupt business practices) Meyer *at al.* (2009). Where institutions are strong in developed economies, their role, though critical, may be almost invisible. In contrast, when markets malfunction, as in some emerging economies, the absence of market-supporting institutions is 'conspicuous' (McMillan 2008).

Institutional differences are particularly significant for firms operating in multiple institutional contexts (Globerman and Shapiro 1999; Meyer and Tran 2006). Formal rules establish the permissible range of entry choices (e.g., with respect to equity ownership) but informal rules may also affect entry decisions. Thus, legal restrictions may limit the equity stake that foreign investors are allowed to hold (Delios and Beamish 1999) and informal norms, such as norms concerning whether bribery is acceptable, may favour locally owned firms over the foreign enterprises (Peng 2003). In other words, because the transactions costs of engaging in these markets are relatively higher, international firms have to devise strategies to overcome these constraints (Peng 2008).

Institutions also provide information about business partners and their likely behaviour, which reduces information asymmetries—a core source of market failure (Arrow 1971; Casson 1997). In many emerging economies, weak institutional arrangements may magnify information asymmetries so firms face higher partner-related risks (Meyer 2001) and need to spend more resources searching for information (Tong, Reuer, and Peng 2008). The strengthening of the institutional framework thus lowers costs of doing business (Estrin 2002; Bengoa and Sanchez-Robles 2003; Bevan, Estrin, and Meyer 2004) and influences foreign entrants' mode decisions by moderating the costs of alternative organizational forms (Williamson 1985). In consequence, the relative costs associated with different entry modes are affected by the institutional framework (Henisz, 2000; Meyer 2001). In particular, a collaborative mode like joint ventures (JVs) provides a means to access resources held by local firms, including resources such as networks that may help to counteract idiosyncrasies of a weak institutional context (Delios and Beamish 1999).

However, the need for a partner may decline with the strengthening of the institutional framework (Meyer 2001; Peng 2003; Steensma et al. 2005). For example, as the regulatory environment in an emerging economy improves, more sectors will be opened to FDI and foreign entrants will face fewer formalities, permits, and licenses. Hence, a reduction of restrictions on FDI may reduce the need for a local JV partner as an interface with local authorities (Gomes-Casseres 1990; Delios and Beamish 1999; Peng 2006). Similarly, improved regulatory frameworks may reduce the need to rely on relationships of a local JV partner when dealing with local businesses (Oxley 1999; Meyer 2001).

An independent entry mode is an entry mode that is particularly sensitive to the efficiency of markets, especially financial markets and the market for corporate control (Antal-Mokos 1998; Peng 2008). Many of the resources and organizational structures of local firms are built around nonmarket forms of transactions, and are therefore harder for potential acquirers to evaluate (Tong *et al.* 2008). This raises the complexity and transaction costs of undertaking the due diligence and contract negotiations necessary for the use of a mode like acquisitions and post-acquisition restructuring (Peng 2006). Thus, costs and risks increase when institutional frameworks are weaker. Combining these arguments, the conclusion can be drawn that foreign entrants may need access to local resources in emerging economies to overcome inefficiencies caused by weak institutions. Yet, at the same time, weak institutional frameworks make it more difficult to access these resources via market transactions (which inhibit independent entry) and raise the costs of acquiring local firms (which make acquisitions challenging). In contrast, collaborative modes like joint ventures (JVs) provide a means to access local resources where arm's length market transactions are difficult.

2.3   Transaction Cost Theory

As noted by Meyer *et al.* (2009) in trying to determine foreign entry mode strategies, most existing literature has focused on the characteristics of the entering firm, in particular its resources and capabilities (Barney 1991; Anand and Delios 2002) and its need to minimize transaction costs (Anderson and Gatignon 1986; Hill, Hwang, and Kim 1990). Transaction cost analysis belongs to the "Institutional Economics" paradigm which has supplanted traditional neoclassical economics. In as much as this new view takes a macro-level focus on institutions country level legal and regulatory frameworks etc. this is only an expansion on the traditional transaction cost research (exemplified by Williamson 1985). The major contributions of the traditional view still remain valid and provide very important insights into understanding transaction costs. As earlier mentioned in section 2.1.1a, transaction cost analysis has its origin in the seminal work of Coase (1937), with later significant contributions by Williamson (1975, 1981). This theory explicitly views the firm as a governance structure. Coase's (1937) initial proposition was that firms and markets are alternative governance structures that differ in their transaction costs. In his view, transaction costs are the "costs of running the system" and include such *ex ante* costs as drafting and monitoring contracts and such *ex post* costs as monitoring and enforcing agreements.

Williamson (1975, 1985, 1996) has however, added considerable precision to Coase's general argument by identifying the types of exchanges that are more appropriately conducted within firm boundaries than within the market. He has augmented Coase's initial framework by suggesting that transactions include both the direct costs of managing relationships and the possible opportunity costs of making inferior governance decisions, basing this on the interplay of two main assumptions of human behaviour (bounded rationality and opportunism) and two dimensions of transactions (asset specificity and uncertainty).

As described by Rindefleisch and Heide (1997:31) 'bounded rationality is the assumption that decision makers have constraints on their cognitive capabilities and limits on rationality'. So, in as much as decision makers often intend to act rationally, this intention may be circumscribed by their limited information processing and communication ability. They further added that 'according to TCA, these constraints become problematic in uncertain environments, in which the circumstances surrounding an exchange cannot be specified *ex ante* (i.e., environmental uncertainty) and performance cannot be easily verified *ex post* (i.e., behavioural uncertainty). The primary consequence of environmental uncertainty is an adaptation problem to changing circumstances; also, the effect of behavioural uncertainty results in a performance evaluation problem.

Opportunism is the assumption that, given the opportunity, decision makers may unscrupulously seek to serve their self-interest, and that it is difficult to know *a priori* who is trustworthy and who is not (Barney 1990). Williamson (1985:47) defines opportunism as "self-interest seeking with guile," and suggests that it includes such behaviours as lying and cheating, as well as more subtle forms of deceit, such as violating agreements. Opportunism poses a problem to the extent that a relationship is supported by specific assets whose values are limited outside of the focal relationship. According to Barney (1990), TCA does not assume that all social actors are opportunistically inclined, only that some actors behave opportunistically, and it is difficult and costly to identify opportunistic actors ex ante.

2.3.1 TCA concepts and their effect on governance structures

In the TCA approach, the properties of the transaction determine what constitute the most efficient governance structure—market, hierarchy or alliance (Williamson 1975). The primary factors producing transactional difficulties have been earlier set out in the section above to include bounded rationality and opportunism, as well as asset specificity and uncertainty. The effect each of these concepts has on the governance structure is now considered in the following sections.

2.3.1.1.   Bounded rationality

This has been explained to mean that certain physical limits exist on the human ability to process information. Decision makers are intentionally rational, but only limitedly so; some of these limits include such shortcomings as: overconfidence, competitive blind spots, and improper valuation of gains and losses (Zajac and Bazerman 1991). According to McIvor (2009:47) 'bounded rationality refers to the cognitive limitations of the human mind, which increases the difficulties of understanding fully the complexities of all possible decisions'.

In this case, an adaptation problem is created when a firm whose decision makers are limited by bounded rationality has difficulty modifying contractual agreements to changes in the external environment. The associated transaction costs include the direct costs of communicating new information, renegotiating agreements, or coordinating activities to reflect new circumstances. A failure to adapt involves an opportunity cost of maladaptation (Malone 1987). So bounded rationality and uncertainty act as antecedents of the adaptation problem; equally so, a problem of performance evaluation arises as well.

In asking for increased autonomy and local embeddedness of subsidiaries in order to benefit from collective learning and to realise innovation advantages associated with linkages to valuable sources of information and knowledge, (Mudambi and Navarra 2004; McDonald, Tuselmann, Voronkova, and Golesorkhi 2011) warn that this could have a detrimental effect on the performance of MNCs if the subsidiaries have too much autonomy and/or they become too embedded in their host locations, especially if opportunistic, rent-seeking behaviour by subsidiary managers (made possible by asymmetric information) permits the inappropriate allocation, or the over-use, of the MNC's resources. In such a case, the subsidiary managers suffer from bounded rationality rather than opportunism (Verbeke and Greidanus 2009). This according to (McDonald, Tuselmann, Voronkova, and Golesorkhi 2011) leads to

"asymmetric evaluations of the cost and benefits by subsidiary and parent company managers, even when evaluations arise from symmetric information on the available options. The valuations placed on increasing autonomy and local embeddedness by parent company managers may, therefore, be different from that of the managers of subsidiaries, because of differing perceptions of the net benefits of strategic and operational options".

2.3.1.2.   Opportunism

Transaction cost analysis views this behavioural uncertainty as arising from the difficulty associated with monitoring the contractual performance of exchange partners (Williamson, 1985). As noted by Rindfleisch and Heide (1997) there appear to be few secondary measures of behavioural uncertainty because such measures are difficult to extract from secondary data. Gatignon and Anderson's (1988) study used the level of international experience as a measure for performance assessment in a foreign market entry context.

A governance problem that has been identified from the literature is *safeguarding*- this arises when a firm deploys specific assets and fears that its partner may opportunistically exploit these investments. Therefore, just like asset specificity discussed in the next section, opportunism also acts as an antecedent of the safeguarding problem McIvor (2009). 'Transaction cost analysis proposes that, because of the opportunistic behaviour of trading partners, high levels of asset specificity increase the cost of safeguarding contractual agreements' Rindfleisch and Heide (1997:44).

2.3.1.3.   Asset specificity

This refers to the transferability of assets that support a given transaction. Assets with a high amount of specificity represent sunk costs that have little value outside of a particular exchange relationship (Williamson 1985). Six main types of asset specificity are identified by Williamson, (1991b) namely: (1) site specificity (2) physical asset specificity (3) human asset specificity (4) brand name capital (5) dedicated assets, and (6) temporal specificity. Rindfleisch and Heide (1997) write that there is a greater focus on human specific assets because TCA studies involve contexts in which human investments represent a substantial and important cost of doing business and secondly, human specific assets lend themselves to a wide variety of measurement approaches, both directly through secondary data sources, such as sales reports, and indirectly through survey instruments.

When faced with the need to safeguard specific assets invested in an exchange relationship, early TCA work claimed that a firm generally seeks to minimize its transaction costs through vertical integration (Williamson 1985). Several other studies on entry modes (Frazier and Roth, 1990; Erramilli and Rao 1993) also support this finding that asset specificity is related to the use of higher levels of control in foreign markets.

2.3.1.4.   Uncertainty

As theorized in the TCA literature, environmental uncertainty refers to "unanticipated changes in circumstances surrounding an exchange" (Noordewier, John, and Nevin, 1990:82). High levels of environmental uncertainty increase the costs of adapting contractual agreements. Williamson (1985) posits that, when faced with the need to adapt to an uncertain environment, a firm will seek to minimize its transaction costs through vertical integration. Not many studies support this position because others see some type of environmental uncertainty acting as a disincentive to vertical integration. Some studies like Walker and Weber (1984) equally suggest that the effect of environmental uncertainty may be multidimensional and that different dimensions may have different effects. Specifically, research studies show two areas of its operationalization; the most commonly held perspective emphasizes the unpredictable nature of the external environment, whereas the second view examines both unpredictability and complexity. Klein (1989) looked at these two dimensions adding that they both have opposing influences on governance structures. It is posited that whereas unpredictability encourages firms to form hierarchical mechanisms, changeability has just the opposite effect. Klein (1989:257) defined uncertainty- dynamism as "the rates at which changes in the environment occur", and complexity as "the degree to which the respondent perceived the environment as simple or complex".

There is an important question of which perspective provides the appropriate conceptual domain for TCA investigations. As a response to this, Klein 1989 write that the answer should be found on theoretical grounds, suggesting that the context in which the investigation is carried out domestic or international should provide an insight into which perspective is important (e.g. complexity is manageable in the domestic context). Rindfleisch and Heide (1997:42) added that "if a researcher has reason to expect that key elements of the external environment could possibly act as a disincentive for hierarchical modes of governance, a multidimensional operationalization as suggested by Klein 1989 is in order. The new institutional economics view therefore adds a macro-level view to Williamson's focus micro-analytical aspects such as opportunism and bounded rationality (Meyer *et al.* 2009). The idea is to try and determine what drives transaction costs in different economies.

2.4   Justification for use of the Institutional and Transaction Cost perspectives.

The New institutional theory as explained in the earlier sections has been identified as an attractive framework for the study of firm internationalisation because it acknowledges variations in the saliency of institutional norms across different countries that can affect organisational strategies. International retail firms face different conditions in different markets and their success depends on their ability to adapt and gain legitimacy in the host market. Also, as a result of the fact that internationalising firms look to reduce their transaction cost based on the entry strategy chosen and the need to expand on the unit of analysis in the original framework of transaction cost analysis (TCA) – individual transaction of the firm as well as the need to consider the macro-level influence of institutions on transaction costs, have all been the reasons for the combined use of both theories in this study.

Scholars (Anderson, Hakansson, and Johanson 1994; Hakansson and Snehota 1995) noted that the governance of a particular transaction may be influenced by other actors within an inter-organisational network, either directly or indirectly. As suggested by Hakansson and Snehota (1995) interactions or exchange episodes may influence how a new transaction is organised. Studies have shown (Heide and Miner 1992; Parkhe 1993) that the time dimension within a given relationship is governed because of either the past history of inter-organizational relations or incentive structure created by the expectation of future transactions. Also, Meyer at al. (2009) noted that traditional transaction cost research (exemplified by Williamson 1985) has focused on micro-analytical aspects such as opportunism and bounded rationality. As a result, questions of how macro-level institutions, such as country-level legal and regulatory frameworks, influence transaction costs have been relatively unexplored, remaining largely as 'background'. All of these views are additions to the original TCA framework.

Therefore, the New Institutional theory used here as a complementary theory in this study provides some insight into these added dimensions. The main premise of the theory as earlier discussed is that organisational decision making may be influenced as much by differences in institutions which can be conceived as 'shift parameters' that alter the slope or intercept of transaction costs such that in transition and emerging economies context, transaction costs are particularly high owing to the 'weak institutions' and high uncertainty (Meyer and Peng 2005). For example, the lack of information systems and effective courts raised search and monitoring costs, and constraints on opportunistic behaviour may become ineffective (Swaan 1997).

The need for combined use of these theories in this study is based also on the views expressed by Rindefleisch and Heide (1997:30) that a particular manifestation of recent interest in transaction cost analysis is a large number of empirical applications in this area conducted by marketing scholars. A reason for this they mentioned is transaction cost's substantive focus on exchange which makes it relevant to a wide range of marketing phenomena amongst which include foreign market entry strategy (Anderson and Coughlan, 1987; Klein, Frazier, and Roth 1990).

All of the above reasons are summed up as several implications and methodological challenges derivable from these theories that have accounted for their combined use in this present study as acknowledged by (Wright *et al.* 2005). They are as listed below:

(a) Relative to developed economies, available evidence shows that TCs are even harder to measure in developing and transitional economies which lowers the predictive power of the theory.

(b) The need to identify which types of TCs are of particular concern to the type of business under investigation (in this case international retail operation).

(c) Relationships are hard to model and predictive power of conventional models is weak.

(d) The need for an understanding of the contextual measures (direct and/or indirect) that drive TCs.

59

(e) Businesses need to adapt to each institutional context. How are the organisational forms designed for flexibility?

(f) Rapid institutional changes interact with organisational change how is this managed?

(g) What measures capture countries' informal and formal institutions and what are their impacts on retail firm entry strategy?

Park and Sternquist (2008:289) noted that 'internationalisation advantages exist in the retail sector because retailers need to keep their ownership advantages within. Internalisation advantages are especially important for innovative retailers because innovations, if shared with external parties, will be vulnerable to the potential loss of long-term revenues... the greater the ownership asset, the more advantageous to the retailer it is to retain the asset within the firm'. Furthermore, the tacit nature of unique capabilities makes transferability to external parties difficult. Cultural or business practice differences add to the difficulty or uncertainty of transferring organisational skills to a foreign market.

From the entry mode perspective, internalisation advantages have been conceptualized as contractual risks (Nakos and Bouthers 2002). Contractual risks refer to the risk of disseminating proprietary know-how meaning that when firms perceived low advantages from internalising foreign operations, they tended to use non-equity modes of entry. Retail managers' perceptions of internalisation advantages (contractual risks) are critical for the choice of an entry mode.

2.5   Entry mode and Retail Internationalisation success

As can be clearly seen from the available literature, foreign market entry has been a popular topic in international business research during the last couple of decades (Gripsrud and Benito 2004:1672). Entry modes as well as choice of foreign markets are analysed in a number of empirical studies (Datta *et al* 2002; Mitra and Golder, 2002; Huang and Sternquist 2007). Retailers active in international markets may choose between several modes, each of them carrying different implications in terms of costs, speed of entry, flexibility, control, financial engagement and risk

(Picot-Coupey 2006). Various other studies (Alexander and Doherty, 2004; Blomstermo et al, 2006; Huang and Sternquist 2007) have shown the importance of the mode of entry to the success of an international retail firm making it a "frontier issue" in international business operations.

Retailing is a service industry where international expansion and cross-border activities have become much more pronounced in recent times. Various researchers in this area have tried to look into foreign market entry by retail firms in a bid to answer very important questions such as: which countries are being selected when a retailer goes abroad? Again, they have tried to ascertain what factors explain the pattern of foreign expansion pursued by retailers. Previous studies have tended to look at such decisions from either economics perspective (Hennart 1982; Dunning 2000) or internationalisation process model perspective (Andersen 1993; Johanson and Vahle 1977; Luostarinen 1979) based on the behavioural theory of the firm. This classical approach to the analysis of international retail expansion has been to discuss 'push' and 'pull' factors (Kacker 1985). Some of the pull factors being: Low growth rate in wages in the foreign market, attractive real estate portfolios, homogeneous domestic market, stable political attitude to business, etc. On the other hand, some of the push factors include: Competitive pressures, Domestic market: small and saturated, Overproduction/excess capacity, Unsolicited foreign orders, Extend sales of seasonal products, Proximity to international customers/psychological distance. (Evans *et al.* 2008) referred to these same variables as PROACTIVE and REACTIVE MOTIVES of Internationalisation.

In all of these, however, it is interesting to note the findings from the study conducted by Alexander (1990) on UK International retail firms. From this study, the UK retailers placed considerable importance on the following factors as their reason for expansion: Niche opportunities within the market, size of the market, the level of economic prosperity within the market, retailer's operating format, retailer's product lines, as well as under-developed nature of retailing in new market. It was surprising to see relatively low scores being credited to factors such as saturation in the home market, favourable labour climate in the new market, favourable laws and tax regulations, along with favourable exchange rates.

This therefore shows that the primary reason for expansion was essentially economic prosperity in a large market where there existed niche opportunities for the retailers' offering. The relative importance ascribed to niche opportunities and low rating of saturation indicate that retailers are prepared to cross frontiers to reach the most appropriate markets rather than exploit marginal opportunities in their home territory. Evans *et al.* (2007:260) noted that "it is evident from extant literature that retailers do not simply internationalise in response to declining sales or market share in the domestic market. A multitude of factors are likely to play a role in driving both this decision and the business strategy adopted in foreign markets". It is also very interesting to note that these findings in the study by Alexander are also supported by findings in the studies by William (1992); Quinn (1999); as well as Vida *et al.* (2000) where they all stressed the importance of these same proactive factors mentioned by Alexander.

2.5.1 Forms of entry into international markets

Having considered the major models/methods of International market selection, it is right now to look at some approaches to the choice of entry mode. The question to be asked here is: What kind of strategy should be used for the entry mode selection?

Petersen and Welch (2002) write that there are three basic classifications of market entry modes namely: Export modes, Intermediate modes (Collaborative), and Independent (Hierarchical modes). Retail firms however use either of two modes: Independent modes, or Collaborative modes. The choice of foreign entry mode is critical and related to control which allows service firms to supply timely and good quality services to international clients, which protects reputation (Blomstermo et al; 2006:212). Control is crucial as it ensures achievement of the ultimate purpose of the organisation. Also, determines risk and returns, the amount of relational friction between buyers and sellers, and ultimately, the performance of the investment abroad (Barkema *et al.* 1996; Barkema and Vermeulen 1998; Khoury 1979).

It is evidently clear that a firm's choice of its entry mode for a given product/target country is the net result of several, often conflicting forces. Hollensen (2007) suggested that the need to anticipate the strength and direction of these forces makes the entry mode decision a complex process with numerous trade-offs among alternative entry modes. Generally speaking, the choice of entry mode should be based on the expected contribution to profit. The following four groups of factors are believed to influence the entry mode decision:

(1) Internal factors
(2) External factors
(3) Desired mode characteristics
(4) Transaction-specific behaviour.

The following sub factors play very important parts in determining the foreign market entry mode choice as the major internal variables (Blomstermo *et al.* 2006): -Firm size, -International experience, and -Product/service. The size of the firm is clearly an indicator of the firm's resource availability; increasing resource availability provides the basis for increased international involvement over time. This is why most large scale firms can afford to consider the use of the hierarchical model and SMEs use export because they do not have the resources necessary to achieve a high degree of control or to make these resource commitments. Also, the International experience of managers and thus the firm, also affect the mode choice. Experience, which refers to the extent to which a firm has been involved in operating internationally, can be gained from operating either in a particular country or in the general international environment. International experience reduces the cost and uncertainty of serving a market and, in turn, increases the profitability of firms committing resources to foreign markets. Lastly, the nature of the product (merchandise) of the retail firm also affects its decision concerning the mode of entry to use (Hollensen 2007:299).

The external factors involve variables like: Socio-cultural distance between home country and host country: Socio-cultural differences between a firm's home country and its host country can create internal uncertainty for the firm, which influences the mode of entry desired by that firm. The greater the perceived distance between the home and host country in terms of culture, economic systems and business practices, the more likely it is that the firm will shy away from direct investment in favour of joint venture agreements (Sarkar and Cavusgil 1996). This is because the latter institutional modes enhance the firm's flexibility to withdraw from the host market, if they should be unable to acclimatize themselves comfortably to the unfamiliar setting. Therefore, it follows that when the perceived distance between the home and host country is great, firms will favour entry modes that involve relatively low resource commitments and high flexibility.

The Country risk/Demand uncertainty, market size and growth, political and economic environment of the host market, direct and indirect trade barriers, in addition to intensity of competition, and the number of relevant intermediaries available in the host market, all affect the entry mode method to be used by the international retail firm (Driscoll 1995).

The different entry mode choices have different characteristics. The risk averse nature of the decision maker for the firm equally affects the entry mode. If risk averse, they will prefer export modes (e.g. indirect and direct exporting) or licensing (an intermediate mode) because they typically entail low levels of financial and management resource commitment (Hill *et al.* 1990). As earlier mentioned, the amount of control needed by management over operations in international markets also affects the choice of entry mode. Modes of entry with minimal resource commitments, such as indirect exporting, provide little or no control over the conditions under which the product or service is marketed abroad.

Wholly-owned subsidiaries (hierarchical mode) provide the most control, but also require a substantial commitment of resources (Anderson and Gatignon 1986; Root 1994). This is very closely related as well, to the flexibility of the entry mode method. Management must also weigh up the flexibility associated with a given mode of entry. The hierarchical modes (involving substantial equity investment) are typically the most costly but the least flexible and most difficult to change in the short run. Intermediate modes (contractual agreements and joint ventures) limit the firm's ability to adapt or change strategy when market conditions are changing rapidly (Anderson and Gatignon 1986; Klein 1989).

Lastly, the tacit nature of knowhow of the firm influences the choice of entry mode. When the nature of the firm-specific know-how transferred is tacit, it is by definition difficult to articulate. This makes the drafting of a contract (to transfer such complex know-how) very problematic. The difficulties and costs involved in transferring tacit know-how provide an incentive for firms to use hierarchical modes. Investment modes are better able to facilitate the intra-organisational transfer of tacit know-how. By using a hierarchical mode, the firm can utilise human capital, drawing upon its organisational routines to structure the transfer problem. Hence, the greater the tacit component of firm-specific know-how, the more a firm will favour hierarchical modes (Gronhaug and Kvitastein 1993).

2.5.2 Entry methods - Intermediate/Collaborative entry modes

Intermediate entry modes are primarily vehicles for the transfer of knowledge and skills. They differ from hierarchical modes in the way that there is no full ownership (by the parent firm) involved, but ownership and control can be shared between the parent firm and a local partner

(Whitelock, 2002). The most common form of entry in this method includes a variety of arrangements such as: licensing, franchising, and joint ventures.

2.5.2.1.   Licensing

This is an agreement wherein the licensor gives something of value to the licensee in exchange for certain performance and payments from the licensee (Doherty, 2000). The licensor may give the licensee the right to use one or more of the following: A patent covering a product or process, manufacturing know-how not subject to a patent, technical advice and assistance, occasionally including the supply of components, materials or plant essentials to the manufacturing process, marketing advice and assistance, the use of a trade name/trade mark. Licensing involves a much greater responsibility for the national firm, because more value chain functions have been transferred to the licensee by the licensor (Zhang *et al.* 2007).

2.5.2.2.   Franchising

Franchising is a marketing-oriented method of selling a business service, often to small independent investors who have working capital but little or no prior business experience. This concept was popularized in the United States, where over one-third of retail sales are derived from franchising (Young *et al* 1989:111). A number of factors have contributed to the rapid growth rate of franchising. First, the general worldwide decline of traditional manufacturing industry and its replacement by service-sector activities has encouraged franchising. It is especially well suited to service and people-intensive economic activities.

There are two major types of franchising: Product and trade name franchising: This is very similar to trade mark licensing. Typically, it is a distribution system in which suppliers make contracts with dealers to buy or sell products or product lines. Dealers use the trade name, trade mark and product line. Examples of this type of franchising are soft drink bottlers like Coca-Cola and Pepsi. Business format 'package' franchising: In this case there is a relationship between the entrant (the franchisor) and a host country entity, in which the former transfers, under contract, a business package (or format) that it has developed to the latter. The package can contain the following: trademarks/names, copyright, designs, patents, trade secrets, business know-how, geographic exclusivity, store design, market research, location selection, etc. McDonalds, Burger King, Pizza Hut, use this format.

2.5.2.3. Joint Ventures/ Strategic alliances

A joint venture or a strategic alliance is a partnership between two or more parties. In international joint ventures, these parties are based in different countries. A number of reasons are given for setting up joint ventures (William 1992) including the following: Complementary technology or management skills provided by the partners can lead to new opportunities in existing sectors (e.g. multimedia, in which information processing, communications and the media are merging), many firms find partners in the host country can increase the speed of market entry, many less developed countries, try to restrict foreign ownership, global operations in R&D and production are prohibitively expensive, but are necessary to achieve competitive advantage.

The joint venture can be either a contractual non-equity joint venture or an equity joint venture. In a contractual joint venture, no joint enterprise with a separate personality is formed. Two or more companies form a partnership to share the cost of investment, the risks, and the long term profits. An equity joint venture involves the creation of a new company in which foreign and local investors share ownership and control. Thus, according to these definitions, strategic alliances and non-equity joint ventures are more or less the same (Hollensen 2007).

2.5.3 Entry methods - *Hierarchical modes*

The final group of entry modes is the hierarchical modes, a situation where the firm owns and controls completely the foreign entry mode. Here, it is a question of where the control in the firm lies. The extent/amount of control that the head office can exert on the subsidiary will to a large extent depend on the number and which value chain functions are to be transferred to the market (Hollensen 2007). This again depends on the allocation of the responsibility and competence between head office and the subsidiary, and how the firm wants to develop this on an international level. If a producer wants greater influence and control over local marketing than export modes can give, it is natural to consider creating own companies in the foreign markets. The most commonly used forms of the hierarchical modes are foreign sales branch/foreign sales subsidiary.

2.5.3.1.   Foreign Sales Branch/Subsidiary

Sometimes, firms find it relevant to establish a formal branch office, to which a resident salesperson is assigned. A foreign branch is an extension and a legal part of the firm. A foreign branch also often employs nationals of the country in which it is located. If foreign market sales develop in a positive direction, the firm may consider establishing a wholly-owned sales subsidiary. A foreign subsidiary is a local company owned and operated by a foreign company under the laws of the host country (Root, 1994).

The sales subsidiary provides complete control of the sales function. One of the major reasons for choosing sales subsidiaries is the possibility of transferring greater autonomy and responsibility to these subunits, being close to the customers. Another reason for establishing sales subsidiaries may be the tax advantage. This is particularly important for companies headquartered in high-tax countries. With proper planning, companies can establish subsidiaries in countries having low business income taxes and gain an advantage by not paying taxes in their home country on the foreign-generated income until such income is actually repatriated to them. The precise tax advantages that are possible with such subsidiaries depend upon the tax laws in the home country compared to the host country. In deciding to establish wholly-owned operations in a country, a firm can either acquire an existing company (acquisition) or build its own operations from scratch (Greenfield investment).

2.6   Market-oriented influence on entry strategy and firm success

The findings from previous studies (Narver and Slater 1990; Leelapanyalert and Ghauri 2007, *Zou et al.* 2009) lend support for a market orientation approach to retail internationalisation. This approach suggests the need to understand customers and competitor firms from the host market in order to adapt the source of competitive advantage accordingly (Bianchi 2002). Market orientation involves the generation and dissemination of market intelligence that is composed of information about customers and competitors and sharing of this information among all functions in the organisation and rapid managerial action in response to this information. Along this line therefore, Kohli and Jaworski (1990:3) define market orientation as "the organisation wide generation of market intelligence, dissemination of intelligence across departments and organisation wide responsiveness to it". It is expected therefore that with the differences in host market conditions, international retailers will collect, process, and disseminate organisation wide information pertaining to host market customers and competitors in order to respond and adapt to new conditions and increase performance and success; the ease with which this is done and the level of organisational understanding of these conditions determine their mode of entry into such foreign markets.

Apart from customers and competitors, market orientation has also been suggested to consider additional agents like suppliers, government and its agencies, agents and networks, etc. Retail internationalisation has often been stressed to involve the firms to be embedded in its social environment and to consider the effect of these other social agents. The importance of the social external environment has been mentioned by these studies drawn from institutional economics (North 1991). Research on retailing has also suggested that retailers' practices are affected by pressures from their institutional environment (Arnold *et al.* 1996; Handelman and Arnold 1999). These studies show that retailers aim to gain legitimacy in their host market and for this, they must be prepared to adapt to changes and pressures from the external environment.

The link has been established that the method of entry used by a retail firm to a large extent determines its success in that market as well as its preparedness to operate based on the dictates of the market its responsiveness to the market. Park and Sternquist (2008) distinguished between 'global' and 'multinational retailers. The former they defined as very specific retailers that have centralised management and expand using a similar concept abroad ignoring national or regional differences; while the latter adapts its retail concept to a foreign market. Very many scholars (Ghauri and Gronhaug 2002; Kshetri 2008) believe that retail practice especially in developing markets (like that of Nigeria used in this study) should be adapted to the local market conditions. This is a potential reason why the findings from these studies reveal that market orientation approach for the retail firms may require the use of some collaborative modes of entry because of the need to understand the local market conditions – an important ingredient for its eventual success. Empirical studies by (Rajan and Pangarkar 2000; Harzing 2002) reveal that global retailers would tend to favour a higher equity entry mode, preferably a wholly-owned subsidiary.

2.7   Chapter summary

This chapter reviews the literature on firm internationalisation examining the internationalisation theories (established streams of the literature) and also looks at retail internationalisation and its theoretical developments. Also, the institutional and transaction influences on firm internationalisation are discussed with an introduction of the institutional economics perspective and its main concepts. Equally examined are the effect of institutions on entry strategies of firms, as well as the transaction cost theory and its effect on governance structures. An important part of this chapter is the justification provided for the combined use of the institutional and transaction cost perspectives for this present study. The final sections of the chapter looked at the importance of entry modes on retail internationalisation success, forms of entry into international markets, and the market oriented influence on entry strategy.

CHAPTER 3: CONTEXTUAL BACKGROUND

Part of the previous sections has looked into the justification for the investigation of entry mode decision strategy into the developing Nigerian market. In this chapter, a closer look is taken into the context for this research (Nigeria) to allow for a proper understanding of the Nigerian market structure, governance, level of development, policies and guidelines, and other important characteristics. The history of retailing in Nigeria before and after independence is traced as well as the effect of the various government policies on retail practice in the country and the general state of the country - politically, economically, socio-culturally, and legally.

3.1   Brief overview of Nigeria

Nigeria is Africa's most populous country and one of the most culturally diverse societies in the world with approximately 250 ethnic groups among its 150 million people (National Population Commission 2007). The country is essentially a mono-sector economy that is highly dependent on oil though the government is trying now to diversify the economy (Ozughalu 2007). The oil and gas sector accounts for over 90% of the country's foreign exchange earnings. According to the (Central Bank of Nigeria annual reports 2011) the country's GDP for 2010 was US$ 206.664 billion (2010 estimate), with the following sector contributions: agriculture 17.6%, industry 53.1%, and services 29.3%. The decline in Nigeria's agricultural and non-oil industrial capacity has continued to exacerbate its dependence on imports. Trading Economics report (2011) show that Nigeria's imports were worth 12.5 Billion USD in the third quarter of 2010. Nigeria imports mainly: industrial supplies (32% of total), transport equipment and parts (23%), capital goods (24%), food and beverage (11%) and consumer goods. Main import partners are: China (17% of total), Albania (11.3%), United States (7.5%), France and Belgium.

Interest rates remain very high (ranging from 13% to 25%) despite government efforts to lower them. A "Wholesale Dutch Auction System" for foreign exchange trading was introduced in 2006, which has helped slow reserve losses while allowing the exchange rate to be more market determined. There are no restrictions to imports except those in the import ban list. There are also no legal barriers preventing entry into business, except the minimum qualifications required by the various professional bodies. Foreign companies seeking to do business in Nigeria are expected to do so with incorporated companies or otherwise incorporate their subsidiaries locally.

In its fifty years since independence, the country has had many years of military rule but since 1999, there has been a gradual return to democratic system of government. Only in April 2011, the general election was conducted with the re-election of the current president for another four years in office. Nigerian's political system remains fragmented and unstable (Olarinmoye 2008). Huge post election violence mainly in the northern part of the country trailed the just concluded April 2011 general elections. Since the return to democracy, the government has aimed at formulating regulations affecting the four major stages of the life of a business namely: starting a business, dealing with construction permits, registering property, and enforcing contracts. These indicators have been used by the government to analyse economic outcomes and identify which reforms have worked, where, and why.

Other areas important to business—such as the country's proximity to large markets, the quality of infrastructure services, the security of property from theft and looting, the transparency of government procurement, macroeconomic conditions, or the underlying strength of institutions—are also been addressed. All of these are part of the Nigeria Sub national Investment Climate Program, which supports state governments in improving their business environments. This program is the Nigerian government's response to its National Economic Empowerment and Development Strategy (NEEDS) and the Country Partnership Strategy between it, the U.K. Department for International Development (DFID), and the World Bank Group, which aim to create momentum for reform through dialogue between the private and public sectors in participant states, drive investments and non-oil growth in these states, and reduce income poverty through shared sustainable economic growth in Nigeria's non-oil sector.

3.2 History of Retailing in Nigeria – Pre-colonial & Colonial period

With a population of over 150 million people, Nigeria as a country exhibits considerable diversity in culture, religion, levels of development, income, and patterns of consumption. These patterns can be related to its somewhat turbulent history, from the early nineteenth century Jihad, which brought Islamic reformation to much of the north, through the great changes induced by colonial conquest and decolonisation, to the civil war in the 1960s, long years of military rule, subsequent oil boom, severe recession, and gradual return to democratic governance. Porter *et al.* (2007) had noted that studies done in trying to trace the development of modern retailing in Nigeria are mainly descriptive and impressionistic because of the absence of detailed official statistics. Some available records, however, show that by the nineteenth century, trade especially in northern Nigeria was exceedingly well established. Trade networks across central Sudan extended to this part of Nigeria (Hopkins 1973).

> "The development of modern retailing in the south, especially Lagos, dates from 1852 following on the bombardment of the town by the British which brought about the effective end to slave trading in this part of West Africa…which attracted European merchants. There were five of them by the end of 1852- Sandeman, Scala (an Italian), Grotte (a German), Diedrichsen (agents for Messrs. W. Oswald of Hamburg), and Johanssen. Two more arrived in 1853, namely Banner and McCoskry, and within a decade, there were several others". Greary, (1927) as cited in Mabogunje, (1964:305).

With reference to Proudfoot's (1937) classification of city retail structures in the U.S, made up of: (a) The Central Business District (CBD), (b) The Outlying Business Center, (c) The principal Business thoroughfare, (d) The Neighbourhood Business Street, and (e) The Isolated Store Cluster, Mabogunje (1964:309) observed that "by and large, the retail structure of Lagos shows these five categories". Notable foreign retail stores in operation included: Kingsway stores, Union Trading

Company Stores, A.G. Leventis Stores, G.B. Ollivant Stores, the K. Chellaram Stores, and Bhojson Stores.

There is clear evidence of the variety and complexity of wholesale and retail trade organisation in the accounts of travellers who visited the region. 'Trade was well organised with urban market-places subject to a degree of state control. There was widespread internal organisation of market-place sellers by products, and an associated tendency for special concentration' (Porter *et al.* 2007: 67). Northern Nigerian traders had contact with European trading companies well before the establishment of colonial rule at the beginning of this century (Mabogunje 1964). The Niger Company in particular, had been supplying European goods for some time to all the southern Emirates of the Fulani Empire. After the British expeditionary forces took control in the north in 1902 and 1903, European traders rapidly followed. Small new firms such as the London and Kano Company (established in 1905), and Greek entrepreneurs, led the field buying raw materials with merchandise (European imports) viewed as 'inducement goods' (Pedler 1974:285).

The completion of the railway line to Kano in 1911 and the sudden development of the groundnut trade resulted in a massive influx of European firms in the Kano region. By the close of 1913, eighteen expatriate and three coastal African firms had established trading stores in the city. In Maiduguri, the new capital of Borno, two Lebanese firms were established by December 1914. Then came a representative of the Manchester-based company Paterson-Zochonis in 1915, in 1920 a Greek, Marcopulos, and eventually the giants like the United African Company (UAC) who had ten canteens in Borno by 1937 (Hogendorn, 1978). The company stores dealt in both produce (purchase) and merchandise (sales) Porter *et al.* (2007).

In the 1940s and 1950s, European companies began to withdraw in a somewhat *ad hoc* fashion, from small-scale trading in up-country locations in northern Nigeria. This was a common development throughout West Africa, related to the costs of supervising small trading posts; their low rates of turnover, political pressure for indigenisation in retail trade, and the establishment of produce marketing boards (Williams 1976). The UAC, he further added, closed up most of its outlets over this period. John Holts, another of the major companies similarly withdrew from produce-buying and retailing and pursued a policy of urban concentration and import specialisation. The withdrawal of these firms and many others further intensified the pattern of merchandise trading through indigenous networks.

The construction of un-tarred roads connecting Maiduguri to the new district capitals (established by the British administration) acted as a further spur to growth in some centres. The massive expansion of consumer demand and merchandise trade in the colonial period meant that permanent, principally retail, stores became a viable proposition in many urban centres often run by stranger-traders: Lebanese, southern Nigerians, and even some Tripolitan Arabs (who had remained in the country after the demise of trans-Saharan trade at the beginning of the century) (Aker *et al.* 2010). The permanent shops described above represented only a limited outlet for European merchandise in northern Nigeria, where shop development occurred much more slowly than in the south. They complemented and supplemented the European trading posts by providing some additional services including credit which the European companies were not willing to give (Porter *et al.* 2007). So in spatial terms, the colonial period can be seen to have been characterised by considerable expansion of retail activity, leading to the setting up of permanent stores and other outlets.

3.3 Post-Independence Retailing in Nigeria

The Civil War which took place after Independence (1967-1970) had its effect on retail practice in the country (Oyefusi 2007). However, the oil boom which followed in the 1970s had many more pervasive effects. Urban incomes in the formal sector expanded dramatically. The Udoji pay award of 1974[8] gave public sector wage increases of up to 100 per cent, and the back-dating of this award by twelve months provided capital sums for employees at all levels. The boom continued and its overall effect was a widespread change in consumption patterns (Andrew and Beckman, 1985). For the first time there was a high-income population of a size which could be served directly by large, modern retail outlets. In the rural areas, there was a movement out of farming into trading, transport, and construction, where quick profits could be made. Agriculture stagnated and the agricultural export sector disintegrated. In a mere four years, 1974-78, manufactured goods imports into Nigeria rose from N512.1 million to N1,970.2 million, food imports from N155.2 million to N1,108.6 million; oils and fats from N3.6 million to N81.8 million (Watts 1983).

All of these led to the development of Western-style department stores and supermarkets (Watts 1983). UAC had several of the outlets. The existence of a considerable European population and an increasingly sophisticated Nigerian elite, well acquainted with retailing standards in Europe and (to a lesser extent) North America, made such ventures highly successful. These included A.G. Leventis (a firm which began retailing in the late 1940s) and a number of firms established by Indian families (with Nigerian nationality), including K. Chellaram, and Bhojsons. Others like the Bata Shoe Company, C.F.A.O. Stores, Kaycee Departmental Stores, Kingsway Chemists, G.B. Ollivant, and the chemist shops of the West African Drug Company (owned by John Holts) all were in operation (Mabogunje 1964; Onokerhoraye 1977). With the fall in oil prices, Nigeria's oil boom collapsed. Export earnings halved between 1981 and 1983, and the crisis subsequently deepened. Foreign exchange was increasingly insufficient for the imported inputs which local industries need to continue production. Factories closed temporarily or permanently and staff redundancies in

---

[8] Chief **Jerome Oputa Udoji** (1912–2010) was a Nigerian administrator, lawyer and businessman who was head of service in the former Eastern Region of Nigeria. In 1972, he headed a civil service commission to review standards of service and compensation within the civil service. The commission came up with this salary review for the public service.

private companies were soon followed by wage cuts and retrenchment in the public sector. This inevitably affected the health of the retail sector. (Porter *et al* 2007). One of the principal department store retailers in Nigeria – UAC's 'Kingsway stores' adopted a policy of very rapid withdrawal from the department store type outlet into new and developing interest – fast food. Leventis stores which were about the largest retailer also withdrew from the market and so did K. Chellaram, a retailer built on small supermarket outlets.

3.4 Government policies and regulations

The role of the government has been extremely significant for retail development in Nigeria (Nwokoye 1981). Ewah et al. (2010:6) noted that social, economic, technological, demographic and natural forces have contributed to the development of retail outlets in Nigeria creating major changes in the structure of retail competition. There are quite a number of government policies that directly affect the business practice generally in Nigeria and retail practice particularly; some of these include:

3.4.1 The Import Tariff

In September 2008, the Government of Nigeria announced a new tariff policy beginning in 2008 to run up until 2012 (CBN Report, 2009) which marked its second attempt at harmonizing its tariff with its West African neighbours under the Economic Community of West African States (ECOWAS) Common External Tariff (CET). The new tariff policy places imports into one of five tariff bands, namely, zero duty on special medicines not produced locally, industrial machinery and equipment (industrial machineries and equipment only attract zero duty if imported during the first year of the company's operation); 5-percent duty on raw materials and other capital goods; 10-percent duty on intermediate goods; 20-percent duty on finished goods; and 35-percent duty on luxury goods and finished goods in infant industries that the government would like to protect. The new tariff policy reduces the number of prohibited imports from 44 items to 26 items.

In the area of import requirement and documentation also, the Nigerian government commenced the implementation of a "Destination Inspection" plan on January 1, 2006. Under the destination inspection scheme, goods destined for Nigeria's ports would be inspected at the point of entry rather than at the point of shipment, which was hitherto the practice. Three companies, namely, Cotecna; SGS; and Global Scan, have been awarded a seven-year contract to act as inspection agents at Nigeria's seaports, border posts, and airports (CBN Report 2010). Bans prohibit the import of various goods including meat, fresh fruit, cassava, pasta, fruit juice in retail packs, toothpicks, soaps and detergents, biscuits, corn, pork products, vegetable oil, sorghum, millet, beer and non-alcoholic beverages and sugar confectionaries, textiles, plastics, and barite (see appendix for the full Import prohibition list).

3.4.2 Product Certification & Conformity Assessment

The Standards Organization of Nigeria (SON) registers and regulates standard marks and specifications. The National Agency for Food and Drugs Administration and Control (NAFDAC) provides testing and certification of imported and domestically produced food, drug, cosmetic, medical, water and chemical products. These organisations have information regarding conformity assessment.

3.4.3 Conversion and Transfer policies

The Foreign Exchange Monitoring Decree of 1995 opened Nigeria's foreign exchange market. In February 2006, in accordance with its plan to liberalize the foreign exchange market, Nigeria adopted a Wholesale Dutch Auction System (W-DAS) which gives banks more control of the foreign exchange market, though the Central Bank still retains its supervisory role over the market (Adamgbe 2006).

Foreign companies and individuals can hold domiciliary accounts in banks. Account holders have unlimited use of their funds, and foreign investors are allowed unfettered entry and exit of capital.

There is a $4,000 quarterly Personal Travel Allowance for foreign exchange and a $5,000 quarterly Business Travel Allowance per individual. Foreign exchange for travel is usually issued in travellers checks by commercial banks while some authorized dealers also issue pre-paid cards that can be used on Visa machines worldwide.

3.4.4 Performance Requirements/Incentives

Nigeria regulates investment in line with the World Trade Organization's Trade-Related Investment Measures (TRIMS) Agreement. Foreign companies now operate successfully in Nigeria's service sector, The Securities and Exchange Act of 1988, amended in 1999 and renamed the Investment and Securities Act, forbids monopolies, insider trading, and unfair practices in securities dealings (Nnona 2006). To meet performance requirements, foreign investors must register with the Nigerian Investment Promotion Commission, incorporate as a limited liability company (private or public) with the Corporate Affairs Commission, procure appropriate business permits, and (when applicable) register with the Securities and Exchange Commission. Manufacturing companies are sometimes required to meet local content requirements. Expatriate personnel do not require work permits, but they are subject to "needs quotas" requiring them to obtain residence permits that allow salary remittances abroad. Foreigners must obtain entry visas from Nigerian embassies or consulates abroad, seek expatriate position authorization from the Nigerian Investment Promotion Commission, and request residency permits from the Nigerian Immigration Service.

The government of Nigeria (GON) maintains many different and overlapping incentive schemes. The Industrial Development/Income Tax Relief Act No. 22 of 1971, amended in 1988, provides incentives to pioneer industries deemed beneficial to Nigeria's economic development and to labour-intensive industries, such as apparel (Suswam 2011). Companies that receive pioneer status may benefit from a non-renewable 100 percent tax holiday of five years (seven years if the company is located in an economically disadvantaged area). Industries that use 60 to 80 percent local raw materials may benefit from a 30 percent tax concession for five years, and investments employing labour-intensive modes of production may enjoy a 15 percent tax concession for five years. Additional incentives exist for the natural gas sector, including allowances for capital investments and tax-deductible interest on loans. The GON encourages foreign investment in agriculture, mining and mineral extraction (nonoil), oil and gas, and the export sector. In practice, these incentive programs meet with varying degrees of success.

For foreign organisations involved with technology transfer, the National Office of Industrial Property Act of 1979 established the National Office of Technology Acquisition and Promotion (NOTAP) to facilitate the acquisition, development, and promotion of foreign and indigenous technologies (Ukpabi 2009). NOTAP registers commercial contracts and agreements dealing with the transfer of foreign technology and ensures that investors possess licenses to use trademarks and patented inventions and meet other requirements before sending remittances abroad. With the Ministry of Finance, NOTAP administers 120 percent tax deductions for research and development expenses, if carried out in Nigeria, and 140 percent deductions for research and development using local raw materials. NOTAP recently shifted its focus from regulatory control and technology transfer to promotion and development. With the assistance of the World Intellectual Property Organization, NOTAP has established a patent information and documentation centre for the dissemination of technology information to end-users. The office has a mandate to commercialize institutional research and development with industry.

3.4.5   Government Policy on Protection of Property Rights

The government of Nigeria recognizes secured interests in property, such as mortgages. However, the recording of security instruments and their enforcement are subject to the same inefficiencies as those in the judicial system. The World Bank's publication, 'Doing Business 2008', Nigeria was ranked 51 of the 178 countries surveyed for registering property, requiring 14 procedures and 82 days at a cost of 22.2 percent of the property value. In 2005, Nigeria was classified as the least efficient of 145 countries surveyed, requiring 21 procedures and 274 days, at a cost of 27.2 percent of the property value. Fee simple property rights are rare. Most property involves long-term leases with certificates of occupancy acting as title deeds. Transfers are complex and must usually go through state governor's offices. In the capital; of Abuja, the Federal Capital Territory cancelled and began a process of reregistering all property allotments, refusing to renew those it deemed not in accordance with the city master plan. Buildings on these properties have frequently been demolished, even in the face of court injunctions. Therefore, acquiring and maintaining rights to real property are a major challenge.

Nigeria is a member of the World Intellectual Property Organization (WIPO) and a signatory to the Universal Copyright Convention, the Berne Convention, and the Paris Convention (Lisbon text). The Patents and Design Decree of 1970 governs the registration of patents, and the Standards Organization of Nigeria is responsible for issuing patents, trademarks, and copyrights. Once conferred, a patent conveys an exclusive right to make, import, sell, or use a product or apply a process.

The Trademarks Act of 1965 gives trademark holders exclusive rights to use registered trademarks for a specific product or class of products. The Copyright Decree of 1988, based on WIPO standards and U.S. copyright law, makes it a crime to export, import, reproduce, exhibit, perform, or sell any work without the permission of the copyright owner. In 1999 amendments to the Copyright Decree incorporate trade-related aspects of intellectual property rights (TRIPS) protection for copyrights, except provisions to protect geographical indications and undisclosed business information. Four TRIPS-related bills and amendments have been forwarded to the National Assembly. An amendment to the Copyright Act has been forwarded to the National Assembly. The bills would establish an Intellectual Property Commission, amend the Patents and Design Decree to make comprehensive provisions for the registration and proprietorship of patents and designs, amend the Trademarks Act to improve existing legislation relating to the recording, publishing, and enforcement of trademarks, and provide protection for plant varieties (including biotechnology) and animal breeds.

Patent and trademark enforcement remains weak, and judicial procedures are slow and subject to corruption. Relevant Nigerian institutions suffer from low morale, poor training, and limited resources (Waziri 2011). A key deficiency is inadequate appreciation of the benefits of Intellectual property protection among regulatory officials, distributor networks, and consumers. The over-stretched and under-trained Nigerian police have little understanding of intellectual property rights. The Nigerian Customs Service has received some WIPO-sponsored training, but officers who identify pirated imports are not allowed to impound offending materials unless the copyright owner has filed a complaint against a particular shipment, which happens rarely. Companies do not often seek trademark or patent protection, the enforcement mechanisms of which they consider ineffective. Nonetheless, recent efforts to curtail abuse have yielded results (Waziri 2011). The Nigerian police and Customs in conjunction with the Economic and Financial Crimes Commission have raided compact disc replicating plants, enterprises producing and selling pirated software and videos, and a number of businesses have filed high-profile charges against Intellectual property violators. Most raids involving copyright, patent, or trademark infringement appear to target small rather than large and well-connected pirates. Very few cases have been successfully prosecuted. Most cases are settled out of court, if at all. Primarily, the Federal High Court, whose judges are generally broadly familiar with intellectual property rights law, handles those adjudicated in court.

3.4.6   Foreign-Trade Zones/Free Ports

To attract export-oriented investment, the GON established the Nigerian Export Processing Zone Authority (NEPZA) in 1992. NEPZA allows duty-free import of all equipment and raw materials into its zones. Up to 25 percent of production in an export processing zone may be sold domestically upon payment of applicable duties. Investors in the zones are exempt from foreign exchange regulations and taxes and may freely repatriate capital. Of the very many export processing zones established under NEPZA, just two, in Calabar and Onne, function properly. In 2001, both were converted into free trade zones **(Calabar and Onne free trade zones)**, thereby freeing them from the export requirement. As a result, investment is quickly moving into Calabar, almost exclusively in industries that add value to imports. Another free trade zone, the **Tinapa Free Trade Zone** owned by the Cross River state government was commissioned during the first quarter of 2007. Oil and gas companies use the Onne free port zone as a bonded warehouse for supplies and equipment and for the export of liquefied natural gas.

Recently, the Government has encouraged private sector participation and partnership with the Federal Government and state and local governments under the Free Zones scheme. This has resulted in the establishment of specialized Zones like: **Lekki Free Trade** Zone - private initiative of a Singaporean holding company and the Lagos state government, and **Olokola free trade zone** between Ogun state and Ondo state in South-west Nigeria. Ondo and Ogun State Governments conceived the idea of developing a deep-seaport and Free Zone (FTZ) around Olokola in the coastline areas of Ondo and Ogun State. The project is proposed to be private sector led with a maximum of 40% government participation. Both of these free trade zones are still under construction and not yet operational. Up north in the country are other free trade zones still under development such as: **Kano free trade zone**, **Maigatari Border Free Trade Zone** located in Maigatari, which is a town at the borderline between Jigawa State in the northwest and the Republic of Niger, and the **Banki Border Free Trade Zone** which is located between the borders of Borno State in the northeast and the Republics of Chad and Cameroon, a project of the Borno State Government. All of these Zones have large expanses of land and easy access to international airports and some seaports as well. They are also equipped with police posts for security, pre-built warehouses for warehousing and storage of raw materials and good internal and external road networks. Other infrastructure that has been made available to these zones includes efficient telecommunication facilities, uninterrupted electricity and water supply, and central transit warehousing at major ports.

3.5   The political context of Nigeria

In the literature, very many scholars have acknowledged the importance of the political environment in the business practice especially in developing countries like Nigeria. In its fifty years since independence, the country has had a very turbulent political history with military interventions and failed democratic experiments. It is probably only in the last decade that some relative stability has been enjoyed politically.

In Roe's (2003) study which was based on an encompassing survey of seven countries, including the UK, USA, France, Germany, Italy and Japan, he provides evidence which indicates that politics interfere with firms' ownership structures and boardrooms' behaviour. While Roe's evidences were not gathered from developing countries, they nonetheless remain relevant. Indeed, the political environments of developing countries offer a more in-depth perspective, where managers and directors of large organizations constantly strive to reap maximum benefits from political office holders. Following independence, Nigerians, until about a decade ago, have lived predominantly within a political environment characterized by military dictatorship, incessant political turbulence and violence, political assassinations and elections marked by massive vote rigging, a situation that is believed to have been exhibited with the present national elections of April, 2011 which this researcher thinks led to the post election violence experienced especially in the northern part of the country. It is therefore not surprising that the past decades of unrest in the Nigerian polity have had serious implications for business conduct. A favourable and conducive atmosphere is needed for businesses to thrive. Indeed, organizations that are impeded by political turmoil and thus unable to function properly are less valuable to investors; therefore dampening political turmoil or insulating an organization from its effects constitutes a strong force in shaping an organization's ownership (Roe 2003).

This further brings to the fore the need to understand the correlations between a country's polity and business operations, especially foreign direct investments. Politics affects a firm in many ways, since it determines who owns it and the external finance it is able to obtain. It determines its growth and profitability potential and ultimately how authority is distributed within the firm (Roe 2003). It is believed that where the political structure of a country is strong and just, this helps to shape the behaviour of the firms and helps also to ensure the organisations operate according to the dictates of the law and ethically too. Indeed, in Nigeria, it is generally uncontested that top politicians (directly or indirectly) hold majority stakes in many organizations, which allows them to nominate board members and management. As a result, they are able to stifle the organization to suit their political interests and in other situations, use their political powers to benefit the organization. With such a setting, it is therefore not uncommon for some multinationals to compromise their ethical standards in order to do business. A good example is the recent conviction of Siemens and Halliburton for bribing a number of top government officials in Nigeria in order to win telecommunication and oil contracts. However, politically motivated corporate corruption takes different shapes and forms. Unlike Siemens which seemingly bribed government officials directly Punch News (2009), MNCs often pay bribes via "consultants" who negotiate the deal and win the business/contract. Consultants therefore act as the medium through which the bribes are paid to the corrupt government officials.

Nigeria has a high 'political instability index' (Fagbadebo 2007). The political structure of the country is polarised along ethnic lines such that the country runs its own peculiar style of democracy that is based on zoning rather than the popular wish of the populace[9]. (Salawu and Hassan 2011:28) noted that:

> "About five decades after Nigeria gained independence, the Nigerian diverse social structure in terms of her heterogeneity has not changed significantly. The diversity nature of the society has made identification with the 'nation' a difficult task. Today,

---

[9] : Rotation between the North and South of the country in the case of who becomes the President

identification is easier at both family and ethnic levels. A consequence of this is that many of the citizens may never develop a proper concept of nation. This kind of ethnic group relation signifies a negative dimension and which may mean much for the Nigerian political system".

The recent post election violence has been along this line with the loss of many lives and property mainly in the northern part of the country especially in the states where one of the presidential candidates originates from (The Guardian, 2011). Indeed, the private and public sector evolved and continues to evolve in an environment of systemic political corruption. The Nigerian polity strives amidst corruption and illegality thus inhibiting good business practices. Large organizations including multinationals can only triumph and remain competitive with significant political will and support. It has also become common for corrupt politicians and ex-office holders to become elected as board members, thus hindering good corporate governance, more so as they often bring their entrenched public corruption behaviour into the private sector (Adegbite and Nakajima 2009).

3.6   The economic context of Nigeria

Taking into account the remarkable rise in oil prices in recent times, there have been favourable forecasts of improved economic conditions in the country. However, despite her oil riches and promising economic fortunes, Nigeria is bedevilled by myriad economic problems which are entrenched in the political and economic structure of the country as well as in the psychology of the people Langer et al. (2009). Indeed, Nigeria advances but uncertainties abound. While other developing countries experience the same problems of harnessing their resource rich economy as Nigeria (Country Focus 2006), the efficiency of markets and consumer participation in the Nigerian economy is enormously limited by the lack of durable networks, stable electricity supply, potable water, efficient telecommunication facilities, as well as safe and efficient roads, railroads, and ports (Country Focus 2006). Small and medium enterprises capable of making immense contributions to the economy have been limited by the poor economic infrastructure of the country. Nigeria, with pervasive but inefficient government controls on economic activities and imperfect capital markets, therefore inherit a weak institutional structure. The government is making serious efforts to address these challenges. In 2007 the government initiated a development policy named 'the seven point agenda' which specifically focused on the areas of:

• Sustainable growth in the real sector of the economy
• Physical Infrastructure: Power, Energy & Transportation
• Agriculture
• Human Capital Development: Education & Health
• Security, Law and Order
• Combating Corruption, and
• Niger Delta Development

Nigeria's economy is a contradiction. Its managers claim the economy is growing, but Nigerians think otherwise as millions are unemployed. About 78 million of its 150million people are considered to be very poor (IMF Report, 2005). Presently, inflation and interest rates are growing, a paradox that the economic managers are finding difficult to reverse. In elementary economics, it is believed that when inflation is high, it is controlled by raising interest rate which would in turn discourage borrowing and ultimately help in checking inflation. But currently, the two are on the high side. The current inflationary rate according to the figures from the Bureau of Statistics is 12.8 per cent. Interest rate on the other hands hovers between 18 per cent and 21 per cent (CBN report, 2010).

A close look at the nation's economic development also shows a government that is over spending without visible results and also an economy where credit to the private sector is locked (Ovia 2008). This credit crunch has continued to retard development and worsen unemployment (World Bank Report, 2010). The World Bank says it is concerned about the rate of spending by the government, especially with the 2011 general elections. The warning is that if this continues and the spending is not linked to infrastructure development, it could destabilise the economy. Since the beginning of the year, the spill-over of global economic meltdown continues to hang-on (Oyesola 2010). Despite many laudable reforms, especially by the Central Bank of Nigeria to sanitise and stabilise the financial system and the banking sector, the economy is still slow to come out of the wood.

Just recently, two international rating agencies - Fitch Rating and Standard & Poor gave a contradictory ranking of the country's economic outlook for the year 2010. While Fitch rated the outlook negatively citing over-drawing from the Excess Crude Account and the Foreign Reserves, S&P gave a nod to the country's economic performance. The Excess Crude Account which balanced at $20 billion in January 2009 has been reduced to $3 billion and the foreign reserves down to $32 billion as against $64 billion two years ago (CBN, quarterly report, 2010).

However, compared to what obtained in the dark days of tyrannical military regimes in Nigeria, the last decade has seen some massive economic improvements in Nigeria which has led to the re-emergence of the middle class in the country. As noted by an official of the Nigeria Investment Promotion Council interviewed, "the exponential growth of Nigeria's telecommunications, financial, real estate and energy industries has resulted in the emergence of a fast growing middle class, especially in towns and cities. Many professionals employed in these and other related industries are characterised by their youthfulness, high earning power, and adoption of western lifestyles and culture, including leisure shopping. The products offered by most of these retailers therefore are not new to the consumers".

3.7   The socio-cultural Environment in Nigeria

Nigeria's position in the global economy is diminishing and its relation with the international community is at risk. The lack of adequate infrastructure and the existing problems with corruption make Nigeria less competitive in the international market Ovia (2008). Before the oil boom in 1973, Nigeria's position was comparable to several Asian countries which are now known as the Tiger economies (Versi, 2007:14). Instead of becoming an economic powerhouse, Nigeria's poor policies and corruption led the nation into an economic depression, which resulted in Nigerians having to continually prove their importance in the global market. Although Nigeria has a huge population and an abundance of natural resources, it is overwhelmed with individual wealth and power, taking its focus off building its economy and improving its infrastructure (Versi 2007). In view of its goal to be one of the top 20 economies in the world by the year 2020, Nigeria's main challenge is culture change. This challenge requires Nigeria to create and implement corruption laws, which will reduce the misuse of resources for personal gain. Nigeria has the ability to regain its economic strength, but must make changes in its culture to abolish flaws like corruption.

The country is still lacking adequate social infrastructure and basic amenities of life. Poverty, high rate of unemployment, armed robbery, bad roads, power shortages, amongst other vices, plagues the Nigerian populace. The result is a poor quality of life for majority of the populace, and the consequence of this is a general perception that everyone will have to (and must) "fend" for himself or herself as the government would not. This is the underlying cause of the endemic public and private enterprise corruption in the country. The implication of this is that the burden of citizens' welfare is being gradually bestowed on private corporations which have serious consequences for the burgeoning debate on corporate social responsibility (CSR). In this regard, CSR is evolving as a compulsory corporate philanthropy, especially in the deprived region of the oil rich Niger Delta. "The social structure of Nigeria can be described as "a fertile ground for bribery, corruption, idleness and the contrivance of get-rich quick attitude which are antithetical to hard work and discipline" (Ahunwan 2002: 271).

Again, while business connections can reduce agency conflicts by promoting efficient and informal information transfers, it can also constitute channels for favouritism (Kuhnen 2005). In Nigeria, business connections, especially through personal and family affiliations, interfere with the efficient management of corporations, resulting in serious cases of insider dealing, appointments to corporate directorships based on personal affinities, use of companies' properties by directors, managers and their associates for personal purposes, as well as leasing/selling personal and associates' properties to the company at exorbitant prices. Indeed, as with most developing countries, a corrupt social mind-set has engulfed both public and private enterprises allowing activities such as drug counterfeiting, environmental degradation, bribery, and corruption to become norms, such that doing things right has become an anomaly (Olebune 2006). Nigeria's 2020 vision is based on more than the abolishment of corruption and culture change although they are key elements; it also focuses on improving the management of its resources. Nigeria receives a steady flow of foreign investment for its oil and natural gas but most of its funds are misused instead of being reinvested.

3.8   The legal context in Nigeria

Nigeria has a complex three-tiered legal system composed of English common law, Islamic law, and Nigerian customary law. Most business transactions are governed by "common law" as modified by statutes to meet local demands and conditions. At the pinnacle of the judicial system is the Supreme Court, which has original and appellate jurisdiction in specific constitutional, civil, and criminal matters as prescribed by Nigeria's constitution. The Federal High Court has jurisdiction over revenue matters, admiralty law, banking, foreign exchange, other currency and monetary or fiscal matters. Debtors and creditors rarely have recourse to Nigeria's pre-independence bankruptcy law. In the Nigerian business culture, businessmen generally do not seek bankruptcy protection. Even in cases where creditors obtain a judgment against defendants, claims often go unpaid.

The public increasingly resorts to the court system and is more willing to litigate and seek redress. However, use of the courts does not automatically imply fair or impartial judgments. In the World Bank Report (2008)- 'Doing Business 2008', which surveyed 178 countries including Nigeria, concluded GON efforts have led to improvements in the way business is conducted, but was not among the top ten reformers, a position it occupied in the last publication. Regarding the enforcement of contracts, Nigeria was ranked 93 out of 178 countries surveyed. The report revealed that contract enforcement required 39 procedures and 457 days, the cost of which averaged 32 percent of the value of the contract. The Nigerian court system has too few court facilities, lacks computerized document processing systems, and poorly remunerates judges and other court officials, all of which encourages corruption and undermines enforcement.

Formal rules are the laws and regulations (North 1990) which governs behaviour. The corruption in the larger Nigerian society is seen to have eaten deep into the judicial system as well, such that a lot of bias exists in the legal system especially in the pronouncements of judges and justices in the courts. Without stability, judges become susceptible to the temptations of judicial corruption. "Corruption is based on some circumstances in the life of some people. This includes early deprivation in life and with an opportunity to acquire material things, any means justifies the end. It is also based on greed and above all, on lack of patriotism". The country of Nigeria has faced a fair share of dealings with judicial corruption and even to this day with the implementation of a fairly new government; the country is still trying to weed out the influences from the continually changing governments of the past. The development of corruption in the executive and legal branches has made its impact on the country.

Time and instability over decades has allowed corrupt government officials to have the opportunity to use their power to pressure the judicial branch officials to get their way. Opportunity and influence can cause a judge in Nigeria to lean toward the temptation because of a contribution of multiple factors they face in the legal system. Contributing factors include poor "compensation for judges, understaffing, poor equipment, bribery, special settlements, and a host of developmental factors decrease the reliability and impartiality of the courts". The compensation for judges is not very strong compared to money from bribes. The lowest ranking judge, like the Judge State Customary Court of Appeal makes an annual salary of $500.00 USD, and the highest judge position in the country, the Chief Justice of Nigeria does better but only makes an annually salary of $2,000.00 USD. Most bribes triple these salaries and have influenced court decisions in favor of the ones with money and power, Udobong, (2007). In October 2004, Nigerian judges, including Supreme Court judges, were arrested on charges of corruption including charges of accepting over thirty nine million naira (N39m) in bribes BBC News, (2004).

To battle against the widespread corruption and change the country's image, the Nigerian Judicial Council (NJC) has stepped in to correct the gross inadequacies brought on by the spread of corruption in the system and has decided to team up with the Independent Corrupt Practices Commission (ICPC) and Economic and Financial Crimes Commission (EFCC). All these organizations are working together in order to remove the entangled hold of corruption on the Nigerian legal system in hopes that it can one day develop into an independent and transparent judiciary system that the people would have pride in, UN Report (2003). In time, the Nigerian federal judicial commission hopes that it will be able to develop and complete their goal of fine-tuning their procedures to ensure that they have developed quality judges who are morally and intellectually strong enough to resist the temptations of corruption when they are appointed to the superior courts. This goal will take time but time allows everything to have the opportunity for change.

Nigeria needs a legal system which reflects and tackles the peculiar challenges posed by the institutional environments described above. This system must nonetheless remain competitive in attracting both domestic and foreign investments by not stifling the independent dynamism that underlies modern capitalism. The generality of the company law in Nigeria has traditionally laid down the "rules of the game" for the internal operation of the corporation (encompassing certain issues such as shareholder rights and the organizational structure) as well as its external relationships (such as the wide range of contracts that corporations make with various external actors including service users/customers, suppliers, distributors, and joint venture partners) which are underpinnings of good business practice.

Nevertheless, what Nigeria lacks, is the devotion and culture capable of enforcing these formal rights (Ahunwan 2002). In Nigeria, there has been a traditional disregard for the rule of law

(Ahunwan 1998), although recent governmental commitment, especially through the setting up of anti-corruption bodies, is creating a general awareness that the law is there to govern and must therefore be allowed to. While the current focus of governmental campaigns appears to concentrate on public office holders, it is, however, expected that the trend will proceed to confront some of the deep rooted and highly complex corruption perpetrated by managers, directors, and chief executives alike, as a result of laxity in law enforcement. As reported by Adegbite and Nakajima (2009) *"The problem in Nigeria is that of enforcement which is silent except when there is a public outcry"*.

The legal system is expected to set out the rules of the game and help protect businesses. As noted by Dimgba (2010), there is the urgent need for the Nigerian legal system to have competition law because of its importance in the liberalisation and development of the Nigerian economy. Though the retail sector of the Nigerian economy is just developing, experts like Megwua (1983); Dimgba (2010) believe that setting the structure now will help in the future to overcome some problems in the operations and activities of organisations. Some sectors of the economy like cement market, downstream petroleum sector, mobile telecommunications market, and pay-television market are already experiencing some difficulties as a result of the absence of competitive laws and regulations.

Megwa (1983) also noted that the foreign investors especially, believe that their investments in Nigeria are far from safe and not protected despite the existence legislations (both local and international). One example mentioned is that as contained in the constitution, the government may not nationalise, expropriate or take an investor's property, moveable or immovable, without enactment of a separate law and payment of adequate compensation. The fear of the investors is that the appropriate or adequate amount of compensation is to be determined by the court and it is not clear whether the court should determine the amount of compensation based on book value, fair value, replacement cost or going concern value or all of the above. Such important elements that go to determine the amount of foreign investment in the country are still not clearly laid out in the Nigerian situation.

3.9   Chapter Summary

This chapter has provided a good overview of the context for this present research – Nigeria. A brief overview of the country is first provided; explaining most of its important features and characteristics especially how this relates to business in the country. History of retail practice in Nigeria is traced before and during the colonial period, as well as post-independence retail practice in the country.

The various policies and regulations governing retailing and business generally in the Nigerian market are discussed so also the economic, political, socio-economic, and legal systems in the country. This present study recognises the importance of the effect of the wider institutional environment in business practice, hence the use of the institutional theory. This chapter has provided some better understanding of the institutional environment of the Nigerian market which will allow for a better understanding of the findings and arguments from this present study.

CHAPTER 4: CONCEPTUAL FRAMEWORK

Some sections of Chapter Two of this thesis discussed the importance of combining institutional theory and transaction cost analysis in the study of retail internationalisation particularly, the entry mode strategies of international retail firms operating in developing markets. The main objective of this chapter is to apply these frameworks to a specific context of retail internationalisation – entry mode strategies in a bid to help answer the research questions as set out for this study. This chapter draws from the literature on institutional theory; transaction cost analysis and international retailing, and proposes a conceptual framework for examining the entry mode choices of international retail firms. This framework addresses the effect of company characteristics and the host institutional environment on the firm's choice of market entry. The underpinning dimensions of both theories acknowledging that retail operations are socially embedded and differ across countries due to differences in the institutional environment, proposes that the entry mode choice of an international retail firm are affected by how well the retailer's practices are in line with the host market conditions as well as the resources and capabilities available to the internationalising retail firm.

4.1. Introduction

International entry mode strategies have been explained as attracting the interest of researchers in international business and practitioners alike, because of their importance to the survival of foreign oriented firms. Entry mode has also been identified as one of the core components of the internationalization concept as such research on firm's internationalization process will to a large extent include the international entry-mode choice. Second, the choice of the correct entry mode for a particular foreign market is one of the most critical decisions for firms in international marketing (Wind and Perlmutter 1977). Third, the theoretical contributions have been more advanced in the area of foreign entry mode than in other topics of the firm's internationalization process (Alexander and Doherty 2009). Several frameworks identifying different constructs that influence the entry mode decision have been developed and empirically tested. It is, however, interesting to note that despite the very many theoretical developments, existing literature on foreign market entry has not reached an agreement on which conceptual framework and constructs should be used to explain a firm's foreign market entry mode (Anderson 1997). Hill et al. (1990) emphasized the need for a unifying conceptual framework within which different factors can be placed and the relationships between them analysed.

Some of these frameworks are as discussed earlier in Chapter Two of this thesis. A common denominator that is extracted from all of these frameworks is the fact that very many factors come into play in the determination of the market entry mode choices of international retail firms, which can be broadly classified as internal (company related) and external (environmental related) with some of these only acting as moderators in the eventual decision process. Wu and Zhao (2007: 184) noted that "To achieve the objective of internationalization, a company should take three factors into account and then choose appropriate entry modes. These three factors are firm factors, environmental factors and moderators". Sekaran (1992) defines a conceptual framework as a logically developed, described, and elaborated network of associations among concepts that have been identified through theoretical and empirical research. The relationships between the independent concepts, the dependent concepts, and where applicable, the moderating or intervening concepts, are elaborated, usually with an indication of whether the relationships are positive or negative.

Available literature shows that scholars hold a variety of views in regard to the phenomenon, foreign entry modes (Musteen *et al.* 2009; Slangen *et al.* 2009). This study is based therefore on the perception of the researcher based on knowledge gained from various theories developed in the field so far. The framework developed in this study is therefore an indication of how this researcher perceives the phenomena being investigated (market entry mode choices), and an understanding of the factors influencing the process.

4.2   Firm characteristics and entry strategies

This study is hinged on the TCA especially the extended version (which uses the firm level as unit of analysis, instead of individual transaction, and also puts in non-transaction cost benefits flowing

96

from increased control or integration, such as co-ordination of strategies in multinational corporations (Kobrin 1988, Hill et al. 1990), to extend market power (Teece 1981), and to obtain a larger share of the foreign enterprise's profit (Anderson and Gatignon 1986) as well as the institutional economics view. The TCA has been seen to be especially effective in explaining vertical integration decisions, and predicting entry mode (including the hybrid forms) for not only manufacturing firms but service firms as well (a section which retail firms come under) Erramilli and Rao (1993). The modified TCA predicts a positive relationship between asset specificity and propensity for high-control entry modes. The strength of this relationship is, however, contingent upon the influence of moderating factors, such as external uncertainty, internal uncertainty and firm size.

As earlier discussed, firms exist because there are transaction costs of using the price mechanism. These costs arise in connection with defining property rights, negotiating, monitoring and enforcing contracts. Doherty (1999) writing on entry mode strategies of firms noted that:

> "Internalization theorists focus on the transaction costs arising from 'natural' market imperfections, that is imperfections that are due to the fact that the neo-classical assumptions of perfect knowledge and perfect enforcement are not realized (Teece 1981; Dunning and Rugman 1985). Given market imperfections, transaction costs can become so high that it is more efficient for the firm to create and use an internal market than to incur the prohibitive transaction costs of the external market (Hill and Kim 1988). Consequently, internal co-ordination (i.e. the firm) is used because of the incentive to bypass imperfect external markets".

"Unanticipated changes in circumstances surrounding an exchange" are environmental uncertainties Noordewier, John, and Nevin, (1990:82) identified as affecting governance mechanisms. High levels of environmental uncertainty increase the costs of adapting contractual agreements. As noted also by Williamson (1985) that when faced with the need to adapt to an uncertain environment, a firm will seek to minimize its transaction costs through vertical integration. So the high cost of monitoring contracts, which in international retailing can come in several forms, favour the use of an independent entry mode by the international retailer.

Entry by acquisitions or JVs takes the form of pooling resources between a foreign entrant and a local firm. In contrast, Greenfield projects do not provide access to resources embedded in local firms. The choice of entry mode thus depends on whether and to what degree foreign entrants require such resources. In developing economies, investing firms usually require context-specific resources to achieve competitive advantages (Delios and Beamish 1999; Meyer and Peng 2005). Strategic management literature on entry strategies has focused on the characteristics of resources to be transferred (Kogut and Zander 1993) and the characteristics of the investing firm (Anderson and Gatignon 1986; Hennart and Park 1993). This suggests a need to complement this literature by considering the characteristics of these sought of resources. However, the likelihood of facing malfunctioning markets varies with the characteristics of the resources sought. A key distinction in the literature is between *tangible* assets (such as real estate) and *intangible* assets (such as brands).

The transaction cost literature has analysed entry strategies with respect to the assets, especially knowledge based assets, which an investor would transfer to the new subsidiary (Anderson and Gatignon 1986; Hennart and Park 1993). A contract would be preferred if the resource contributions of at least one partner can be sold in a reasonably efficient market (Buckley and Casson 1998). Three arguments have been put forward to suggest that certain types of resources are less suitable to market exchange. While this has typically focused on resources to be transferred, Doherty (2000), Meyer and Peng (2005), extend this line of thought by suggesting that the logic of the argument equally applies to resources *sought*. First, *information asymmetries* are a classic source of market failure. The market for information is prone to failure because buyers cannot assess the quality of the information prior to the exchange. However, once the information is known to both parties, buyers no longer have the incentive to reveal their true valuation of the information (Arrow 1971; Akerlof 1970). The prevalence of information asymmetries between buyers and sellers thus has long been a core motivation for the internalisation of transactions within firms (Buckley and Casson

1976; Casson 1997) and for the choice of a JV (Buckley and Casson 1998; Brouthers and Hennart 2007) or an acquisition (Hennart and Park 1993) as a mode of entry.

Second, *asset specificity* is at the core of Williamson's (1985) transaction cost based explanation of organization forms, which has been applied to entry modes extensively following Anderson and Gatignon (1986). Essentially, the more business partners invest in resources specific to a transaction, the more they create interdependencies that expose them to potential opportunistic behaviour (Brouthers and Hennart 2007). This threat may inhibit transactions or encourage firms to internalize operations. Asset specificity arises in FDI in particular from partner-specific learning processes. Third, *tacitness of knowledge* inhibits its transfer unless instructor and receiver interact directly in a form of learning by doing, but this can make the transfer of knowledge very costly (Teece 1977). Such learning by interpersonal interaction is difficult to organize via markets, and may be encouraged more effectively within organizations (Kogut and Zander 1993). In consequence, interactions that involve the exchange of tacit knowledge may be internalised, again favouring acquisition or JV over Greenfield entry. All three lines of the argument are more relevant for intangible assets than for tangible assets (Bruton, Dess, and Janney 2007). Asset specificity can, in principle occur when resources are either intangible or tangible, while information asymmetries and costs of tacit knowledge are challenges that arise from knowledge-components of resources, which are likely to be higher for intangible assets. Entrants may thus prefer to acquire another firm with the pertinent resources, but where such acquisitions are not feasible—for instance in contexts with weak institutions—they are more likely to opt for JV. Therefore, scholars like (Bruton, *et al.* 2007; Musteen *et al.* 2009) would argue that *the high cost of negotiating and monitoring contracts in the international market will call for the use of an independent mode of market entry for foreign retail firms.*

The arguments suggest that institutions discriminate primarily between JV and acquisition/ Greenfield, while resource needs primarily discriminate between Greenfield and JV/acquisition.

99

(Kogut and Singh 1988; Chang and Rosenzweig 2001; Elango and Sambharya 2004) note that not enough theoretical arguments for effects separating the various entry modes have been provided. However, how do the institutional and resource effects *interact* with each other?

Firm are known to have assets both tangible and intangible. Experts have written that the possession of intangible assets such as managerial technology and retail formats by retail firms are inherently difficult to protect and this difficulty becomes even more acute in developing international retail markets (Alexander 1997; Burt *et al* 2008). Given the presence of significant intangible assets in international retailing markets, and the focus on managerial technology and trading relationships, the view here is that w*here an international retail firm has a number of intangible assets like unique retail concepts, technology, and brand, it will enter foreign markets with the independent mode of entry.*

4.2.1   Environmental factors and entry strategies

Retailers' international expansion leads to the transfer of retail management technology or the establishment of international trading relationships across regulatory, economic, social, and cultural boundaries (Alexander 1995). In this sense, the external environment including cultural, legal, political, and economic factors affects retailers' decisions as to where, when, and how to expand into foreign markets (Vida & Fairhurst 1998).

4.2.1.1.   Formal institutional structures

North (1990:3) defines institutions as "the humanly devised constraints that structure human interaction". Similarly, Scott (2001:33) defines institutions as "regulative, normative, and cognitive structures and activities that provide stability and meaning to social behaviour". In this sense, institutions can be broadly classified as formal and informal ones. Variables such as: the legal, political and economic systems in a country define the formal institutional factors whilst other variables like: market size, cultural and retail market distance, market development stage, habits and inertia, etc. all make up the informal institutional factors. Ingram and Silverman (2002) write that there is need to bring these variables to the forefront in order to gain a deep understanding of

100

strategic behaviour and firm performance even in developed economies and that its deficiency becomes more striking when probing into emerging economies (Narayanan and Fahey 2005). In other words, when markets work smoothly in developed economies, "the market-supporting institutions are almost invisible", according to McMillan (2007), who goes on to argue that when markets work poorly in emerging economies, "the absence of strong formal institutions is conspicuous".

Legal regulations in the home and host country represent the strongest environmental pressures faced by organizations (Scott 2001). Governments might formulate policies and laws regarding retailing. For example, European governments have strict regulations on land planning (e.g. PPG6 in England), pricing (e.g. Loi Galland in France), store opening hours (e.g. Ladenschlussgesetz in Germany), and store size requirement (e.g. Loi Raffarin in France). These rules not only stimulate many European retailers' aggressive expansion into other countries but also slow down foreign retailers' expansions (e.g. Wal-Mart) in European markets (Huang and Sternquist 2007). A country with a strong rule of law is defined as one having ''sound political institutions, a strong court system, and provisions for orderly succession of power'' (PRS Group 1996). The rule of law is codified by a country's governance infrastructure, which represents ''attributes of legislation, regulation, and legal systems that condition freedom of transacting, security of property rights, and transparency of government and legal process'' (Globerman & Shapiro 2003:19). Thus, the host country's governance infrastructure reduces retailers' uncertainty about what legal protection they can expect from the legal system.

However, the rule of law is a double-edged sword. On the one hand, rules establish a stable structure to reduce uncertainty (Meyer 2001). On the other hand, foreign countries' restrictions can be barriers to retail firms (Vida *et al.* 2000). In a new situation, a rule or absence of a rule can become a constraint, a limiting factor (Common 1931). When a country's governance structure is weak, its protection function is undermined. A weak governance structure usually results in political

101

and economic instability—a common phenomenon in a developing or emerging economy (Hoskisson, Eden, Lau, & Wright, 2000). Globerman and Shapiro (2003) find that countries that fail to achieve a minimum threshold of effective governance are unlikely to receive any foreign direct investment (FDI). Countries with a weak governance infrastructure have to improve to be able to attract foreign investment. The example of China's experience in attracting foreign investment illustrates this phenomenon. As cited by Tse *et al.* (1997), in the absence of laws and regulations, foreign investors were less willing to come to China. In the past two decades, China has introduced dozens of laws and regulations that reduce the level of risk and uncertainty for foreign firms. These rules increase the confidence level of foreign firms investing in China. In addition, Meyer (2001) finds that entrants are more likely to establish WOS in transitional economies such as Eastern Europe that have progressed furthest in institutional reform. Therefore, it is predictable that as the host country's governance infrastructure gets stronger, retailers are more likely to commit more resources. However, if, along with the strengthening of the governance structure, the rule of law gets more and more restrictive, retailers may perceive the environment as unfavourable again, and as a result, postpone entry or prefer entering using low resource modes. Yiu and Makino (2002) posit that the multinational companies choose a JV over a WOS when the regulations of the host country get more restrictive.

As early as 1970, Hollander, in his book "Multinational Retailing," suggested that retailers' international exploration could be stimulated by government policies in either the home or host country. Government regulations and restrictions may force firms to look abroad for growth (Dimitratos, Lioukas, & Carter 2004). The comparison of internationalization activities of European retailers and US retailers may be an illustration of the influences of home country government regulations on retailers' foreign expansions. For example, Germany and France, while being the largest markets in Europe, have very stringent restrictions on the retail sector. These government regulations partially account for the fact that retailers from France and Germany have been most active outside their home countries. In 2004 and 2005, half of the Top 20 retailers with largest sales outside their home countries were from these two countries (Badillo & Kidder 2007; Naro 2005). European retailers are also among the earliest to internationalize. For example, Carrefour was founded in 1959 and has been in the international area since 1969. In contrast, the United States has the most lenient retail regulations of any country in the world.

This advantage partially explains why the US retailers have been relatively inactive and slow to expand internationally compared to their European counterparts. For example, Wal-Mart, while being the world's largest retailer, is a latecomer to the international arena, having begun its foreign expansion in 1991 in Mexico, almost three decades after its founding in 1962 (Arnold *et al.* 2001). In 2005, US retailers dominated the list of the largest single-country operators and captured seven of the Top 10 slots (Badillo & Kidder 2007). Similar to European retailers such as Metro AG and Auchan who were forced to look beyond domestic borders for growth because of the stifling regulations in their home countries (Naro 2005), Japanese retailer Sogo's enthusiasm for overseas expansion was also attributed in part to the limitations placed on the opening of new stores in Japan (Sternquist 2007). In these cases, retailers seeking growth in other countries usually had unutilized resources ready to invest.

When a retailer considers expanding into a certain country, it first takes into account this country's regulations on foreign investment, if there are any. There are two primary types of regulatory forces, imposition and inducement (Grewal & Dharwadkar 2002). Imposition is coercive, which means that retailers have to follow the law. For example, the Large-scale Retail Store Law (LSRS) in Japan significantly impeded the expansion of Toys 'R' US (Evans & Mavondo 2002). Retailers in Germany have to follow at least four major strands of regulation: mandated union representation on corporate boards (*Mitbestimmung* or co-determination), restricted store hours (*Ladenschlussgesetz*), constrained pricing flexibility (GWB) and limits on big box retail construction (Badillo, Naro, & Spiwak 2005). India currently bans foreign retail direct investment, preventing foreign retailers such as Wal-Mart, Carrefour, and Tesco from investing in and operating their own stores. If a retailer perceives the regulations of the host country as unfavourable, the host country market becomes less attractive to the retailer, and therefore, no entry or later entry will be preferred. Further, in some cases where market entries are decided in spite of unfavourable situations in the host country, low control entry modes that involve relatively low resource commitments are often adopted (Kim & Hwang, 1992). In the case of India, as a result of regulations imposed by the government, many foreign retailers now have entered India through franchise agreements (Wonacott 2006), a low-control and low resource commitment entry alternative. On the other hand, a host country may provide strong inducements in order to attract firms (Hollander 1970; Meyer & Scott 1992). For example, Hollander (1970) reports that the Argentine government once issued a decree providing tax and import benefits for supermarkets, sparking the entry of the US firms into the Argentine supermarket industry. In China, many special economic zones (SEZs) along the coast provide tax incentives and lower foreign exchange restrictions for potential overseas investors, attracting foreign firms who are motivated to reap the benefits of investment in China (Grewal & Dharwadkar 2002; Ma & Delios 2007). In such a case, a retailer choosing low control entry modes may be limited in its gains or may have to share benefits with other parties. To avoid these situations, the retailer may choose high control entry modes whenever possible. Using a longitudinal sample of 2998 foreign business activities in China between 1979 and 1993, Tse *et al.* (1997) conclude that foreign firms operating in China prefer WOS or JV to licensing.

4.2.1.2.   Informal institutional structures

Normative mechanism gives priority to moral beliefs and internalized obligations as the basis for social meaning and social order (Scott & Christensen 1995). In this conception, organizational behaviour is guided by not only self-interest and expedience, but also an awareness of one's role in a social situation and a desire to behave appropriately in accordance with other's expectations and internalized standards of conduct (Scott 2001). According to Simon (1959), decisions are socially and culturally determined. The cultural distance that exists between the home and host country

104

affects the choice of foreign expansion form (Kogut & Singh 1988). A great deal of research supports the existence of significant cultural similarities between the home and host country will result in high control entry modes (e.g. Gatignon & Anderson 1988; Kim & Hwang 1992). In the case of significant cultural distance, retailers may perceive high risk in entering a foreign market and feel intense pressure deriving from the need to serve customers who differ culturally from those to whom the retailer has become accustomed.

Accordingly, they may prefer no entry. Alternatively, retailers may choose to enter countries with cultures that are similar to the home market before entering countries with dissimilar cultures (Vida 2000). Thus, UK retailers have favoured Ireland; French retailers have favoured Spain; and Japanese retailers have favoured Hong Kong and Taiwan (Sternquist 2007). In these cases, retailers may choose high control modes because a high level of understanding of norms and values already exists; therefore, local partners are less necessary.

Norms in a society influence organizational and individual behaviour (Simon 1959). International retailers are subject to norms from not only the national culture, but also the retail industry in the host country. Thus, in addition to cultural distance, retail market distance is one of factors affecting retailers' internationalization decision-making (Gripsrud & Benito 2005). Retail market distance may be defined as the difference between the market conditions of the home market and that of the foreign market in the host country. Two aspects may be involved. One is target customer preference, and the other is retail practice. For a retailer who sells consumer goods, the difference in consumer preferences between target customers from the home and host countries is probably one of the most important factors to take into consideration. The boundary-spanning role of retailers requires that retail offerings be adapted in the new environment (Vida et al., 2000). McDonald's, when expanding into India, had to eliminate meat from its menu. Toys "R" Us changes its merchandising selections in the overseas stores. About 20% of its merchandising assortment is chosen for local consumer interests; for example, it introduced porcelain dolls for the Japanese market and wooden toys for Germans (Sternquist 2007). A given retail format may also need to be adapted to new consumer environments in order to "fit" into local situations (Pellegrini 1991). In Argentina, Wal-Mart did not initially adapt its retail format to the local consumer preference and learned valuable lessons there (Cited in Mitra & Golder 2002). Similarly, Carrefour's hypermarket failure in the US resulted partially from its merchandising assortments and low-key French advertising approach that did not meet American consumers' preferences (Tordjman 1988).

Moreover, retail management practice in the foreign retail industry represents another kind of norm to which retailers must conform. Ignoring the norm may result in failures. An example is the case of Sephora as illustrated by Sato (2004). Sephora was established in 1973. Since 1993 they have begun to develop large cosmetics stores with a self-service selling system and have been quite successful in Europe and the US In 1998, Sephora entered into the Japanese market with a WOS—Sephora Japan. It was a retail chain of the high-class cosmetics stores with a self-service selling system. However, Japanese cosmetic manufacturers always supply retailers with luxury cosmetics on the condition that the manufacturer salespersons must explain the products to consumers face-to-face. Sephora's entry into Japan had a major disruptive impact on the Japanese cosmetics distribution system. Japanese manufacturers opposed Sephora's operation and refused to supply the products. As a result, Sephora had to close all its stores in Japan in 2001 because of the lack of a full range of merchandise.

Retailers expanding into a foreign market that has a high level of retail market distance compared to its home market may experience normative pressures. In order to mitigate the normative pressures and "legitimately fit" into the new environment, retailers may choose adaptation, a salient feature of the normative mechanism (Scott 2001). However, adaptation is a long term and accumulative process. Retailers may seek local partners to accelerate the process; hence, low control entry modes may be preferred. With the help of local partners, the foreign retailer gains isomorphism legitimacy through adaptation. On the contrary, a high level of retail market similarity requires less adaptation, and less likelihood of local partners.

There is increasing evidence that a firm's business activities are influenced by its home society characteristics (Kogut & Singh 1988; Tse *et al.* 1997). According to Hofstede's (1980) typology, four major dimensions of the national culture may have impact on retail firms' behaviours. Power distance refers to how well societies tolerate inequality. Societies with small power distance indices advocate relative equality in organizations and institutions. On the contrary, retailers from countries possessing large power distance attributes are more likely to prefer high control in their relationships with others. Retailers from large power distance cultures may seek control by adopting high control entry modes when expanding overseas. Tse *et al.* (1997) find that foreign firms from high power distance countries prefer equity-based entry modes to non-equity entry modes.

A culture with the characteristic of individualism focuses on free competition and leadership. Retailers from individualistic societies tend to take initiatives independently of others. Therefore, they are more aggressive and prefer early entry and high control to maximize the return. Uncertainty avoidance means risk averse. Firms from a low uncertainty avoidance culture tend to be more venturesome and take more risks. They are more likely to engage in exploration of novel and risky situations. High-resource commitment involves new or ambiguous circumstances, and thus, are more risky decisions for retailers. In contrast, low-resource commitments are less risky and therefore, are more preferred by retailers from high uncertainty avoidance societies. For example, Pan and Tse (2000) find that firms from high uncertainty avoidance cultures favour non-equity modes instead of equity modes.

The fourth cultural value dimension identified by Hofstede was that of masculine versus feminine values. This dimension indicates the extent to which dominant values in a society tend to be assertive and look more interested in things than in concerning for people and the quality of life.

The Masculinity and Femininity dimension describes how Masculine cultures tend to be ambitious and stress the need to excel. Members of these cultures have a tendency to polarize and consider big and fast to be beautiful (Rinne, et al, 2010). Firms from such cultures would want the independent mode of entry. Feminine cultures on the other hand consider quality of life and helping others to be very important; in this case, small and slow are considered to be beautiful (favouring the use of collaborative entry modes). Feminine cultures emphasize people, the quality of life, helping others, preserving the environment, and not drawing attention to oneself" (Nakata & Sivakumar, 1996: 64).

There is also a fifth cultural dimension, long-term versus short-term orientation; and following the study by Minkov (2007), a sixth cultural dimension, indulgence versus restraint, have since been added to Hofstede's list of cultural dimensions (Hofstede, Hofstede, & Minkov, 2010). Thrift and perseverance are associated with a long-term orientations, whereas respect for tradition and fulfilment of social obligations are associated with a short-term orientations. It is most likely therefore to see firms from countries with short-term orientation favouring the collaborative mode of market entry. Indulgence refers to a tendency toward the free gratification of human desires. On the opposite pole, restraint refers to the belief that gratifying one's desires needs to be curbed and social norms regulated. So just like the case of firms from countries with short-term orientation, this restraint dimension would make the firms to adopt the collaborative modes of market entry whilst firms from cultures with the indulgence dimension would prefer the use of the independent entry mode strategy.

In another dimension, today and tomorrow's choices are said to be shaped by the past (North 1990:7). Not only is the decision socially determined, it is also historically located (Simon 1959). Decisions are not independent they are inseparable from the result or performance linked to previous decision-making Forest & Mehier (2001). The cognitive mechanism explains why a global retailer such as The Body Shop generally uses the same entry mode during international expansion. From a cognitive perspective, organizations possess habits and inertia. As Porter (1990:580) notes:

"Firms would rather not change. Past approaches become institutionalized in procedures and management controls". According to North (1990), organizations tend to use investment modes consistently. For instance, Lu (2002) observed a strong tendency of intra-organizational imitative behaviour among Japanese multinationals as to foreign entry mode choice; this intra-organizational imitative behaviour is called "parent isomorphism" by Davis *et al*. (2000:243). The primary way that the internal institutional environment can influence entry mode choice is through organizational imprinting, which means that once a practice or decision has been chosen and implemented, the likelihood of alternatives being considered and used in future decisions will be reduced (Lu 2002). Frequently, organizational habits and inertia preclude rational changes Grewal & Dharwadkar (2002). Over time, the decisions are institutionalized and become taken for granted Yiu & Makino (2002). Therefore, we posit that the imprinting influence of the entry mode used by a retailer in its earlier entries will result in the same entry mode in later entries especially when the situations are similar to the past.

Again, it has been observed that firms do not exist in isolation but are connected to each other in a network context, Anderson (2002). As such, the decisions of firms are influenced by others' actions. Prior decisions or actions by other firms increase the legitimacy of similar decision and actions. Uncertainty encourages imitation (North, 1990). Firms tend to follow similar firms (such as competitors) that they perceive to be more legitimate or successful than themselves in order to reduce uncertainty Grewal & Dharwadkar (2002). Further, firms can learn from not only their own experience but also the experience of others and from what is happening in their surroundings Sengupta (2001). Strategic choice theories suggest that imitation can be a strategic response to competitor activities, whereby late movers take advantage of the fact that the risk and the costs associated with a new situation have been absorbed by the first-movers Lieberman & Montgomery (1988). A retailer can decide which country to enter by following other retailers. China has been one of the most popular investment destinations in the world for more than one decade.

One motivation for foreign firms investing in China is to follow their competitors' move to China, Grub & Lin (1991). Meanwhile, "organizations within the same population facing the same set of environmental constraints will tend to be isomorphic to one another and to their environment because they face similar conditions", Dacin, (1997:48). When considering a totally unknown foreign area in which little similarity to previous practices is found, retailers will naturally avoid or try to postpone the consideration of the market entry first. However, if the retailer decides to expand into this new area and has no past experience to rely on, the retailer may resort to other retailers' experience—that is, the retailer will mimic others' expansion behaviours. For example, Ahold's expansion into Latin America was inspired by "the super-normal 'first mover' returns on the investments of Carrefour in emerging markets such as Brazil and Argentina" Wrigley & Currah (2003:226). Carrefour entered Brazil in 1975 and Argentina in 1982 through JV. Ahold's entry into Brazil (1996) and Argentina (1998) also used JV modes. There are two major mimic behaviours: frequency-based and trait-based, Haunschild & Miner (1997). Frequency-based imitation refers to the tendency to imitate the behaviours that have been adopted by large numbers of other retailers, whereas trait-based imitation focuses on the decisions or practices adopted by other successful retailers. Usually, more prestigious firms are more likely to be imitated. For example, Lu (2002) found that more successful companies are more frequently imitated by others in Japan—a phenomenon called "follow the leader" syndrome. Both frequency and success may provide justifications for a retailer to use an entry mode used by other retailers entering into the same area.

4.3   Combined effect of environmental factors and firm resources on entry strategies

Meyer *at al.* (2009) explained that to understand how the two dimensions of institutions and resources interact, a consideration of two extreme cases is important. They noted that if institutions are very weak and thus fail to ensure even modest efficiency of markets, foreign entrants would not be able to rely on markets to access local resources. Under such conditions, acquisition may be prohibitively costly because of the inefficiency of financial markets. Moreover, in this situation it is likely that the resources of the acquired firm could not be properly valued, and their integration

110

would be challenging. Hence, foreign entrants in need of local resources would prefer the creation of a new entity in partnership with a local firm, with both partners contributing selected resources and sharing control.

The above situation would apply to both tangible and intangible resources. In the opposite extreme case, where strong institutions make markets highly *efficient*, foreign entrants would probably be able to use contracts to arrange most transactions. Thus, Greenfield entry becomes highly feasible. In this situation, acquiring resources in the form of tangible assets would not posit substantial challenges. However, the three sources of market failure outlined earlier would still affect transactions in intangible resources. For example, transactions in goods or services with a high content of knowledge would be potentially subject to information asymmetries (Buckley and Casson 1998), asset specificity (Williamson 1985), or costly transfer of tacit knowledge (Kogut and Zander 1993). However, under strong institutions, the market for corporate control is relatively efficient and enables firms to engage in acquisition. Hence, we expect that under strong institutions, acquisitions would be more likely to be used when foreign entrants seek intangible resources held by local firms, while Greenfield operations are appropriate when relatively fewer local resources are required, or when resources are tangible and can be acquired or accessed using market transactions. Meyer *et al* (2009) conclude that overall, it is expected that a significant moderating effect of intangible resource needs on the institutional effect that is opposite to the direct effect, while the corresponding moderating effect of tangible resources may not be significant.

4.4   Conceptual Model of International Retailers' choices

Following from the above discussions therefore, the view is that the entry mode choice chosen by an international retailer as it considers entry into an emerging market is largely determined not only by the characteristics and resources of the firm, but also by the various formal and informal rules in practice in the host market. The eventual success of such a firm can be seen as the ability of the retail firm to gain legitimacy from all the relevant social actors in the field of retailing in such host markets. This differs from a purely market orientation approach where retailers focus mainly on consumers and competitors as the relevant social actors. Although consumers are usually key social actors for retailers in every country, other social actors must also be considered for the survival of the retailer in the host market. All of the above views and arguments are summarised and presented in the conceptual model below:

Figure 4.1 Conceptual Model of Entry mode Choices of international retailers.

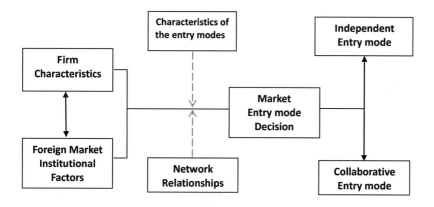

4.5. Understanding the model

The above framework summarises the views of scholars (Driscoll 1995; Erramilli, & Rao, 1993; Kim *et al.* 2002; Wu and Fang Zhao 2007; Tseng and Lee 2010) who all agree that a diverse range of situational influences could bear on a firm's desire for certain entry mode choice. The emphasis is that there are no optimal foreign market entry modes under all conditions. Therefore, a firm cannot just consider an institutionalizing mode; it needs to consider the characteristics of modes, the firm factors, environmental factors and other factors when it chooses entry mode. This framework shows factors that influence the entry mode choice of an international retail firm are firm specific, and also environmentally determined. The factors from these two broad sources interact and are

112

moderated by such other factors as the characteristics of the mode, and network relationships in the market.

The firm characteristics therefore include such factors as experience of the firm, the possession of some unique advantages, firm strategy, resources, etc. Socio-cultural conditions, demand, competition, political and economic conditions, legal system and rule of law, level of market development, etc all come under the foreign market institutional factors whilst the moderating factors relates to the characteristics of the desired mode such as: the control it affords, level of dissemination risk, resource requirement, amount of flexibility, corporate policies, etc. A careful consideration of the effect of each of these influences will lead a firm into deciding on the method of entry to use which could eventually be either the independent entry strategy –e.g. wholly owned subsidiary or the collaborative mode e.g. franchising, joint ventures, licensing, etc. Figure 6.1 contains a detailed breakdown of this framework.

4.6.   Chapter Summary

This chapter started by restating the importance of understanding the strategies needed for foreign market entry and acknowledges that very many theoretical contributions on the frameworks and constructs for foreign market have been developed. However, the fact also remains that there is no consensus as to which framework/constructs should hold in explaining entry mode strategies. Scholars like Hill *et al.* 1990; Anderson, 1997 have called for a unifying conceptual framework that considers the relevant factors and analyses the relationship between them. The above notwithstanding, a common feature of all the frameworks is that internal company factors, external environmental factors, as well as some moderating variables all influence the entry mode strategies of the firms.

The relationship between firm characteristics and entry mode is explained; so also are the important environmental factors (formal and informal), and other moderating factors discussed. The combined effect of these broad areas of influences on entry strategy are equally discussed after which a conceptual framework is formulated that summarises and captures the relevant factors needed for consideration in retail internationalisation.

CHAPTER 5: RESEARCH DESIGN AND METHODOLOGY

The relevant methodological issues pertaining to this present research are addressed in this chapter. The first parts of this chapter look at the research philosophy underpinning this present research and sets out the research design. Other aspects of this chapter considers the research methodology, description of the methodology, evaluation of the case studies, and also an in-depth overview of the qualitative analysis process; importantly, the various levels of coding on the data and how they are validated using Nvivo are explained with data from the fieldwork so as to set out the framework for the analysis.

5.1   Research Philosophy (Epistemology, Ontology and Axiology)

Research philosophy relates to the development of knowledge and the nature of that knowledge. The philosophy adopted contains important assumptions about the way in which a researcher views the world. These assumptions underpin the research strategy and methods chosen as a part of that strategy (Saunders *et al* 2007). They further add that the three major ways of thinking about research philosophy are: Epistemology, Ontology, and Axiology.

Epistemology concerns what constitutes acceptable knowledge in a field of study. Ontology is concerned with nature of reality. This raises questions of the assumptions researchers have about the way the world operates and the commitment held to particular views. Two aspects of ontology important to researchers are: Objectivism- which portrays the position that social entities exist in reality external to social actors concerned with their existence. The second aspect, Subjectivism holds that social phenomena are created from the perceptions and consequent actions of those social actors concerned with their existence (Saunders et al. 2007). Axiology, on the other hand, is a branch of Philosophy that studies judgements about values. It expresses the role that the researcher's own value play in all stages of the research process in order to give credible results. Heron (1996) argues that our values are the guiding reason of all human action. He further goes on to state that researchers demonstrate axiological skill by being able to articulate their values as a basis for making judgements about what research they are conducting and how they go about doing it; especially in such areas as: choosing one topic rather than another, making a choice of philosophical approach, choice of data collection technique, etc.

Researchers in the management sciences are often faced with the fundamental philosophical challenge of deciding whether to adopt the positivist orientation, and pursue quantitative research paradigm; or embrace the phenomenological school of thought, hence do qualitative research; or selectively combine (triangulate) the best of both approaches in a particular research.

Positivism is a research philosophy that holds that the goal of knowledge is simply to describe the phenomena that we experience. The purpose of science is simply to stick to what we can observe and measure. Knowledge of anything beyond that, a positivist would hold, is impossible. It refers specifically to the philosophy espoused by Auguste Comte (1853) and generally to later philosophies which are based on the fact that human thought proceeds through three stages: theological, metaphysical, and positivistic. The first, theological, involves trying to explain all phenomena through the direct operation of supernatural beings and divine forces. The second, metaphysical, is similar to the first, but those supernatural beings have become more abstract and less anthropomorphic. In the final, positivistic, both supernatural beings and metaphysical abstractions are abandoned in favour of naturalistic, empirical explanations.

According to Positivism, sense perceptions are the only admissible basis for knowledge and thought. Everything outside of natural phenomena or properties of knowable things is excluded, and so highly speculative metaphysics and theology are rejected. Science forms the boundaries of human knowledge, and, as a consequence, positivism expresses great hope for the ability of science to solve human problems. It holds that meaningful knowledge about the real (external) world should be gained through observations and measurements, conducted by objective rather than subjective methods (Easterby-Smith et al. 1991).

According to Easterby-Smith (1991); Patton, (2002), the major characteristics of positivism includes:

- The researcher keeping a distance from what is being observed (independence)
- Allowing objective criteria, rather than personal beliefs and interests, to guide the choice of what is studied, and how (value-freedom)
- Seeking to identify causal explanations and fundamental laws behind regularities in human social behaviour (causality)
- Starting with initial hypotheses, and subjecting same to deductive tests using collected observations (hypothetico-deductive)
- Breaking down concepts such that facts can be measured quantitatively (operationalization)
- Reducing problems to their simplest possible elements to enhance understanding (reductionism)
- Making samples large enough to enable generalisation about observed regularities in human social behaviour (generalisation); and
- Seeking comparisons across samples (cross-sectional analysis)

It is worthy of note that things have changed in our views of science since the middle part of the 20th century. Probably the most important has been our shift away from positivism into what we term *post-positivism*. Post-positivism, is not a slight adjustment to or revision of the positivist position -- post-positivism is a wholesale rejection of the central tenets of positivism. A post-positivist might begin by recognizing that the way scientists think and work and the way we think in our everyday life are not distinctly different. Scientific reasoning and common sense reasoning are essentially the same process. There is no difference in kind between the two, only a difference in degree. Scientists, for example, follow specific procedures to assure that observations are verifiable, accurate and consistent. One of the most common forms of post-positivism is a philosophy called *critical realism*. A critical realist believes that there is a reality independent of our thinking about it that science can study.

Phenomenology on its part is a philosophical discipline originated by Edmund Husserl who developed the phenomenological method to make possible a descriptive account of the essential structures of the directly given (Smith and Thomasson 2005). According to Creswell (1998), Phenomenology emphasizes the immediacy of experience, the attempt to isolate it and set it off from all assumptions of existence or causal influence and lay bare its essential structure. Phenomenology restricts the philosopher's attention to the pure data of consciousness, uncontaminated by metaphysical theories or scientific assumptions. Husserl's concept of the life-world — as the individual's personal world as directly experienced — expressed this same idea of immediacy. With the appearance of the *Annual for Philosophical and Phenomenological Research* (1913 – 30), under Husserl's editorship, his personal philosophizing flowered into an international movement. Its most notable adherents were Max Scheler and Martin Heidegger (McPhail, 1995; Moran & Mooney 2002).

So phenomenology sees reality as socially constructed and not objectively or externally determined. Therefore based on the premise that human actions arise out of the meanings people attach to their experience, phenomenologists focus on understanding why people have different experiences. The key to explaining human behaviour in this case, lies within the individual and not some external causes. The fundamental task is therefore to uncover meanings, not gathering facts and measuring how often certain patterns occur. Golafshani (2003) mentions the following as essential characteristics of phenomenology:

- The researcher's involvement in what is being observed
- Development of ideas and theories based on post hoc analysis of collected data (induction)
- Examination of the full complexity of the data (systems view)
- Use of multiple methods to establish different views of the phenomena; and
- Intensive investigation of small samples, over time (longitudinal analysis).

Easterby-Smith *et al* (1991) outline these major differences between the two philosophical positions as summarised in the table below.

Table 5.1 Positivist versus Phenomenological Paradigms

	Positivist paradigm	**Phenomenology paradigm**
Basic Beliefs	- The world is external and objective - Observer is independent - Science is value-free	- The world is socially constructed and objective - Observer is part of what is observed - Science is driven by human interest
Researcher should:	- Focus on facts - Look for causality and fundamental laws - Reduce phenomena to simplest elements - Formulate hypotheses and test them	- Focus on meanings - Try to understand what is happening - Look at the totality of each situation - Develop ideas through induction from data
Preferred methods include:	- Operationalizing concepts so that they can be measured - Taking large samples	- Using multiple methods to establish different views of phenomena - Small samples investigated in-depth or over time

Source: Easterby-Smith et al. (1991), Management Research

This present study utilises the qualitative research approach with an exploratory research purpose based on search of the literature, as well as interviewing experts in the subject area of retail internationalisation and entry mode strategies.

5.2 Research Design

The research questions set for this present study, nature of the problem investigated, and the decision to use the qualitative research method have all informed the scope of this present research and nature of the data collected. The qualitative research methods has moulded the research design so as for it to be responsive to the respondents and also to the context of a developing market like Nigeria. No reliable list of foreign retailers in Nigeria exists; the only important thing is that there are presently, not many foreign retail firms operating in the country. Available records show the existence of nineteen foreign retail outlets operating in various parts of the country.

Following the recommendations of Yin (1989), Eisenhardt (1989), and Stake (2000), evidence for this investigation was collected from a variety of data sources, including secondary sources such as company documents and press articles, participant observation on retail practices, and interviews with experts. These data collection techniques produced rich information and descriptions of the cases. This researcher experienced the problem expressed by experts (Erramilli and Rao 1993; Driscoll and Paliwoda 1997; Ekeledo and Sivakumar 1998; Moore 2000) concerning the difficulty in collecting data on international operations. Information is provided reluctantly as internationalisation is considered as a strategic, hence sensitive issue. Moreover, international developers are mainly senior managers in high positions with busy timetables. In this context, given the difficulty in conducting in-depth interviews with international retailers, special care was to be provided to cross-validate the data from the interviews as such, this present research utilised a four-step research design.

Firstly, data on retail operation mode decisions was collected from the Federal Ministry of Commerce and Industries Nigeria. This government institution regulates and provides expertise to retail and manufacturing firms operating in the country. Data was also obtained from other agencies of the government whose activities impacts in some way on the retail practice in the country; such agencies include: The Corporate Affairs Commission – responsible for the incorporation of businesses in the country, as well as the National Agency for Food and Drug Administration and Control (NAFDAC) - responsible for overseeing the quality of consumable products imported, manufactured, and sold anywhere in the country. Various secondary data relevant to this study was gathered from these agencies.

Secondly, interviews with key decision-makers were conducted in the selected retail companies. Retail internationalisation is known to be a strategic marketing decision. The respondents in the selected retail firms were chosen based on their knowledge and personal involvement in the operation mode decisions of the firms: these architects of the foreign expansion plans included top level executives in these firms like the [C.E.Os] and the export and international marketing managers of the firms and other board members of the firms, as well as their managers heading the operations in the Nigerian market. The interviews lasted between 60 to 90 minutes, were recorded and fully transcribed. As a result of limited finance available to the researcher, and the diverse geographical location of the head offices of these international retail firms, some of the interviews were done over the phone. The purpose of the interviews was to seek knowledge on various aspects of the internationalisation process of the firms, especially their entry mode strategies, their selection of foreign markets, and how the internationalisation process started. The interview guide was pre-tested in order to allow for clarifications or further explanations by key informants. The interview guide was designed around several potentially important constructs suggested by the research problem and the literature in international management and international retailing, as well as the underpinning theoretical frameworks for this study.

Thirdly, both internal and external secondary source materials were collected from the retail firms and analysed. Internal reports on store networks and international expansion plans, as well as pictures of stores in foreign countries were studied for each of the case studies. An extensive research in newspapers and magazines, on company websites, as well as in company annual reports were also looked into.

Lastly, participant observation was used in the data generation as well. Observation as a data collection tool entails listening and watching other people's behaviour in a way that allows some type of learning and analytical interpretation. The main advantage is that we can collect first-hand information in a natural setting, Ghauri and Gronhaug (2002). The non-participatory observation method was used for this study in triangulation with the other methods of data collection, so as to have a rich and balanced source of data.

This four-step methodological design contributed to yielding valid and reliable findings. Concerning the analytical procedure for data analysis, findings were derived by performing a separate analysis by data source for each case-study as this helps improve the research reliability (Eisenhardt 1989), before tracing back similarities and differences in results between cases. Hence, a case-study methodology combining in-depth interviews and internal and external secondary data analysis was developed in order to refine the conceptual model of factors affecting the operation mode choice by retail firms. The Nvivo software was used in the data analysis. Figure 5.2 below sets out an outline of the design for this present research.

Figure 5.1 Outline of Research Plan adapted from Eisenhardt (1989) and Yin (2003)

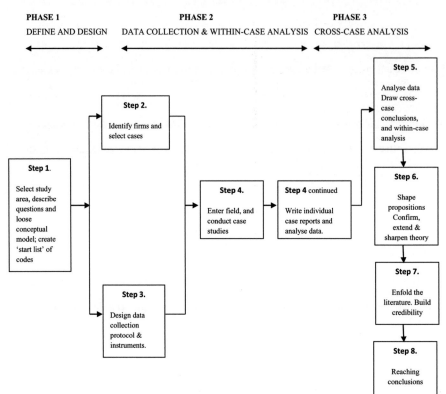

5.3   Research Methodology

According to Zalan and Lewis (2004) the purpose of methodology is to demonstrate the grasp of the theory of methods and to lay out general methodological considerations consistent with the research problems, ontological and epistemological positions and underlying theories. This present research considered greatly the following three important aspects:

(1) Research methods used in previous studies in this area of research and their limitations

(2) Justification of the methodology used by focusing on its advantages over other methodologies; and

(3) A brief description of the methodology.

Zalan and Lewis (2004) further added that the choice of methodology is determined not only by the ontological and epistemological stance of the researcher, but also by (1) the objectives of the study, (2) the nature of the research problem; and (3) the theoretical frameworks that inform the study. These should be the primary concerns and will often shape the ontological and epistemological stance adopted by the researcher. The researcher thus needs to discuss how the chosen methodology is driven by each of these considerations (*this present research took all of these into consideration*). The use of the qualitative method for this present study is also as a result of the views of experts (Guba and Lincoln 1994; Heron 1996; Easterby-Smith 2002; Saunders *et al.* 2007) that qualitative methods offer a unique advantage when the researcher is trying to observe, describe, and explain dynamic processes such as international negotiations, or decision making by top management teams, which are best captured in close proximity to the phenomenon. As Silverman (2005:115) stated, no research method is intrinsically better than any other; everything will depend upon one's research objectives.

As noted by Alexander (1990a, 1990b) where recent insights into why and how retailers choose entry modes are available in the literature, such insights have been developed through the use of in-depth qualitative research rather than the observational and quantitative research that characterises early work such as Treadgold (1988). This present study therefore, follows the call by Doherty and Alexander (2004) that if research on international retailing is to address new issues and begin exploring old accepted frameworks such as those on entry mode strategy then one key way to address this is through qualitative research which will be able to access and interpret the complexities and interrelationships of factors that impact on the decision-making and implementation process. In their view, quantitative approaches on retail entry modes have been able to help establish and provide understanding and identify major research questions in this area of retail internationalisation and entry strategies therefore, qualitative methods are needed to answer these questions, address new issues, and explore the old accepted frameworks.

124

The research method used to find answers to the research questions in this present study is the **case study methodology**. Case study methodology is chosen because it allows for the possibility of studying a retail organisation in its host environment in a natural setting, which provides the benefit of obtaining rich insights into these complex processes which are usually difficult to assess by quantitative techniques. This methodology was chosen also based on the views expressed by Saunders *et al.* (2007) that a case study strategy can be a very worthwhile way of exploring existing theory. A well structured case study strategy can enable the researcher to challenge an existing theory and also provide a source of new research questions.

5.3.1. Description of Methodology

Yin (1994:13) defines case study as "an empirical enquiry that investigates a contemporary phenomenon within its real-life context, especially when the boundaries between phenomenon and context are not clearly evident". According to the author, no attempt is made to isolate the phenomenon from its context, and it is of interest precisely because of its relation to its context. This is one reason why case studies have been widely used in the area of management, information systems and retailing (Sparks 1995).

In the context of this thesis, the multiple case study approach is chosen because this approach seems to be particularly appropriate when theoretical developments are limited, phenomena are context-dependent and when it seems necessary to enrich and reconfigure the elements derived from the literature review to define a model (Robson 2002). The issue is then explored through a multiple case-study approach as it constitutes a useful analytical tool when there is a need to identify common elements to deepen the knowledge of the research subject. It lays the groundwork for the construction of a 'composite portrait' (Stake 1995).

For several researchers, case study is a type of research strategy. It is an alternative to other research strategies such as experiments or historical studies (Yin 1994). However, other researchers do not agree with this approach. For example, Stake (2000:435) states that "case study is not necessarily a methodological choice but a choice of what is to be studied, by whatever method". Stake (2000:436) emphasized what can be learned from a single case rather than the method of inquiry, and defines case study as "both a process of inquiry about the case and the product of that inquiry. The focus of this thesis follows both Stake (2000); in that it considers case study as a research process and what is learned about the phenomenon to be studied, and Yin (1989); in that the case will be studied in its natural setting through a set of procedures and techniques, in order to obtain information about the processes and relationships with the environment.

Case study research can include both single and multiple case studies, which can be used for exploratory or explanatory purposes (Yin 1994). Specifically, Stake (2000) explains that case studies can be intrinsic, instrumental or collective (more than one case). Intrinsic case studies are developed when a particular case in itself is of interest to the researcher, and not for theory building purposes. Instead, instrumental case study is developed when a researcher examines a particular case for obtaining insight of something else, of a more general phenomenon. The case is of secondary interest and the main purpose is to advance the understanding of that other interest. Finally, collective case study refers to an instrumental study expanded to several cases. It is important to state that one reason for embarking on the multiple case study methodology for this present research is that it is convenient for investigating 'how' or 'why' type of research questions (Yin 1994). In this thesis, the theories have already specified some clear research questions. The multiple case studies then are used to determine whether a theory's propositions are appropriate or whether some alternative set of explanations are more relevant. Thus, this multiple case study research will support, extend or challenge the theories.

5.3.2. Evaluation of the Case Studies

This present research considered the multiple case study research under an interpretive approach to generating knowledge. Following Klein & Myers (1999), the foundation assumption for this interpretive research is that knowledge is gained, or at least filtered, through social constructions such consciousness, and shared meanings. These are important dimensions used in this present study. In addition to the emphasis on the socially constructed nature of reality, this present research also acknowledges the intimate relationship between the researcher and what is being explored, and the situational constraints shaping this process. This research is aimed at producing an understanding of the social context of the phenomenon and the process whereby the phenomenon influences and is influenced by the social context a view expressed by Walsham (1995).

In trying to reduce the possibility of getting wrong responses and answers, due care was taken by the researcher in this present research to pay considerable attention to two particular emphases on research design namely: **Reliability and Validity.** To ensure reliability, the researcher considered the extent to which the data collection techniques or analysis procedure would yield consistent findings. The researcher assessed this, by looking at the three questions posed by Easterby-Smith *et al.* (2002):

- Will the measures yield the same results on other occasions?
- Will similar observations be reached by other observers?
- Is there transparency in how sense was made from the raw data?

The researcher also made efforts in every available way to ensure reliability by ensuring that the respondents chosen from the various case study firms are top management level staff and board members involved in making such strategic decisions as internationalisation and entry strategies. Efforts were equally made to be sure that the right persons are the ones selected; and in conducting the interviews, a well structured format was used so as to be sure that the same yardstick is used for all the respondents with due diligence also taken in interpreting the data. This is in line with what

Robson (2002) identified as four threats to reliability, namely: subject or participant error; subject or participant bias; observer error and observer bias.

The researcher in this present research also ensured that the findings are really about what they appear to be about *which is the major concern of research validity.* The view of the researcher is that if the validity or trustworthiness of this present research can be maximized or tested, then more "credible and defensible result" (Johnson 1997:283) may lead to generalizability, which is one of the concepts suggested by Stenbacka (2001) as the structure for both doing and documenting high quality qualitative research. Therefore, the quality of a research is related to generalizability of the result and thereby to the testing and increasing the validity or trustworthiness of the research. This present research therefore considered the issue of generalizability **(external validity)** of the findings from the study. There is the need to emphasize here that the purpose of this present research is not to produce a theory that is generalizable to all populations. The task is simply to try to explain what is going on in this particular research setting, Nigeria (in terms of the entry mode decision choices of the foreign retailers). The researcher hopes to test the robustness of the conclusions from this study by exposing them to other research settings in a follow-up study.

5.4. Sampling procedure

This present research used the **purposive theoretical sampling technique** which allows for choosing cases in terms of the theory on which the research is based, choosing 'deviant' or 'extreme' cases, and changing sample size during research (Bryman 1988). The non-probability purposive sampling (purposeful sampling) as well as the theoretical sampling techniques were the main sampling methods used for this present study. The Purposive sampling techniques involve selecting certain units or cases ''based on a specific purpose rather than randomly'' (Tashakkori & Teddlie, 2003:713). Sampling special or unique cases—employed when the individual case itself, or a specific group of cases, is a major focus of the investigation (rather than an issue). The aim here is not to select a mere representative sample but a sample that possesses certain characteristics (Teddlie, and Yu, 2007).

Theoretical sampling on the other hand, is the process of data collection directed by evolving theory rather than by predetermined population dimensions (Strauss, 1987). It is stressed here that theoretical sampling "involves . . . much calculation and imagination on the part of the analysts . . ." (Strauss, 1987: 39). As theoretical constructs evolve, precise information is sought to refine emerging ideas. When doing theoretical sampling, researchers must determine what data sources (e.g., groups of people, documents, bodies of literature) could yield the richest and most relevant data, and what cases (e.g., individuals, particular settings, specific documents) drawn from these sources are most likely to provide empirical indicators needed for category development (Draucker, et al, 2007). This procedure was used for this present study.

The cases selected for this study needed to meet some earlier set criteria which were important for the research. They first must be foreign firms – 'foreign' meant the firms are corporations owned and incorporated outside Nigeria but authorized to do business in the country. Secondly, the firms must be retail firms falling under either the food/grocery or non grocery categories (table 6.1 shows the category of the retail firms used for the study). Thirdly, the firms must have operations in Nigeria or be contemplating starting off operations in the country (like the case of Wal-Mart – a good example of the extreme or 'deviant' case). Lastly, the firms must use or be planning to use the independent entry mode or any of the collaborative modes of entry; this is important because since retailing involves some level of contact with the customers this therefore will exclude the firms that are mainly into export of their products into Nigeria.

The selection of the case studies was also guided by the underpinning theories for the present study namely: the institutional and transaction cost perspectives. Initial sampling decisions were based on these perspectives though the researcher realises that once data are collected and coding begins, the research can be led in "all directions which seem relevant and workable" (Draucker et al, 2007). This present study followed Glaser's (1987) recommendations for data collection strategies related to theoretical sampling, which includes staying open by using different interviewing styles, sites, or participants; follow up on recurring patterns in participant data; and asking key participants (in this case top level retail executives) to give more information on categories that seem central to the emerging theory. This present study also involved jotting down ideas from the perspectives that direct data collection, and analyzing secondary data (i.e., data collected for any purpose) as a source of comparative analysis.

5.5. Sampling method, recruitment and ethical considerations

The strategic nature of the subject under investigation meant that the right information can only be obtained from some key informants in the retail firms used for this study. This researcher made several calls and sent out letters to the top management staff of the retail firms seeking their permission and asking for their assistance to be part of research. After identifying the potential interviewees, the next step was to further screen the identified persons so as to select the most eligible. Yin (2003:78) states that the "goal of the screening procedure is to be sure that you identify cases properly prior to formal data collection". This involved explaining the research purpose and procedure to the potential interviewees and seeking their consent for the conduct of a formal interview. At the end, an average of three top executives was selected from each of the twelve retail firms chosen for the study.

As with forms of research with human subjects, qualitative research requires ethical considerations to be taken care of during the research process (Patton, 2002). This research study was conducted in accordance with the ethical regulations laid out by the University of Strathclyde: Ethical Codes of Practice. In this case, the researcher submitted a research outline to the Department of Marketing Ethics Committee prior to the commencement of field work for the research detailing the procedure to be followed to ensure that the research conforms to the University standards. This document was approved by the Ethics Committee.

This present study took into consideration the views of Fontana and Frey (1994) in respect of ethical considerations in interviewing namely: informed consent and right to privacy. In this present study, the procedure of informed consent was followed at every stage of the process. The numerous recruitment phone conversations sort the consent of the interviewees and so did the recruitment letter (see Appendix 1). At a time before starting an interview, the research once again explained the purpose of the research study, explained who will use the information and how the information would be used. At this stage the researcher explained the issues of confidentiality and anonymity to the interviewee and got their verbal consent on tape as well; this is in line with the suggestion of Warren (2002) to avoid the contradiction of having signed consent forms on one hand and promising confidentiality and anonymity on the other hand. The interviewees were assured of confidentiality and anonymity on any papers that was to be produced from this present study.

A structured interview guide (see Appendix 2) was developed for this study. The aim of this approach is to ensure that each interviewee is presented with exactly the same questions in the same order so as to ensure that answers can be reliably aggregated to be able to draw comparisons. This process according to (Bryman, 2006; Kvale, 2008) provides insight into declarative knowledge used, maintains a focus on the given issue, provides detailed information on the issue, and also provides structural relationships of the concepts. The guide outlined the set of issues to be explored with each interviewee. The interview guide was developed to reflect the themes of the research objectives presented in Chapter 1. Again, the themes of the research objectives emerged from the literature review and conceptual chapters. The interview guide was structured into four sections that covered such areas as: the type of arrangement used by the retail firms, the various company and Nigerian market characteristics, the transfer of technology, and the host and home country policies as it affects their entry mode strategies. Importantly, the interview guide was pre-tested with five top executives of retail firms here in the UK with operations in other developing markets; this was tape recorded and transcribed by the researcher to check for any inconsistencies or difficulties in understanding the questions. This enabled the researcher to make some minor amendments which eventually led to the development of this research instrument with which rich data were generated for this research study.

5.6.   Overview of the Qualitative research Process – Data Management

Qualitative research is always known to have a very huge size of generated data sets that may overwhelm the researcher if not properly organised and managed. Throughout the course of this study, three concurrent flows of activity as suggested by experts (Miles and Huberman 1994, Lacey and Luff 2001) were embarked upon: data reduction, data display, and conclusion drawing/verification. Boeije (2010) referred to this as segmenting the data into parts and reassembling the parts again into a coherent whole. As shown in section 5.7.1 the aim of reassembling the data is to look for patterns, search for relationships between the parts, and finding explanations for what is observed.

5.6.1 Data Reduction

Data reduction is known to occur continuously throughout the life of any qualitative oriented research. 'It refers to the process of selecting, focusing, simplifying, and transforming the data that appear in written-up field notes or transcriptions' (Miles and Huberman, 1994:10). For this project, the data reduction started when the researcher decided (though without full awareness), the conceptual framework, number and type of cases, the research questions, and data collection method to choose. This process led to writing summaries, coding, teasing out themes, making clusters, making partitions, and writing memos. Data reduction therefore, became a part of the analysis that sharpens sorts, focuses, discards, and organises data in such a way that final conclusions can be drawn and verified (Tesch 1990). For this present study, the process of data reduction started writing summaries of each case, documents, and observations; this is captured using the contact summary sheet and document summary forms as explained below. However the most important aspect of the data reduction in this study was coding the data; the process used is explained in section 5.6 below.

5.6.1.1.   Contact Summary Sheet

After a field contact, the researcher took time out to make sense out of the contact; to be able to do this; a contact summary sheet was used. This is just a single sheet with some focusing or summarising questions about a particular field contact. The field notes are reviewed and the questions answered briefly to develop an overall summary of the main points in the contact. The major questions in the summary sheet are:

- What people or situations were involved?
- What were the main themes or issues in the contact?
- Which variables in the initial framework did the contact bear on most centrally?
- Did the contact address any of the research questions?
- What new speculations or hunches about the field situation did the contact suggest?
- What should the researcher do for the next contact and what type of information should be sought?

The contact summary sheet is filled out as soon as the researcher corrected, reviewed, and wrote up the field notes usually after just a couple of days after the contact when the event was still fresh and most of what was discussed could still be remembered. This is suggested by Lofland and Lofland (1984).

Figure 5.2.   Contact Summary Form

Type of contact: Mgt.......................... ....

              Who, what group   Place   Date

Phone.. ....

      With whom, by whom   Place   Date

Site...   Date Coded.................................

SALIENT POINTS   THEMES/ASPECTS

5.6.1.2.   Document Summary form

Quite a wide range of documents were picked up by the researcher during the field work for this study: meeting agendas, company annual reports, budgets, brochures, newspaper articles, gazettes, etc. These documents provided very useful facts about the many cases studied; so to better clarify and summarize the content of these documents, a document summary form was designed and used.

This form helped to put the documents in context, explaining the significance of each document and a brief summary which allowed for the researcher's reflective commentary. These documents were also coded especially important parts in order to allow for easy retrieval and to aid in the final analysis as suggested by Carley (1990) and Weber (1990).

Figure 5.3.   Document Summary form

Document Form	Site..
	Document..............................
	Date obtained.......................

1. Name and description of document

2. Event or contact, if any, with which document is associated.

3. Significance or importance of document

5.7.   The Coding process

The transcribed data from the interviews, field notes, documents and observations showed that the interviewees have answered the various questions in different order such that topics of relevance can be found all throughout the data, and often multiple parts pertaining to the exact same theme are found in different places. So the pieces that are believed to belong together are combined. A method that was used in this present study was the constant comparison of the data generated from each case studied. This enabled the researcher to describe the variations that are found within this topic of study and also to indicate in which situations different variations manifest themselves. It was observed that each time the cases were analysed and compared, new codes were formulated and the content of some existing category changes; this process was repeated until no new insights were gained for further development of the categories. As suggested by (Draucker; et al. 2007; and Boeije 2010) this present study started with open coding – leading to the creation of a list of codes, then moved into axial coding – setting up a list of categories, before finally using the selective coding – that led to the development of the framework for analysis.

Firstly, a system of categories and concepts is created with the intention of gaining knowledge into this subject under investigation (entry mode decisions of the foreign retail firms) and ultimately of answering the research questions. Armed with an insight into this research area under investigation, some current research issues, common explanations for the phenomena as provided by the interviewees and an awareness of the theoretical perspectives used a set of codes - **'coding scheme'** emerged from the data.

At this stage (just as shown in Appendix 4) all the transcribed data were read very carefully and divided into fragments. The fragments were compared among each other, grouped into sections dealing with the same subject, and labelled with a code. The codes were validated at this stage when no new codes are needed to label fragments that appeared in the remaining parts of the data.

The second step in the coding involved coding around several single categories or axes (a process Boeije 2010 described as 'axial coding). The purpose here is to determine which elements in the research are the dominant ones and which are the less dominant ones; the data at this stage is reduced and reorganized - synonyms are crossed out, redundant codes are removed and the best representative codes are selected. This determined the properties of the categories by showing the

135

indicators as recognised in the data and regularities or patterns emerged which rose above the level of the single text fragment aimed at explaining larger parts of the data and bringing the different parts back together. As in the earlier step, this stage was validated when the distinction between the main codes and sub-codes became clearly established meaning the definition and properties of each category (axis) are clear such that no further adjustment was needed.

The last stage of the coding involved looking for connections between the categories in order to make sense of what was happening in the field; Lofland and Lofland 1995 described this as the hunt for the core concept. The aim at this stage was to determine important categories formulating the theoretical model, reassembling of the data in order to answer the research question and realize the research aim. This process involved interpreting and positioning findings in the existing literature, thinking about the answers to the research questions and drawing conclusions. Validation at this stage was ensuring consistency between the data and the descriptions thus far and a fit with the theoretical model. Importantly, this stage involved answering some vital questions (suggested by Boeiji, 2010) as listed below:

- Which themes have turned up repeatedly in the observation?
- What is the main message the interviewees have tried to bring across?
- How are the various relevant themes related?
- What is important for the description (What) and the understanding (Why) of the interviewees' perspectives and behaviours?

All of the above procedures are further explained in the next section.

5.7.1. Preparing the data for Analysis (within & cross case analysis)

All the interviews conducted for this study were tape recorded and fully transcribed by the researcher and carefully uploaded into Nvivo8- the software for data analysis. The interview transcripts were saved as word documents; so also were the field notes in form of memos and observations. Each interviewee had a full transcript of the interview which was saved separately; in order to be able to identify the source of the transcripts; the interviewees from each of the retail firms interviewed were assigned some special codes which represented the file names for the interview transcripts. For example, the interview transcript for the Business Development Manager for Game Stores was saved as G-BDM; the one for the General Manager of Shoprite was saved as SH-GM; whilst the one for the major franchisor for KFC in Nigeria Devyan International was saved as K-Devyan CEO. This procedure was used for all the thirty nine (39) interviewees across the twelve (12) international retail firms studied.

The next step involved importing these documents (the interview transcripts for all the interviewees, and the field notes) into Nvivo. Figure 5.4 below shows the Navigation and List view screen in Nvivo after the documents were imported and coded. As shown in this figure, the transcript for the Shoprite General Manager (one of the first interviews conducted) was coded – using open coding (*breaking down the data into fragments and assigning a code*) and it had eighty-six (86) codes that came up under seventeen nodes (17) from the axial coding (Appendix 3 shows the open coding for this interview transcripts and Appendix 4 provides the full transcript for this interview and the coded fragments are shown in yellow (*this is the standard format in Nvivo*). The same open coding was done for all other transcripts at the end of which a total of 392 codes emerged (**coding scheme).** This represented the within case analysis.

The cross case analysis then involved moving into the next level of coding (axial coding). Boeije (2010:108) describes this as "a set of procedures whereby data are put back together in new ways after open coding, by making connections between categories". As earlier explained, it involved coding around several single categories or axes this was done to determine whether the codes developed thus far cover the data sufficiently, check whether each fragment has been coded properly, decide which code is most suitable if synonyms have been used to create the codes, look for evidence for distinguishing main codes and sub-codes, and to see whether a sufficiently detailed description of a category can be derived from the assigned fragments. This stage required the theoretical sensitivity of the researcher and an awareness of the major aims of the study to be able to develop and define the categories and at the same time determine the relationships between the categories. These categories were coded as the case nodes as shown in figure 5. below. These categories therefore provided the framework for the analysis; a third stage of coding often referred to as 'selective coding'.

Notice from this table that the 'Names column' is thirty nine (39) – *showing the number of interview transcripts. The References column shows the number of common codes across all the transcripts for each category. The Nodes column shows the number of nodes the codes were coded at.*

Figure 5.4   Open coding schemes of interview transcripts

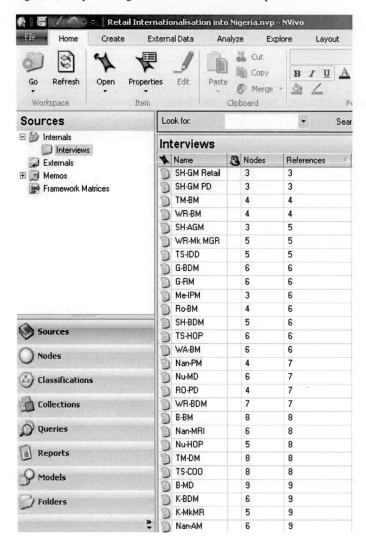

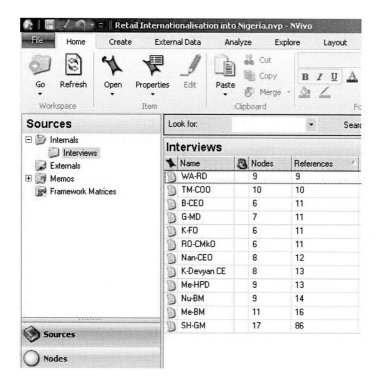

The within and cross case analysis was made easy by the design of the contact summary sheet and document summary form which was used to highlight the data collected from each interviewee immediately after the field work as the data is transcribed. This procedure was immensely helpful at the axial coding stage. It formed part of the field notes and was imported and important parts coded in Nvivo. The sections below explain how each of these documents was used.

5.7.2 Conclusion Drawing and Verification

From the start of the data collection for this project, the researcher was very careful in noting regularities, patterns, explanations, possible configurations, causal flows, and propositions maintaining openness. All of these helped in drawing the final conclusions which needed also to be verified; the meanings emerging from the data had to be tested for their plausibility, their sturdiness, their confirmability- that is their validity. Therefore, the final stage of the coding process (*selective coding- which involved looking for connections between the categories in order to make sense of what was happening in the field; and reassembling of the data in order to answer the research questions)* led to introducing queries on the data.

In Nvivo, queries allow you to question your data, help discover patterns in the data, test hunches, create and validate theories. Different forms of queries are available on Nvivo but for this present study, the **coding queries** were used. In this situation the queries were used to refine the coding so as to answer specific questions especially the research questions set out for the study. For example, the data is questioned to find out what each of the interviewees thought of the various categories making up the analytical framework for the study. A summary of their views is as presented in Chapter six – Data presentation, Analysis and Findings.

5.7.3. Data Display

Using the extended text has often been the most frequently used form of data analysis in most qualitative research projects. It is clear that humans are not very powerful as processors of large amounts of information; our cognitive tendency is to reduce complex information into selective and simplified forms that may be easily understood. Extended text can overload humans' information processing capabilities (Faust 1982) and preys on their tendencies to find simplifying patterns.

The data display in this research project include the use of charts, and networks designed to assemble organised information into an immediately accessible, compact form that allowed the researcher to see what is happening and either draw conclusions or move on to the next step of analysis the display suggests may be useful. Creating these visuals is a way of raising awareness about the possible gaps in the available knowledge and stimulating thinking about how to fill these gaps helping to develop interpretations. Appendix 5 for example shows a model developed from coded interview data with the Shoprite General Manager the full transcription of which is contained in Appendix 4. The figure better captures the various coding categories for this case (*the interviewee – Shoprite GM)* on the weighting factors: Firm characteristics, informal & formal institutional factors, as well as the external moderating factors.

5.8. Interviews Locations

Regarding the locations of interviews, the researcher used a flexible policy to suit the moment, and also to suit the wishes of the targeted individuals. The researcher used both formal and informal communication styles in order to make the necessary arrangements to conduct the interviews. Table 5.2 below provides more details about the locations of interviews conducted in this research.

Table 5.2   Interview location

Interview Locations	Frequency
Interviewees office	24
Interviewees House	2
Hotel's Café	5
Telephone	8
Total	**39**

As contained in the table above, a larger proportion of the interviews were conducted in the office of the respondents 24 of the interviews representing 61.5% were in the office, 2 (5.1%) interviews were carried out in the homes of the interviewees, and another 5 interviews (12.8%) were done in the café of the hotels where the interviewees stayed. Eight interviews (20.5%) were over the phone because the interviewees as a result of their busy schedule could not be reached at the time for the field work. It is important to note also that even for the respondents that were interviewed face to face, a number of telephone calls were put through to them by the researcher in seeking clarification to some points raised during the interview and also to obtain additional information.

5.9. Interview Duration

The time or the duration for conducting interviews varied for each interview, this difference is linked to a large extent to the place the interviews were conducted. Some of the interviews in the offices had to be stopped for a little while just to allow the interviewees attend to some pressing issues related to their office; this came in the form of official phone calls, and reports from subordinates and managers. The table below shows the time spent on the process of conducting the interviews in this study.

Table 5.3   Duration of Interviews

Interview Duration	Frequency
Less Than One Hour	4
One to Less than Two Hours	26
Two Hours and Above	9
Total	**39**

Only 4 interviews representing (10.3%) were concluded within the hour. 26 other interviews representing (66.7%) were concluded between one and two hours, whilst another 9 interviews (23%) went beyond two hours to be concluded. Most of the interviewees in this case had so much to talk about that the researcher found interesting and relevant so no attempt was made to cut them short. The researcher encouraged the interviewees to freely express their views.

5.10. Conclusions

This present research has utilised a qualitative research approach mainly because of its suitable based on the context used for the study, the nature of the research questions and objectives set, as well as the type of data needed to be generated in addition to the purpose of the research. Amongst others, the very many benefits derivable from this use of such a research approach namely: a focus on natural settings; an interest in meanings, perspectives and understandings; an emphasis on process; and a concern with inductive analysis have all been influential factors for this choice of research approach.

In an attempt to ensure validity and reliability from the findings of this present research, the researcher had used the main methods employed in qualitative research, most of which are observation, interviews, and documentary analysis in some form of triangulation. Adequate care was taken to overcome the major problems encountered in conducting qualitative research. Qualitative research in any form is demanding, typically presenting a mass of confusing and

143

intricate data taking up valuable time and requiring skill to make sense of the huge mass of data. Doherty (1999) noted that research on the internationalization of retailing has focused on descriptive studies. This present study has been more of an exploratory one in trying to explain what goes on in the Nigerian market in terms of the entry strategies used by the foreign retail firms. A great deal of qualitative material comes from talking with people whether it is through formal interviews or casual conversations. In conducting formal interviews for this present research, the researcher had taken time to:

- to develop empathy with interviewees and win their confidence;

- to be unobtrusive, in order not to impose one's own influence on the interviewee.

The best technique for this is the unstructured interview but as a result of some limitations such as time and cost, this present research has used a structured guide for the interviews, especially in relation to the various top level respondents chosen from the retail firms. In as much as qualitative research seeks to generalise about general issues, representative sampling is desirable. This researcher, however, recognises the views expressed by Bryman (1988) that representative sampling cannot always be achieved in qualitative research because of:

(a) the initially large exploratory nature of the research;

(b) problems of negotiating access and;

(c) the sheer weight of work and problems of gathering and processing the data.

It is further added that often, one has to make do with an opportunity sample in those areas where access is offered. The purposive theoretical sampling technique because of its characteristics which is suitable to this present research has been used. In this case, the basis of the sampling has been made clear and no inappropriate generalising claims is made for the findings. It is believed that a follow-up study may be able to better establish a theory that can lead to a better generalisation. Quite importantly also, the field work process has been outlined and discussed with a clear

144

indication of the data management process especially the coding process and method of validation of the codes and the procedure for drawing conclusions; all of these have set out the framework for data analysis as contained in the next chapter.

CHAPTER 6:   DATA PRESENTATION, ANALYSIS, AND FINDINGS

This chapter presents the findings of the empirical research. After a description of the international retail firms in Nigeria used for this study, the firms are assessed based on their method of entry into the Nigerian market. This evaluation looked at a number of firm and environmental characteristics. The analyses investigate major dimensions/constructs of the institutional and transaction cost theories underpinning this research for the firms, from the perspective of this developing Nigerian market: influence of asset specificity on entry mode selection, external/internal uncertainty, free-riding potential, effect of competition, cultural and retail market distance, population, etc.

Equally assessed are the influence of the legal system in the host market on the entry mode choice, the political system in place, and the government policies (imposition/inducement) in addition to the practice of the individual firms in terms of their habits/inertia and imitation tendencies. It is important to mention again that all of the above areas have been covered in the interview guide designed around several potentially important constructs suggested by the research problem and the literature in international management and international retailing. A summary of the flow of the data analysis is as shown in the figure below.

Figure 6.1: Outline of the framework for data analysis

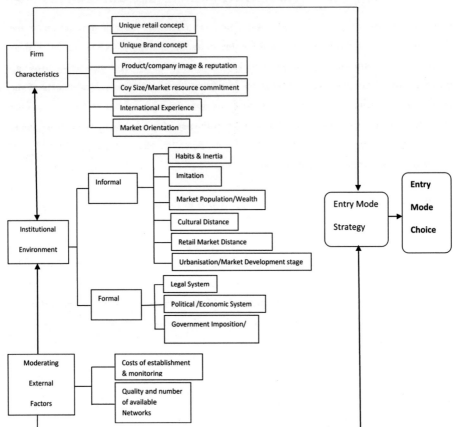

6.1. Introduction

In the previous chapter, such issues as the research design, sampling method, data collection method, and the fieldwork process were discussed. In that chapter, it was stated that the multiple case study methodology is to be used for this study. As a brief recap, a total of twelve international retail firms operating in the Nigerian market were chosen for study. In-depth interviews were conducted with some key decision makers in these firms as well as other key officers in some regulatory agencies of government like: The National Agency for Food & Drug Administration and Control (NAFDAC), The Nigeria Investment Promotion Commission, and The Standards Organisation of Nigeria. The statutory functions of these organisations affect retail practice in the country. Also a lot of secondary data were equally collected.

The following sections first profiles the retail firms used for this study, after which the major findings based on analyses of information provided by some of the key decision makers of these firms interviewed and the collected secondary data are presented in line with the objectives and focus of this research: what entry mode choice is used by international retail firms in entering the developing Nigerian market, what major determinants (from the organisational and environmental environment) influence the retailers' entry into the Nigerian market, as well as the extent to which these variables affect their entry mode decisions.

6.2. Case Analysis - Profile of Responding Retail Firms

NANDOS
Nandos is operating in Nigeria under a franchise arrangement from South Africa with UAC of Nigeria Plc. UAC Restaurants is the division of UAC of Nigeria in charge which was created as a result of the merger of the two restaurant business of UAC – Mr Bigg's and Menu Masters division.

Nandos opened its first outlet in October 2005 in Lagos and since then five more outlets have been opened across the major cities of Lagos and Abuja. According to the Business Development

Manager, Africa Lawrence Rock, UAC Nigeria Plc is a "master licensee for the brand who in turn has the ability to franchise the brand out in their territory". So far, all the outlets are owned by the UAC Plc.

The area manager Abuja Joseph Ekechukwu disclosed that Nandos aims to set up offices in all 36 states of Nigeria pointing out that before the end of 2011, the organisation will establish more new outlets, thereby increasing the number of its workers.

UAC of Nigeria Plc has a rich and varied history of successful enterprise that pre-dates the geographical entity called Nigeria. The rump of the Company's early days can be traced to the activities of European traders and commercial activities.

UAC was first incorporated in Lagos, Nigeria under the name Nigerian Motors Ltd on April 22, 1931 as a wholly-owned subsidiary of the United Africa Company Ltd. (a subsidiary of Unilever), which later became UAC International. The name was changed to UAC of Nigeria Limited on 1st March, 1973 and UAC of Nigeria Plc was adopted in 1991. In addition to UAC Restaurants, the company's other subsidiaries include: UAC dairies, UAC foods, UACN Property Development Company Plc (UPDC), and Warm Spring Waters Nigeria Limited. It has majority stakes in the following other companies: Grand Cereals and Oil Mills Limited (GCOML); Spring Waters Nigeria Limited (SWAN), Opticom Leasing Company Limited, CAP PLC, UAC Registrars Limited and GM Nigeria Limited as a joint venture with General Motors Corporation of Detroit USA.

Nando's is a casual dining restaurant chain originating from South Africa. Founded in 1987, Nando's operates in 34 countries and on five continents. The restaurant is named after Nandie, the son of Fernando Duarte, a Portuguese national from Mozambique living in South Africa. He and a friend, Robert Brozin, bought a restaurant called *Chickenland* in Southern Johannesburg, in 1987. This became the first Nando's restaurant

Nando's has a total of 30 outlets in Zimbabwe, Malawi, Swaziland, Kenya and Botswana. However, the bulk of its business is in South Africa, where it owns 180 outlets. The group also owns a further 160 outlets in Europe and Australia.

Source: Company reports and field notes

KFC

In Nigeria, KFC opened its first outlet at the City mall in Onikan, Lagos, Nigeria. The brand was brought to Nigeria, via Devyan International Nig. Ltd (formed from a joint venture between RJ Corp of India and Chellarams Plc) and an agreement with Yum Restaurants International (YRI), who are the franchise owners of the KFC brand.

Marc Schreuder, the Chief Executive Officer of Devyan International said the tripartite partnership, was born out of the recognition of Nigerians' crave for excellent and quick service along with quality foods without leaving the country shores. Bruce Layzell, the business development manager of Yum Brands added that the quality of service from KFC outlets in other parts of the world is what they will offer in Nigeria.

Chellarams Plc is a well known and trusted provider for both the consumer and industrial goods markets in Nigeria. The company's strong international reputation and professional infrastructures makes it a preferred business partner and place of employment. Established in 1923, Challarams possess immense experience in manufacturing, distribution, sales and marketing in Nigeria.

KFC was founded as Kentucky Fried Chicken by Colonel Harland Sanders in 1952, at Louisville, Kentucky USA though the idea of KFC's fried chicken actually goes back to 1930. It is now a global fast food restaurant. The company adopted the abbreviated form of its name in 1991.

150

Sanders sold the entire KFC franchise operation in 1964 for US$2m and since that time, the chain has been sold three more times: to Heublein in 1971, to R.J. Reynolds in 1982 and most recently to PepsiCo in 1986, which made it part of its Tricon Global restaurants division, which in turn was spun off in 1997, and has now been renamed Yum! Brands.

Source: Company reports and field notes

GAME STORES - (A subsidiary of Massmart Holdings Ltd).

Game stores have successfully entered the Nigerian market and are looking at expanding the brand with an outlet in The Palms shopping centre in Lagos, Nigeria. The company is operating its own store in Nigeria where it sells a variety of products such as house wares, furniture and electronics. Game operates out of 90 stores in 11 African countries. Game's Director for Africa, Richard Fuller, noted that the product range offered in Nigeria is similar to that found in their South African stores. Only around 35% of the products he said are currently bought from local Nigerian suppliers, partly because of a ban on the importation of certain products such as furniture, plastics and textiles. Fuller says they do extremely well on furniture bought from local suppliers and that import restrictions have not affected sales in any way.

Massmart is a managed portfolio of nine wholesale and retail chains, each focused on high volume, low margin, and low cost distribution of mainly branded consumer goods. This group has a South African ownership and operates in 14 other countries in Sub-Saharan Africa through four divisions comprising 290 stores. The group is the third largest distributor of consumer goods in Africa. It was founded in 1990 and listed on the JSE on the 4th July, 2000. Deloitte's 2010 *Global Powers of Retailing* places Massmart Holdings at 166th position in the global retail ranking.

Game stores are a subsidiary of Massmart Holding. The first Game store opened in Durban South Africa in 1970. The group's other brands include: Dion Wired, Makro, Builders warehouse, Builders Express, Builders Trade Deport, CBW, Jumbo Cash & Carry, and the Shield buying group.

151

The group has grown over the years by acquiring other stores like: Shields (1992), Dion stores (1993), CCW stores (1998), Game stores (1998), Jumbo stores (2001), Brown & Weir stores (2002), Builders Warehouse (2003), DeLay Rey, Servistar, federated timber stores (2005), Cambridge Food stores (2008), and Buildrite stores (2009).

Source: Company reports and field notes

SHOPRITE HOLDINGS LTD

This company opened its first Nigerian store in the Victoria Island area of Lagos in 2005. Shoprite is operating its own outlet in the Nigerian market and has its origin in South Africa. The company was founded in 1979 when eight stores in the Cape Town area of South Africa were purchased by Manuel Correia for one million Rand. The next 30 years were marked by various acquisitions and innovative expansion strategies that brought Shoprite to the R59 billion business it is today. The company later acquired Grand Bazaars, quadrupling its outlets. In 1991 the company acquired Checkers. The company's first store outside of South Africa was opened in 1995 in Lusaka, Zambia. That same year the company acquired distributor Sentra, allowing the company to expand into franchising.

In 1997, struggling OK Bazaars was acquired by the company from South African Breweries for one rand adding 157 supermarkets and 146 Furniture stores to the company. In 2002, the company acquired the Madagascar stores of French chain Champion. The same year, the company bought three Tanzanian supermarkets from Score Supermarket and opened its first Hypermarket outside of South Africa in Mauritius. In 2004, the company opened its first store outside of Africa in Mumbai, India. The same year, 14 stores were added with the acquisition of Foodworld, the company also bought South African ticket seller Computicket and opened its first Liquor store.

In the Deloitte report – *Emerging from the downturn: Global Powers of Retail 2010*, Shoprite Holdings Ltd was listed as the largest retailer in South Africa and 130th biggest retailer globally.

152

The company in December 2007 announced an investment of US $80m into the Democratic Republic of Congo for the development of two world class supermarkets in the major cities of Lubumbashi and Kinshasa.

In 2010, Shoprite made the decision to disinvest from India and focus on investment opportunities in the community rich countries of Western Africa in line with its long term growth plan. Today, the Shoprite Group trades with 1146 corporate and 276 franchise outlets in 17 countries across Africa, bringing the total number of stores in the Group to 1422.

Source: Company reports and field notes

NU METRO MEDIA STORES

Nu Metro South Africa owns and operates multiplex cinemas and media stores in Nigeria and Kenya. It retails DVDs; and distributes Hollywood, Bollywood, and Nollywood (Nigerian) product to cinemas in Africa. The first outlet in Nigeria is located at the Palms shopping complex in Victoria Island Lagos.

The Business Development Manager for Johnnic Communications owners of Nu Metro media stores stated that the early success of the Nu Metro Media Store in Lagos, which opened in June 2006, selling books, music CDs and DVDs, was the first proof of the massive pent up demand for world-class retail that exists in Nigeria. Until then, the largely-untapped buying power of Nigeria's 150 million population had gone untested. Before Nu Metro, there was nothing in the retail space that could be described as modern, let alone world-class. For Nu Metro's owners, the push into Nigeria - which includes taking a stake in local newspaper Business Day - has not been without frustration. The company had faced a lot of challenges in trying to establish itself in the Nigerian market. So far, the company is working in collaboration with Silverbirds Nigeria limited, the leading company in entertainment in Nigeria.

Source: Company reports and field notes.

153

METRO CINEMAS

Metro Cinema is a leading Home Entertainment company in South Africa owned by Johnnic Communication, a South Africa-based entertainment outfit. It operates 24 cinema multiplexes across South Africa using the latest technologies. The aim of the company is to bring the most exciting and diverse slate of movies to its customers. Nu Metro films run an office in Nairobi, Kenya which handles the marketing and sales of all Nu Metro Film's titles into both East and West Africa covering countries like: Kenya, Uganda, Tanzania, and Ghana.

The company now operates on Victoria Island in Lagos, Nigeria, under a joint venture arrangement with Silver Birds production Nigeria. According to the Chief Operation Officer of the company, Anthony Ward, "this new cinema hall is aimed toward showcasing internationally-equipped halls, with world class standard. The equipment is the ones that are being used in London, USA, South Africa and Kenya, and we are here in Nigeria to show them that there is the need to have an international standard cinema hall. Our equipment is the one that is being used internationally and we are concentrating on West Africa for now," he said. Ward further added that their sound equipment produces Dolby Digital 1.5 Surround sound, and they are made in Germany with high quality digital sounds. The company he said has been in the entertainment business since 1901 and have been into different parts of the world and now in Nigeria.

"We have spent close to 106 years in this cinema business and we also run media store. We have media store in Silverbird Galleria, we also produce magazines and newspapers, but basically, we have music industry and Compact Disk (CD) production in South Africa and other countries in the world" he said. Nu Metro cinema, which will be competing with other counterparts, he noted, a total sum of $15million has so far been spent on the project having completed the first phase which is the production of West African quality music, the Nigeria road maps and the production of Compact Discs (CDs).

Source: Company reports and field notes

BIG TREAT

Big Treat Plc though a Nigerian company now, started off operations in Nigeria with a Chinese ownership in 1991 with Pamela Wu the Chief Operating Officer as a bakery and confectionary business on Opebi road in Lagos, Nigeria, and has over the years diversified into production of branded milk, supermarkets and fast food business with its turnover between 2006 year end and 2007 year end, increasing by 89%. Currently, the company has over 22 outlets across the country with factories in Lagos, Kano, Kaduna, Port Harcourt, Abeokuta, Aba, Onitsha among others. Big Treat is one of Nigeria's fast food outlets, convenience store marketers and household supermarkets.

The company is expanding its brand now via a strategic partnership with Oando, a Nigerian petroleum company that owns and operates filling stations nationwide. This strategic partnership provides that Oando Marketing offer 58 numbers of its over 500 service stations to Big Treat to expand its distribution bases across Nigeria. This development is expected to further make the Oando service stations a one-stop shop for high quality consumer products.

The expansion plan began with 6 stations in Lagos State by the 25th of September 2008, and then 8 by the end of November 2008, before finally spreading to service stations around the country.

Commenting, Mrs. Lara Banjoko, the Chief Operating Officer, Oando Marketing Limited, said, "At Oando we are constantly seeking ways to improve consumer experience on our forecourt, this partnership therefore excites us as it presents us another opportunity to provide value-added services to our customers. This is just one of the few planned strategies through which we will continue to enhance the one-stop-consumer experience we are known for".

Oando Marketing Limited is the leading oil marketing retailer with over 500 retail outlets and numerous commercial customers cutting across the different geographical zones in Nigeria and operations in Ghana, Togo, Liberia and Republic of Benin.

Source: Company reports and field notes

WRANGLER

Wrangler is a manufacturer of jeans. The brand is owned by the VF Corporation who also own Lee, Jansport, and The North Face, among others. Its headquarters are located in downtown Greensboro, North Carolina with production plants in a variety of locations throughout the world. Wrangler International is now chaired by Dieter Jacobfeuerborn.

The history of the company dates back to 1904 when C.C. Hudson along with some of his friends, incorporated the Hudson Overall Company. Its first factory was built in 1919 and changed its name to Blue Bell Overall Company. So Wrangler Jeans were first made by Blue Bell, who acquired the brand when they took over Casey Jones in the mid-1940s. Blue Bell employed Bernard Lichtenstein ('Rodeo Ben'), a Polish tailor from Lodz who worked closely with cowboys, to help design jeans suitable for rodeo use. This was the origin of Wrangler Jeans. The 13MWZ style, introduced in 1947, is still available worldwide. In addition to this, Wrangler has since introduced several other lines that are more designated towards a specific group. Some examples of this are 20X, Riggs and Aura.

Wrangler is now a global brand with factories around the world. Blue Bell opened a factory in Belgium in 1962 and the Wrangler brand name started to enjoy a successful launch in Europe. By 1973, Wrangler jeans had become an icon of youth culture, synonymous with teenagers the world over. In 1986, Blue Bell merged with the VF Corporation of Pennsylvania, preparing the ground for the global success of the Wrangler brand. Wrangler now has six stores in Nigeria spread around Lagos, Abuja, and Port Harcourt. One of its outlets in Lagos is situated at 'The Palms' shopping complex on Victoria Island with all of its stores providing an ideal family shopping experience for both casual and formal clothing according to its General Manager.

Source: Company reports and field notes

ROCAWEAR

Roca wear was established in 1999 by the American Rap musician "Jay-Z" Shawn Carter and Damon Dash. According to the company records, Roca wear has annual sales of $700 million. The company expanded its brand through licensing pacts to develop lines for children and juniors; socks, and sandals, leather, suede, and fur outerwear; handbags, and belts; lounge wear; headwear, jewelry, and sunglasses as well as co-branded product with Pro-Keds, State Property, and Team Roc.

In March 2007, Jay-Z sold the rights to the Roca wear brand to Iconix Brand Group for US$204 million. Jay-Z will retain his stake in the company and will continue to oversee the marketing, licensing, and product development. In March 2009, the company launched its first social networking site, offering style news, music, fashion, and cultural connections. The company operates in Nigeria under a licensing agreement.

Source: Company reports and field notes

T.M.LEWIN

T.M.Lewin (Thomas Mayes Lewin) is a gentleman's shirt retailer and formerly a UK manufacturer. It was founded in 1898 when Thomas Mayes Lewin opened his first shop in London. The company has grown over the years with a wide range of products for men and women from formal, work and casual shirts, trousers, suits, knitwear, ties, cufflinks, bowties, to other fashion accessories

T.M.Lewin produced shirts and accessories with a history of innovation, with its founder becoming one of the first to make the 'coat-shirt'. This novelty was noted in the London Opinion and Today newspaper in 1905. In 1979 T.M.Lewin & Sons was acquired by the McKenna family and in 1980 Geoff Quinn, the current managing director, joined the company from Turnbull & Asser.

The McKennas and Geoff Quinn took to sourcing the shirts directly from the mills; consequently in 1983 T.M.Lewin acquired Asquith Brown, a shirt manufacturer owned by John Francomb, who subsequently became part of the T.M.Lewin management team. As a consequence of direct sourcing the company grew rapidly in the 1980's. In 1993 Geoff Quinn became managing director following the deaths of both McKenna brothers.

Today T.M. Lewin has 75 stores in the UK and Ireland, and very many concessions with House of Fraser and other stores in Singapore. In Nigeria, the company operates under a licensing arrangement with the licensee operating from an office/warehouse in the Ikoyi area of Lagos Nigeria.

Source: Company reports and field notes.

T-MART SUPERMARKET

T-Mart is an American supermarket and the first international retail firm to commence operation at the mega Business and Leisure resort Tinapa in Calabar where it is located. The Cross River State Governor, Liyel Imoke, on a recent visit to the resort, said the shop is a typical American super store with reasonable prices that can compare with any of its kind anywhere in the world. According to him, "while prices at the shop are as good as in any big stores in the Western world, its services are excellent and of good quality as there is none of its kind in Nigeria or in the West African sub-region".

Head of Operations, T-Mart, Ms Tanya Williams, described the outfit as a big franchise that has recorded a phenomenal business transaction in Tinapa. Williams said since the store commenced operation in mid-November 2009, "the number of customers coming to the store has increased consistently because of excitement from the quality of its goods which are imported from reputable manufacturers in United Kingdom, United States and Dubai." She added that patronage has been tremendous as customers come from far away states and other African countries to buy from the store.

Source: Company reports and field notes

WAL-MART

Wal-Mart Stores, Inc. is an American public corporation that runs a chain of large discount department stores. In 2010, it was the world's largest public corporation by revenue, according to the Forbes Global 2000 for that year. The company was founded by Sam Walton in 1962, incorporated on October 31, 1969, and publicly traded on the New York Stock Exchange in 1972. Wal-Mart is headquartered in Bentonville, Arkansas with operations in 15 other overseas territories.

Wal-Mart operates under its own name in the United States, including the 50 states and Puerto Rico. Wal-Mart operates in Mexico as Walmex, in the United Kingdom as Asda , in Japan as Seiyu, and in India as Best Price. It has wholly-owned operations in Argentina, Brazil, and Canada. Wal-Mart's investments outside North America have had mixed results: its operations in the United Kingdom, South America and China are highly successful, while it was forced to pull out of Germany and South Korea when ventures there were unsuccessful.

Wal-Mart's operations are organized into three divisions: Wal-Mart Stores U.S., Sam's Club, and Wal-Mart International. The company does business in nine different retail formats: supercenters, food and drugs, general merchandise stores, bodegas (small markets), cash and carry stores, membership warehouse clubs, apparel stores, soft discount stores and restaurants.

In 2004, Wal-Mart bought the 116 stores in the Bompreço supermarket chain in northeastern Brazil. In late 2005, it took control of the Brazilian operations of Sonae Distribution Group through its new subsidiary, WMS Supermercados do Brasil, thus acquiring control of the Nacional and Mercadorama supermarket chains, the leaders in the Rio Grande do Sul and Paraná states, respectively. In November 2006, Wal-Mart announced a joint venture with Bharti Enterprises to open retail stores in India. As foreign corporations are not allowed to directly enter the retail sector in India; Wal-Mart will operate through franchises and handle the wholesale end of the operations.

In January 2009, the company acquired a controlling interest in the largest grocer in Chile, Distribucion y Servicio D&S SA and on February 22, 2010, the company confirming it was acquiring video streaming company Vudu, Inc. for an estimated $100 million. Available records show that apart from its South African procurement operations, Wal-Mart has no visible presence in Africa. Therefore, with the procurement of a large retail floor space at the Tinapa Business Resort, it is only a matter of time before the company establishes itself in the African market. A top executive of the company mentioned that their expansion into markets in Africa is slow because they have not been able to develop what he called 'a business strategy for Africa'.

Source: Company reports and field notes.

6.3. Firms' Location & mode of entry into Nigeria

One major objective of this study is to ascertain if any firm characteristics affect the entry mode of the international retail firms into the Nigerian market. Based on the conceptual framework developed for this study and the field studies carried out, the coding system developed a number of themes that aided the analysis; the findings are as presented below:

Table 6.1.   **List of Case study firms & Entry mode used**

Retail Firms	Classification	Entry mode used	Market of origin	Location in Nigeria
Nandos	Food/Grocery	Franchise	South Africa	Lagos, Abuja
Shoprite	"	WOS	South Africa	Lagos
KFC	"	Franchise	USA/India	Lagos, Abuja
Wal-Mart	"	WOS	USA	Calabar
Big Treat	"	Strategic Alliance(Implant)	China	Whole Country
T-Mart Supermarket	"	Franchise	USA	Calabar
Roca	Non Grocery	Licensing	USA	Lagos
Wrangler	"	Franchise	USA	Lagos, Abuja and Port Harcourt
T.M. Lewin	"	Licensing	UK	Lagos
Nu Metro Media Stores	"	Franchise	South Africa	Lagos
Metro Cinemas	"	Joint venture	South Africa	Lagos, Abuja
Game Stores	"	WOS	South Africa	Lagos

From the table above, it is important to firstly state that all the retail firms in Nigeria used for this study confine themselves to a single particular organisational form; this finding is contrary to that by Burt (1991) who mentioned that when active in international markets, grocery retailers use different modes of store expansion and do not stick to a preferred mode. Half of the retail firms investigated is into grocery retailing and the other half are non-grocery retailers. Four of the retail firms in this study operate in Nigeria using the wholly owned subsidiary method of entry. The others use different forms of the collaborative method of entry, ranging from: Franchising, Joint Ventures, to Strategic Partnerships for example, Big Treat uses a form of implant where they have their store outlets at some selected garages (filling station) operated by the oil firm Oando that has over 500 of such stations across the country.

6.4.   Cross Case Analysis

In the following sections, the views of the interviewees from the retail firms chosen for this study are presented. Their views as expressed in the questions asked which were drawn up with reference to the focus/objectives of this study and the major constructs of the underpinning theories of the transaction cost economies and the institutional model are presented below. All of these are aimed at providing the needed answers to the major questions raised in respect of this study, namely:

(i)   What entry modes do international retail firms use to internationalize into the developing Nigerian market?

(ii) What characteristics of the available entry modes affect their entry mode choices

(iii) What major company and environmental factors influence the entry mode choices?

The sections below present the findings from this study, in respect of the research questions stated above. Section 6.5 addresses the first two research questions while sections 6.6 and 6.7 look into the third research question.

6.5   The Nigerian Market and foreign Retail Entry

This present study revealed that most of the international retail firms in the Nigerian market use the collaborative mode of entry rather than the independent entry mode (see Table 6.1). Only three of the retail firms use the independent entry mode while the others use different forms of the collaborative mode, ranging from: licensing, to franchising, joint ventures, and strategic alliances.

The retail executives for the various firms interviewed gave many characteristics of the entry mode that have influenced their final decisions on the method to use. Evidence gathered from this empirical study show the important influence of such characteristics as: involvement/control, investment cost, knowledge dissemination risk, protection of company assets, need for rapid expansion, and returns on investment. The GM of Shoprite when asked stated that:

> "Shoprite has an aggressive expansion policy mainly because our growth has been hampered as a result of the trading ban imposed on South Africa in the days of apartheid. With its abolition, the company expanded into foreign markets. We have a very strong

brand name and reputation, huge size and resources to commit to foreign operation, as well as advanced technologies and innovations to use in these markets.

We waited for Nigeria to return to democratic governance before considering entry in order to reduce the risks involved in operating under a military government where there is no respect for the rule of law and no stability in the system both politically and economically. With a realisation of this in the 1990s, we were the first big retail firm to enter the market; we established our own store using our technologies and innovations in the Nigerian market.

We couldn't find any partner of our size to work and developing a local relationship we felt would be too expensive and costly because it would mean transferring our assets and technologies to the local partner we know only so little about. This situation would need us to incur some additional cost just to be sure the local partner operates within our overall company policies and directions. All of these led to our use of the wholly owned subsidiary in the Nigerian market we wanted the control of our market".

The above views were also mentioned by the Business Development Manager for Game stores another retail giant from South Africa also using the wholly owned subsidiary entry mode. He equally added that the reduced cost of establishing their outlet in Lagos, Nigeria, due to the development of a mega shopping mall like 'The Palms' equally influenced their decision.

The executives of Nandos, KFC, Nu Metro Media stores, Wrangler and others using the franchise system, mentioned that this method has been used as a result of the significant resource commitments of capital, informational, and managerial resources. The need to share the huge financial requirements, limited knowledge of the Nigerian market, as well as having very few managerial personnel to send to Nigeria, all led to their use of the franchise entry mode. An interesting point mentioned by the executives of Nandos and KFC, however, is the fact that they chose their franchise partners based on business relatedness and experience. Their franchise partners in the Nigerian market have the experience and operated similar businesses in Nigeria. Marc Schreuder, the chief executive officer of Devyan International, the major franchisor with Chellarams Nigeria Plc., noted that "we looked out for business relatedness because this enables the accumulation and exploitation of related and relatively homogeneous knowledge on products and markets". The KFC executive equally mentioned that as a result of their business practice, they are very rich in legal and relational resources, and would often prefer contractual entry modes because

163

they already have the appropriate resources for using contractual entry modes and may incur minimal costs during market entry. One executive of Roca interviewed added that the amount of financial, informational, and managerial resources they had available as they considered entry into the Nigerian market, was sufficient for establishing a full ownership subsidiary in the market; however, they feel the resources may not be enough for using the wholly-owned entry mode in such a market. This is because rapid expansion is imperative to the organisation as such, "we need to use shared ownership modes of entry for acquiring complementary resources". This entry mode the organisation has used most frequently in almost all of its other foreign markets.

This executive and others from firms that have used the collaborative mode of entry also mentioned that partner selection in the Nigerian market is a very important area of consideration. They added that besides business relatedness, other important characteristics about the partner are equally looked into. Some of these are related to the task to be performed whilst others are directly linked to the partner to be selected. The following are some of the criteria mentioned by these executives:

- connections to government or non-government organizations (e.g., other firms, trade organizations, etc.);
- regulatory permits, licenses, or patents;
- facilities (location, R&D or office facilities);
- managerial (Quality of HR, leadership) and/or labour (e.g., technical, service) skills.
- transparency of the firm and/or ethical values/ beliefs;
- reputation;
- goals, objectives, aspirations, or synergy potential;
- commitment, seriousness and/or enthusiasm for the partnership;
- favourable past association with the local firm or mutual acquaintances;
- successful partnering record with other firms;
- firm size;

- market share or industry position;

- financial capabilities (assets, ability to raise financing); and

- trustworthiness.

All of the above areas are taken into consideration in deciding the collaborative mode to use so as to ensure the partnering firms can work together effectively. The need to make the choice of the "right" partner that best fit with the operations of these respective retail firms they say is crucial.

Again, fear of the stability of the political, economic and legal system in the country in addition to the level of corruption and state of the rule of law, as well as infrastructural deficiencies were some of the other reasons given by the executives of the retail firms (like T.M. Lewin) that have entered into the market using licensing. They mentioned that instability in the political, economic and legal systems in Nigeria increases the uncertainties faced by businesses, so having reduced commitments and investments, is the only way to guard against potential losses.

6.6. Retail Firms' characteristics & choice of entry mode in the Nigerian market

Ascertaining the choice of entry mode used by international retail firms in entering the Nigerian market is one of the major objectives of this study. The very many frameworks on retail internationalisation recognized the influence of firm specific factors in this area, which is composed mainly of the firms' assets, external and internal uncertainty, free-riding potential etc. (Alexander and Doherty 2009). In a bid to ascertain the effect of these dimensions of the firm characteristics, the decision makers interviewed for the retail firms were probed with over nine questions on: the effect of company characteristics – (size of organisation, effect of competition, unique retail concept, nature and relatedness of products, specialised technology/processes, brand strength/image, unique retail formula, customer service, etc.). Other areas include: International experience of the company, as well as the effect of company reputation just to be able to get their assessment of their firms along these lines. It is important to state that these variables were selected, based on their relevance to the objectives of this study, as well as their link to the theoretical construct on which this study is based.

Data obtained from the interviewees on the effect of these company characteristics as stated above, show that some company characteristics played a major role in determining the entry mode strategy used by the international retail firms operating in the Nigerian market. The possession of related products, the level of competition in the market, as well as the company's product image and reputation, in addition to customer service, size and market resource commitment and international experience were clearly stated by the interviewees as important factors that have influenced their entry mode choice in the Nigerian market.

6.6.1. Unique retail concept

This study revealed that some of the international retail firms in the Nigerian market used different operating formats. The GM for Shoprite mentioned that:

> "as at the time of our entry into the Nigerian market, the level of competition was quite low and competition was virtually non-existent such that there were no other firms giving our incoming operation a significant challenge which enabled us to introduce our retail structure conveniently into the Nigerian market'. He further stated that 'our research had shown that the average Nigerian consumer has an idea of the supermarket/hypermarket format, all we needed to do was to offer to the market a source of differentiation in the delivery of added values which involved the importation of our concept the consumers perceived as new. In doing this, we were very careful so as to be aware of the implications of introducing our store format and to see if there are possible oppositions that will be generated in the market".

Similar views were expressed by some managers in Game stores as well as Nandos and KFC. In his views, the managing director of Game stores mentioned that:

> "Our experience has shown that customers do not wish to be unduly challenged, especially by complex operating procedures and format in the store, although they want something of interest and in some cases want to be involved in the service provision. So, we introduce concepts we know the market would accept".

As a result of this fact, Shoprite has expanded and internationalized from acquisitions; its Business Development manager added that they are always cautious not to radically change the structure in

166

all of its market; allowing the conditions in each market to determine the speed and dimension of the retail concepts introduced. He was quick to add that their retail formats have a grounded history within their domestic markets and they have come to realise that such formats may not fit within a new international context. Therefore, while a distinct format may benefit them in foreign markets where they operate, the main concern is to ensure that such formats have to deliver real benefits to the new retail environment and be distinguishable from existing offerings, otherwise, consumers without an understanding of the format, will be less likely to perceive it as a positive benefit.

Besides the above views, this present research revealed that the foreign retail firms in the Nigerian market really did not decide on their entry mode strategy in the market with a consideration of their retail format. A common feature mentioned by all of the executives of these firms interviewed was that the Nigerian market was waiting to receive the services and products of such foreign firms. The average consumer did not bother about the retail format used; the emphasis was more on the products offered and services delivered. So what the firms ensured was to use a format and retail concept the market understood. As mentioned by the General Manager of Shoprite:

> "The retail format identifies a retailer's capabilities and serves as the unifying component of the competitive plan. The specification of retail service-output levels, operational efficiencies embodied in the retail technology, and the learning and experiences contained in the retail culture, determine the position the retailer secures in the market place".

So, for most of these firms, they have not encountered the usual problems of the transfer of retail formats into foreign markets especially in a developing market like Nigeria. The executives mentioned that in other developing foreign markets where they operate, they have such problems as different consumer preferences, different supply and distribution conditions, government policies, and different domestic retail system as limiting the transfers of elements such as assortment, service, location and price. In addition, technologies and methods geared to the developed home market conditions were found to be inappropriate in such developing markets. All of these were not inhibiting factors for the retail firms in the Nigerian market.

Though not operational in Nigeria, one executive of Shoprite interviewed stated that in some of their stores just established in some other developing markets, some consumers always would want to get some personal service; as such, they would dispense with the use of the self- checkout even when they have very limited time to stay in the stores.

6.6.2. Brand concept

This study reveals that the bulk of the retail firms in Nigeria have come into the country with some unique brand concept. A majority of the retail firms claim to have private labels for some of their products that the consumers have favourably embraced. The use of private label is a relatively new phenomenon in Nigeria. Before now, retailing in the country had been dominated by informal retailers in open markets as well as small, independent and homogenous outfits, who had no resources and the need to use private label products. However, the entrance of foreign retailers into the country has transformed the nature of competition among retailers by placing more emphasis on brand equity and customer loyalty as expressed by the interviewees. The grocery and non-grocery retailers alike have embarked on various differentiation strategies, including the use of private label, in order to build and maintain a strong customer base.

The large supermarkets and department stores have adopted the use of private label on some basic product lines. Pastry products are leading the way, as some supermarkets also own their own bakeries. Notable examples include Big Treat, and Shoprite and Game stores. The executives interviewed noted that many customers who may have visited to buy the branded pastry products end up purchasing other items as well with some of the retail outlets like Shoprite extending the use of private label to other product lines.

In the words of one of the top executives interviewed:
"there is nothing so spectacular about the type of retail services we offer to our customers in the Nigerian market; compared to what we offer in some other of our markets, I'll say we have cut down on some of our provisions. We only very strongly, provide a good brand

image for our products and very clearly promote more of our private labels to the Nigerian consumers"

The Regional Manager of Game stores noted that they are trying to take advantage of the marketing opportunities in the use of private labels by building and maintaining strong and easily recognisable brands. He further added that "the quality of the products we are offering to the customers is what has led to the high level of patronage for our private labels".

The Business Development Manager for KFC mentioned that

"product ranges will need to be adjusted slightly for any market. We are prepared to focus activities around the development of a brand that will be meaningful to consumers in the international environment and differentiate us amongst the domestic and international retail market. We have to be certain that we possess a brand rather than just a label".

The executives of Wal-Mart, Nu Metro media stores, Nandos and some others, expressed the view that their operations are oriented towards their brands. In the words of the Nu Metro executive

"we have an approach that sees the organisation as a whole, oriented towards the creations of the brand, the nurturing of that brand through development, and the sustaining of the brand's identity and evolution once it has been established. Any organisation that is not brand oriented will inevitably end up undifferentiated in the marketplace and this we try to avoid".

The Wal-Mart manager had said they aim at brand orientation "because of its impact on creating merchandise advantages, customer service, trading format, and customer communication advantages". This study also revealed that whilst some retailers like Game stores, and Shoprite have individual brands that the retailers sell in-store where they use one or more brands to address their market segments in the Nigerian market, other retailers like KFC, Nandos, T.M. Lewin, and Wrangler are attempting to be the brand itself and all brands within the store are the retailer brands. The manager of T.M. Lewin mentioned that "building successful brands will enable us to enjoy the importance of 'symbolic' values and distinct brand 'personality'. Thus, we are trying to be able to occupy a place in the consumer's life so as to be able to better build a favourable brand position and sustained brand growth".

In summary, therefore, this study reveals that apart from the private labels introduced by some of these international retail firms in Nigeria, the majority of these firms are offering the Nigerian consumers the same products they are used to only in better quality with additional service delivery and conditions. The Area Manager of Nandos Abuja noted that "Nigerians are used to the concept of fast food, what we have succeeded in doing, is providing the customers with this same concept and an improved menu and service with some added dimensions." This view is supported by the executives of KFC, Metro Media stores and Game stores.

Interestingly, however, when asked if their retail concept influenced their choice of entry mode into the Nigerian market, most of the executives answered in the affirmative that they considered their brand concept important and this directly influenced their entry mode choice into the market. The idea behind this one executive mentioned, was to use a mode that helped to protect their respective brands. Along this line, therefore, whilst firms like Game stores, and Shoprite have used their wholly owned outlets, others like Nu Metro Media stores, KFC, Nandos, T-Mart supermarkets etc. have used franchise arrangements. The available records show that Nigeria's middle class has grown in the last couple of years and many rural areas have evolved into towns and cities with greater economic activities; consequently, a boost for retailing in the country. An official of Nigeria Investment Promotion Council (NIPC) interviewed stated that "the exponential growth of Nigeria's telecommunications, financial, real estate and energy industries has resulted in the emergence of a fast growing middle class, especially in towns and cities. Many professionals employed in these and other related industries, are characterised by their youthfulness, high earning power, and adoption of western lifestyles and culture, including leisure shopping. The products offered by most of these retailers, therefore, are not new to the consumers".

The idea is that where the consumers know the products offered and how to consume them then it becomes easy to sell the products using different means, especially where the market is familiar with the product or service. As stated by a manager of Game stores. "Where the product or the process is complex for the consumers to use, then it would be best to have us explain this to the consumers ourselves for us to be sure of the type of information the consumers receive". The KFC manager, on his part, further added that their operations in Nigeria have been made relatively easy because even before their arrival into the Nigerian market, the average Nigerian consumer already knew about their products, as such, they needed no form of product adaptation in order to fit into the Nigerian market. The Area manager for Nandos mentioned that their products are deemed appropriate for foreign markets if they satisfy the "3C" criteria meaning culture, climate and customer – to be offered to foreign stores, the products must suit the individual environmental and consumer characteristics of each market.

6.6.3. Product/company image & reputation

Following the view of the interviewees on their introduction of private brands in the Nigerian market, the retail firms claim to have developed good product image as well as company image that have enabled them to withstand competition. The interviewees recognise image as crucial to the successful internationalization of their retail format in the Nigerian market. As stated earlier, the firms claimed to have successfully built a consumer franchise by shifting loyalty away from manufacturer brands to their retail stores. Along with the others, a retail firm like Shoprite noted that they have built up their own brand products as a rival to manufacturers' products, on the basis of both price and quality. In consequence, they have also built product ranges that appeal to their customers, which provide them with the ability to convey a distinct message to the consumers in the Nigerian market. In the views of the Abuja Area Manager of Nandos,

> "the dilemma of product and company image requires us to fully understand the transferability of our image and hence our brand. Based on the market we find ourselves, at times we discover that some of our existing offering will not possess a distinct image in the international market. Under such conditions, we consider either to acquire a local operation or developing a new operation for the international market. There is always the challenge of trying to provide an offering that is distinctive in some way."

Having a favourable store image was also another important issue, a bulk of the interviewees interviewed mentioned, as contributing to their operations in the Nigerian market. There was a mixed-bag of ways the retail firms claim to develop a good store image. An executive of Shoprite stated that:

"for our operations in the Nigerian market, just like we have it in all other international markets we serve, provision of high quality goods in a wide assortment, appropriately priced, having a nice store layout that is easy to access; in addition to our convenient locations and returns policy are all factors that have given us a very high store image".

Along this line, the manager for Wrangler mentioned that "our provision of modern styles, and very knowledgeable and helpful staff, as well as good ambience in-store, has raised our store image". This view was supported by the CEO for Big Treat, KFC and Roca who in their response also included other factors like: their reputation in the past, store architecture, method of service delivery, and reliability as reasons for their improved store image in the market.

The executives of these retail firms in the Nigerian market stated that the need to protect the image and reputation of their various companies and brands have influenced greatly their choice of entry method. In their response, the executives of Shoprite, Game stores, and Wal-Mart, that came into the market using the independent mode of entry stated that it was in a bid for them to keep the image and reputation of their firms and products that they have opted to use this mode; they expressed the fear that with the low level of development of the retail sector in Nigeria, finding experienced and credible partners may have been difficult.

Also, for the other retailers in the market who have used some other forms of collaborative entry modes, the fact was made that the experience, dependability and reputation of the partners in the Nigerian market are important considerations that were looked into in the establishment of such business relationships. The executives of KFC noted they came into the market in a joint venture with a highly established firm like Chellarams that has operated in the retail sector in Nigeria for over forty years; the same fact was mentioned by the executives of Nandos, using a franchise arrangement with UAC Nigeria Plc. Pamela Wu the chief operating office for Big Treat also mentioned this point as being the reason for the strategic partnership they established with Oando an oil giant with several retail filling stations across the country. The views of their other counterparts like Roca, T-Mart supermarket and others like Metro Cinemas partnering with Silver Birds Nigeria, are still along the same line.

The Managing Director for Game stores stated that:

> "brand image management is a critical part of our company's marketing program. Communicating a clearly defined brand image enables our customers to identify the needs satisfied by the brand and differentiate the brand from competitors; this has been a key to our product success. Developing this needs-based image strategy helps our brands to create a clear and distinct position within its category. This makes the brand strong in the market; ultimately providing it with a good market image at the same time".

The executives of the other retail firms equally support this view. One of the executives noted that it is the less tangible, more experience-related dimensions of store image which are the most difficult to establish immediately in a new foreign market like Nigeria. The meaning which domestic consumers attach to these dimensions has been built up over a number of years of continued experience to the retailer and competitors, and in the case of consumers in the host Nigerian market, there has been such history of exposure to the store or retailer.

6.6.4. Firm size & market resources commitment

Almost all of the retail firms in operation in the Nigerian market (Wal-Mart, Game stores, Shoprite, KFC, Wrangler, Nu Metro, Nandos, etc.) are very large organisations in measures of employee numbers, sales, ownership of capital equipment, and financial capability. The executives of these firms interviewed noted that the size of their firms had affected their choice of entry method into the Nigerian market.

Having the financial capacity necessary for investment in any international market and the composition of the management of these firms are some other very important dimensions raised by the interviewees. The executives of these firms mentioned their strong and aggressive management with very knowledgeable experts in the field of retailing and international business as playing a key role in their entry mode decision into the Nigerian market. A major finding from this study is that most of the top executives of these international retail firms in Nigeria came in from their respective head offices and have very many years of experience in their established company procedures. The General Manager of Shoprite, for example, before coming to establish the outlets in Nigeria, said he had been outside South Africa since 1998, working in Angola, Madagascar, and Zambia.

As mentioned above, Shoprite and Game stores, two of the biggest international retail firms in Nigeria at the moment, operate in the Nigerian market using their wholly owned subsidiaries. Wal-Mart is also using this entry method (though yet to start operation). A summary of the responses from the executives of these firms show that this method of entry has been used just to allow them to enjoy proprietary advantages which their large size provides them. The records show that Shoprite came into Nigeria in 2004, though opened its store for business in 2005. The Regional Manager noted that at the time of their entry into the Nigerian market, there was just no competition especially from well established firms like theirs; this, he said, motivated them to establish their own outlet just to take advantage of being the first to come into the market. In his words: "in 2004, when we came into the Nigerian market, we saw the size of the foreign business community was very small. There were no other large retail outfits that could compete with us; we therefore decided to utilise our pioneering advantage in the market". The company was equally prepared to commit huge funds into the Nigerian market as a result of the large size of the market and its growth potential.

The executives of these firms further revealed that besides financial strength, their use of the independent entry mode in the Nigerian market has been influenced also by the cheap cost of acquiring retail floor spaces. Both the governments (at Federal and state and local government levels) and private developers have embarked on the development of modern mega shopping infrastructure such as: The Palms Shopping mall in Lagos, TINAPA project in Calabar, Polo Park in Enugu, Ceddi Plaza in Abuja, and others in Port Harcourt, Kano, and other parts of the country. Compared to the cost of putting up their own structures, the executives said the costs of acquiring spaces in these mega shopping malls are relatively cheap. Shoprite and Game both have their outfits at 'The Palms' shopping mall in Lagos. Therefore, all of their other investment is in developing their retail format and merchandise; this, they claim, has greatly reduced their cost of operation in the market compared to the situation in other developing markets where they operate with limited or non-existent retail infrastructures.

Unlike Shoprite, Wal-Mart and Game stores, the other international retail firms in the Nigerian market mentioned that they have used the collaborative entry mode just because of the need to reduce their level of resource commitment in the market. Part of the reasons given was the high cost of losing their investment in the market in the event of failure. This view is close to that expressed by the executives of the other firms that used their wholly owned subsidiaries but operated from rented retail spaces in the newly developed mega shopping malls in some major cities in the country. The bulk of these retail firms in Nigeria operate from these mega shopping complexes. It is observed that high street retailing is not common in Nigeria. An executive of the Nigeria Investment Promotion Commission interviewed said it is because high street shopping operations were severely damaged in the past by the activities of itinerant street traders. This "grey market" was able to trade alongside fixed retail outlets and was able to undercut them on price as a result of informal import systems operating in contraband and "look-alike brands" from neighbouring markets.

In the words of one of the executives for KFC,

"most of our competitors claim to understand consumer tastes, fashion, employment laws and so on, but the fact is you don't understand those things when you enter a new market. You get them wrong and when you get them wrong you can get them seriously wrong that is why we never profess to be retail experts outside of our home market, which is why we always look for a partner".

6.6.5. International experience

When asked how knowledgeable they were in international retail operations and how they assessed and related with other organisations and agents in the foreign markets, the interviewees all had a lot to say on this. The general Manager of Shoprite stated that:

"We operate in seventeen countries across Africa and Asia and have built up the necessary expertise over the years. Our entry mode is based on a business plan which has been tried and tested over the years. We have a standard business plan after taking into consideration the differences in country laws and regulations, supply chain issues, tax, regulatory guidelines, labour, etc."

The Regional manager Africa for Wal-Mart in his response noted that this is the major problem that has affected their entry into most developing markets around the world. In the case of Nigeria, he stated that they are yet to develop what he called an "African strategy", hence the delay in their take off at the Tinapa site where the firm is situated.

The executives of Metro stores, KFC, Nandos, and a few others mentioned that since the retail subsector of the Nigerian economy is still developing; there are not many experienced agents to work with and this has influenced their choice of entry mode. They highlighted the fact that it would be too difficult and expensive to enter into arrangements with local partners that would require some form of training, hence they have sought for collaborative arrangements with some highly experienced organisations like Silver Birds, UAC Nigeria Plc. and Chellarams. The General Manager for Shoprite and the Managing Director of Game stores had mentioned that they have their own specialised buying subsidiaries and supply chain networks, hence their use of the independent entry mode in Nigeria. They claim to be working with a select few suppliers in the Nigerian market. Having to make the suppliers and agents understand their operating procedures and business practices is a risk they mentioned they are not prepared to take, in as much as they have no other established retail firm competing with them in the market.

6.6.6. Market orientation

A manager in Wal-Mart mentioned that "whether the market is psychically close or not, we must analyse the non-domestic market on its own terms and establish a market orientation in our thinking about our new market of operation". In the words of the Nandos Area Manager:

> "Market orientation is our organisational culture 'that most effectively and efficiently creates the necessary behaviours for the creation of superior value' that leads to the generation of increased profits for us. We have designed a system that enables us to gather important intelligence about our customers and markets helps dissemination of the information gathered, and also, enables us to better respond to the challenge of competition".

The following sums up the views of the other interviewees as they mentioned that where they are intending to introduce an operation with an existing format and merchandise range, they will have to consider whether they are prepared to make adjustments to meet the needs of the new market. The head of operations for T-Mart supermarket stated that experience has shown them that only operational experience in a market will really tell them what they need to know, hence they live in the country in question and learn about the new market and then set their strategies.

The figures below summarise the findings, in respect of above firm characteristics, for the retail firms investigated. The table shows the interviewees have indicated that such factors as: International experience, product/company reputation, company size and market resource commitment, and brand concept influenced the entry mode choices of the retail firms. Other factors like the retail concept and market orientation though considered important, were seen not to have really influenced the entry strategy of these firms. The table also shows a classification of the firms according to their method of entry into the market.

Figure 6.2   Summary of findings on firm characteristics

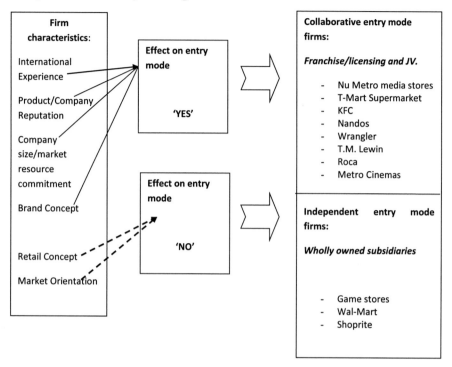

Table 6.2 provides further summary of the above findings by clearly indicating the extent to which data gathered and analysed provide support for the various firm characteristics that have been investigated. The table for example provides that a factor like (a) unique retail concept has not been supported by the empirical evidence from the study with respect to its influence on the entry strategy of the retail firms in Nigeria.

Table 6. 2.   Summary of Findings on Firm Characteristics

Importance of major firm characteristics/factor investigated on entry mode choice	Outcome/findings
(a) Unique Retail concept	Not supported by empirical evidence
(b) Unique Brand concept	Supported by empirical evidence
(c) Market Orientation	Not supported by empirical evidence
(d) International Experience	Supported by empirical evidence
(e) Product/Company Reputation	Supported by empirical evidence
(f) Firm size/Market Resources commitment	Supported by empirical evidence

6.7.   The Institutional Environment and Entry mode choices

So far, the analyses have considered the various company characteristics that have in one form or the other influenced the entry mode choices used by the retail firms in the Nigerian market. Equally important is the fact expressed by experts that some other variables that are external to the firm may play very important roles in its entry mode decisions in international markets. Given that the responding firms in this study operate within a wider environment outside of their home countries, it was useful to explore, as many previous studies have done, the extent to which the external environment influenced the entry mode choice of these retail firms in the Nigerian market, particularly in respect of the major informal and formal variables such as: Habits & Inertia, Imitation, cultural distance, retail market distance, population, economic fluctuation, legal and political systems, government regulations, etc. as classified by North (1990). This line of analysis is pursued in the remaining part of this chapter.

6.7.1. Informal Environmental Factors

In analysing some of the informal forces in the external environment of these firms operating in the Nigerian market in terms of their entry mode choices, the aim was to ascertain if the system used by the various international retail firms now, or that which they have used in the past in whatever way, influences their choice of entry method into the Nigerian market. The other dimension was to equally verify if the system used by their competitors has influenced their choice of entry into the Nigerian market. As classified by experts, the habits/inertia of these retail firms, as well as their imitation behaviour was investigated. Part of this also included a look at the dimensions of the environmental forces, with the underlining principle of trying to ascertain the view as expressed by experts within the conceptual framework of this study that organizational behaviour is guided by not only self-interest and expedience, but also an awareness of an organisation's role in a social situation and a desire to behave appropriately in accordance with other's expectations and internalized standards of conduct. The attempt here was to ascertain how the size and disposable income of the consumers in a foreign market, the differences in retail structure and practices between the home and host markets of a retailer and the different developmental stages of each market, as well as the various cultural variations affect their entry mode choice in the host market. The views of the interviewees are expressed below:

6.7.1.1.   Habits & inertia / imitation in entry mode

The executives of all the responding retail firms investigated in Nigeria agreed that the entry mode they have used in entering the market is as a result of their experience gained in the use of such an entry method in other international markets where they operate. i.e. the method they have used in the past in previous international markets. The General Manager of Shoprite and his counterpart in Game stores mentioned that they have gained a lot of expertise from the very many markets where they operate, especially the fact that most of these markets are equally developing like the case in Nigeria. The executives of Nandos, KFC and Wrangler also stated their entry into the Nigerian market has been influenced by what they have done in the past in entering other developing markets. An important issue worthy of mentioning here is the point made by the General Manager of Shoprite when he noted that besides the expertise they have developed from their operations in other markets, they still take into consideration some peculiarities in the various foreign markets such as: the laws and regulations and supply chain issues. Most of the other interviewees agreed with this view as well.

There is no clear indication to show the imitation of the strategy used by competitors in the entry mode choices of the retailers in the Nigeria market. Only one (1) of the retail firms mentioned this fact; and even within the firm there were some contradictions from the field study. Five (5) top executives of Game stores were interviewed and two of them admitted imitating the strategy Shoprite which started operations first in the Nigerian market had used. The other three executives gave a different view; saying they looked at what their competitor had done but this was not their major influence.

6.7.1.2. Market population/wealth

In the words of the CEO of Big Treat, "the population of a market is important in determining its attractiveness. A large market with high levels of economic activities and disposable income will be attractive to us". The re-emergence of the middle class in Nigeria, who have a high disposable income, coupled with the penetration of telecommunications, banking, and improvements in infrastructure, all of these are some of the reasons adduced by the majority of the interviewees as influencing their entry into the Nigerian market and their choice of entry mode.

The Marketing Manager for Nu Metro Cinemas mentioned that with a population of over 150 million people and a fast growing middle class made up of young professionals characterised by their youthfulness, high earning power, and adoption of western lifestyles, including leisure shopping, this development greatly influenced our decision to enter into the Nigeria market. The Shoprite boss supported this fact when he added that "apart from the change to a democratically elected government, the size of the Nigerian market attracted us in our expansion plan for Shoprite in Africa".

Interviewees for the other retail firms used in the study agree that retailing in Nigeria has benefited immensely from these developments, as the disposable income of the average Nigerian consumer has increased significantly. Non-grocery retailers like (T.M.Lewin, Wrangler, Game and Metro stores) in particular, mentioned that they are experiencing increased patronage from new customers who can now afford some of their big ticket items and patronize them for the sake of quality products and higher standards of services. As a result, there is increased focus on brand equity building by them.

The present position notwithstanding, the Nandos Business Development Manager for Africa further added that the potential for additional growth in the Nigerian market have made them increase their commitment in the market such that since the opening of its first outlet in Lagos in 2005, five additional outlets have been established in

Lagos and Abuja and plans are on for more outlets to be opened with an injection of over One hundred million naira (N100m) investment package for the Nigerian market.

An executive of Game stores further added that "the projection that the population of Nigeria will grow significantly in the near future is an important indication for us to try and establish our position in the market". Another important issue raised in this section, is the fear expressed by the CEO for Big Treat that partly accounted for their use of the method of a strategic alliance. She noted that unemployment levels affect their assessment of different markets; explaining that high unemployment levels will depress retail spending, and this will discourages them from entering a market where unemployment remains a long-term problem. The high unemployment level in the market has fundamentally impacted on their retail development in the Nigerian market.

Lastly, the head of operations for T-Mart supermarket mentioned that "the possessions of the people in a market while not a direct reflection of wealth are an indicator of it". She said the very large number of consumers in Nigeria who own cars was one reason they considered in deciding to site there stores at Tinapa; a location that is far from the city centre, where a large number of the consumers reside besides the excellent facilities provided at the site.

6.7.1.3.   Cultural distance and entry mode choice

Only three (3) of the retail firms (Wal-Mart, Roca, and Wrangler) claim to have some huge cultural differences with the host Nigeria market. A bulk of the other firms claims they have close cultural differences between their home country market and the market in Nigeria. One major explanation for this is the fact that most of these firms are coming in from other markets/countries in Africa with a lot of cultural similarities to Nigeria, the interviewees noted. The executives of Nandos, Shoprite, Game, KFC and the rest from South Africa indicated that the market in South Africa is not very different from that of Nigeria, except that the South African market is better developed and well regulated. In the words of the Managing Director of Game stores

> "The Nigerian market is largely an informal one which made our entry as a multi-national retailer a bit difficult. However, the market can be compared to the South African market which has a well established and highly competitive retail sector. We were faced with the task of changing the retail culture in Nigeria to show our Nigerian customers the benefits of shopping at a large supermarket instead of the open market".

In explaining why their organisation started operations in Nigeria only in 2005, after over 30 years in operation, the interviewees for Shoprite mentioned that " It was easier to focus on those countries closer to South Africa to build up the necessary know-how within Shoprite in terms of supply chain, company procedures and general expertise before expanding our operations further". He equally mentioned that the expertise created by the organisation in terms of the experience gained from operations in other developing markets like Nigeria, has greatly shortened what should have been a huge cultural distance between both markets. Other interviewees like those in KFC, Nandos, Game stores and Nu Metro further corroborate this fact.

Interestingly also, this study reveals that even for the retail firms that claim not to have a close cultural distance with the market in Nigeria, this has not made them adopt the collaborative mode because according to one of the interviewees of these firms, their decision is informed more by the problem of the information transfer process from their home country to the market in Nigeria. They claim to be more concerned with how they will exploit their established processes in the Nigerian market an advantage they are not willing to share with any others in the market. As put by the chief operating officer of Big Treat "We are having a well-established business plan that is perfect for the Nigerian market; this has enabled us to come up with very good product concepts and distribution strategies. We do not intend to transfer this knowledge through any other party in our business operations".

A top manager in Nandos mentioned that "one way we cope with the challenge of cultural differences in the markets we operate, is to adopt entry methods that restrict direct engagement with the market. This way, the company externalizes engagement". Nandos uses mainly franchise and joint venture agreements. This view is supported by the general manager for Shoprite who said that:

> "in the Nigerian market, just as it is in most of our other foreign markets, apart from the chief executives in these markets, we try to ensure that the other individuals on the ground in the international market remain predominantly nationals of that market. We aim at making local personnel predominate once the initial operation has been established, in order to minimize the problems of culture-based mistakes damaging the operation. This is because culture defies comprehensive simplistic characterization".

> "the most important attribute with which we overcome cultural challenges in the marketplace is our ability to keep asking questions, to learn, to take nothing for granted, and not to assume some form of cultural superiority. We acknowledge the fact that it is not in our place to judge but rather to interpret the unfamiliar environment in the market".

The above, are the views of a KFC manager who further added that their organisation is not only very conscious of their own interpretation of cultural phenomenon but also their reaction to it, for they must also live within the confines of their own culture and the values imposed on them by other cultures.

On the part of the managing director for Game stores, he stated that:

"it is important for us to consider social and cultural factors that are closely intertwined in the markets we operate. No matter how skilled a retail firm is in bringing its product to the market, and how developed its internal competencies are, the ability to work with the market is fundamental to a successful operation. It would be naïve of us to conclude that all markets with specific levels of economic development will see the same social developments which is moderated by cultural influences. We measure and characterise the social environment by the artefacts of everyday existence, the physical representation of economic wealth, and the consumers' personal interaction with the social environment"

Equally important according to this executive is the fact that when assessing the market, we look for key indicators that will provide a social picture of the consumer environment into which we might be considering moving.

6.7.1.4.   Retail market distance

The Business Development Manager UAC Nigeria when asked about the nature of retail practice in Nigeria, noted that as a result of the very early stage of development of the retail sector in Nigeria, there seemed not to be too many restrictions in this sector apart from the import prohibition of certain items. This study revealed that the participating retail firms have not experienced any major differences in the retail practice in Nigeria from that of their home countries. One of the interviewees mentioned that "apart from the unregulated nature of the Nigerian market and limited foreign competition, all other features of the market are similar to the situation in our home country". Another respondent from Shoprite had stated that:

"the average Nigerian consumer has developed the habit of seeking western styled goods and culture; this has made it easy for us to serve the market without difficulties. There was no need for us to think of changing our retail format or products in the Nigerian market. The bulk of our products in Nigeria are the same as those in our home market".

Majority of the interviewees agreed with the fact that the use of a retail practice like self service worked very well in Nigeria because the consumers wanted it and boldly embraced the concept as well as the use of private labels for some of their products. Enterprise density was also stressed by the Shoprite executive as an important measure of the retail structure in Nigeria. He mentioned that Shoprite is able to make immediate assessments of an international market, on the basis of enterprise density figures the number of inhabitants per retail outlet; this allows them to make assumptions about the overall condition of the retail structure.

In his words, "a market with a high number of inhabitants per outlet would prove advantageous to our operations that require a developed structural infrastructure in which to operate. He was quick to add that the case of the Nigerian market has offered them considerable opportunities to prepare to manage the problems of operating within a structure and distribution system that does not have the familiar features found in our domestic market though not completely different. As a reward, therefore, for managing these problems, we now have the opportunity to establish our own types of operations in the Nigerian market with the very huge potential that has enabled us gain a substantial market share.

This study also highlighted the importance of market concentration in the entry mode decision choice of the retail firms in the Nigerian market. Even to this time, the number of international retail firms in Nigeria is still very little the size of the market notwithstanding. There are also no well-established local rivals to face the international firms as such competition is not so strong, as a result of which, these earlier entrants are reaping full benefits from the Nigerian market.

6.7.1.5.   Urbanisation/Market development stage

Interviewees in big retail firms used in this study like Nandos, Shoprite, Wal-Mart, Game stores, and KFC all agree that high levels of urbanization are an important factor they consider in moving into international markets. In the words of one of the executives, "modern retailing supports an urbanized environment. Isolated rural communities do not benefit from the same retail facilities as urban agglomerations". One attraction they mentioned that brought them into the Nigerian market is the very large and young Nigerian population as well as the equally large number located in the rapidly urbanised cities around the country.

The managing director for Game stores mentioned that:

"the Nigerian market is attractive to us because it promises to sustain the levels and rate of growth we have previously seen in our domestic market. The advanced retail structures similar to those we are familiar with, have not appeared in the Nigerian markets because of the lack of capital and a fundamental lack of economic development a situation that is rapidly changing. We do not operate under the assumption that because retail formats and operating practices have succeeded in our domestic and advanced retail systems, then less developed retail markets like that in Nigeria will immediately accept our operations. If this was our practice, then we would have been ignoring an important fact that our retail stores have successfully operated in other markets where the competitive structure has been determined by historical conditions that have not been and will not be replicated elsewhere in other markets in the same way".

6.7.2 Formal Institutional Factors

6.7.2.1.   Regulatory Forces

Executives of these retail firms all agree that as international firms, they need to be aware of the regulatory context in which they operate and the impact this has on operations of their respective organisations. The General Manager of Shoprite stated particularly that

"our company needs to be aware of the differences in regulation that we face in the new environments. When assessing the political environment in a new market, we must consider the market on the basis of its destination, type of government the country has; who is in charge of the legislature and the government does it have a one-party state that may offer stability, in that changes of policy may be less likely in the short term. Or multi-party systems of government which may reduce the likelihood of radical policy shifts, but may also lead to comfortable 'arrangements' that do not encourage open government".

Executives of other retail firms like Game stores, KFC, Nandos, Wal-Mart and Nu Metro added that they equally would want to know how long the political system has been in place, what the country's relations are with the International community of states, how the Government approaches fundamental economic issues and hence regulate commercial and financial activity, as well as the legal requirements that are there as far as property rights, including patents and copyrights are concerned.

The large format retailers in this study highlighted that the link between saturated developed markets and retail planning regulations suggest that their focus on emerging markets may be partly caused by such regulations in the developed markets and the relative absence of such restrictions in emerging markets. Other important dimensions they mentioned that are considered include: any restrictions on ownership and the repatriation of profits, available commercial codes in practice especially in respect of takeover activities, and how much information is available to them, as well as the planning or operating employment restrictions in the market.

The executive for Shoprite added that "for us, planning issues may not be a problem, because our operations fit into standard units within shopping malls or other developments. Of greater concern to us is the fact that since labour costs are such a large proportion of our costs, we always would want to find out if there are some hidden costs, such as those of training or redundancy payments, which may amount to considerable expenditure".

6.7.2.2.   The Legal System in the host market

When asked if the strength of the rule of law in Nigeria affected their decision about the mode of entry into the Nigerian market, the bulk of the interviewees said this played a key role in their decision. One of the executives interviewed stated that "yes, we considered the strength of the rule of law in Nigeria especially the effectiveness of the court system in the country. We believe that it was only with the change to civilian rule in 1999 that Nigeria started developing into one of the top economies of the world. We watched the significant in-roads the government made to combat corruption and the reforms made to further strengthen the legal system".

The interviewees equally mentioned the issue of the legal requirements as far as property rights are concerned including patents and copyrights, as well as any restrictions on ownership and repatriation of profits, and finally, the commercial codes operational in the Nigerian market. Almost all the interviewees mentioned that since their firms have one or more distinct merchandise and brands, their products may be replicated where copyrights and patents are not respected. They added that they needed to be conscious of the level of exposure they have to risk as far as their property portfolio was concerned.

The executive for Game stores mentioned that

> "we needed to be sure of the legal requirements in the Nigerian market in respect of foreign ownership of businesses and the government position on repatriation of profits. Our investigation revealed the government's 'Indigenisation decree' used in the past as a way of protecting the local industries and we also looked to see if any restrictions were placed on capital flight from the economy. A confirmation that these were no longer the practice in the market was important to us".

Shoprite's General Manager equally added that "we needed to ascertain if there were any restrictions or regulations on takeover activities in the Nigerian market. Our expansions in most of our other foreign markets have been through acquisitions; so we needed to see if there were any limitations in terms of our expansion". This executive further added that the absence of these restrictions, including that on planning – floor space and layout to a large extent encouraged their use of the independent entry mode in the Nigerian market.

6.7.2.3.   The Political/Economic System in the host market

A manager in Wal-Mart was quick to say that "we know the state still retains considerable power to affect regulations that directly impinge on retail development. So we are particularly exposed to the political environment in which we operate". This view was also echoed by the respondent for KFC who said that:

> "our experience in the past has shown that indigenous retailers are able to invoke political passions and exercise political influence in markets where the arrival of more competitive international operations threatens to disturb the retail structural status quo. We needed to see this was not the case in the Nigerian market. Also with the Federal system of government in the country, we needed to see the local, state, and national government did not exert independent policies, especially in the areas of taxes on incomes and purchases as well as location and expansion".

With respect to the economic aspects of the Nigerian market, the bulk of the interviewees in this study acknowledged the fact that the economic activities in a foreign market require stability as such, the financial insecurity of both the foreign market and their individual firms are considered acute.

An executive of Nigeria Investment Promotion Council (NIPC) mentioned that over the last couple of years, there has been significant progress recorded by Nigeria economically and this has greatly improved the profile of the country in attracting

FDI. The official mentioned that for a very long time until recently, a fundamental weakness of the Nigerian market was economic instability. High inflation had been a significant contributor to that instability. "The retail trade suffered from hyperinflation in its relationship with consumers, operationally and financially. Inflation altered consumers' shopping patterns because wages and salaries lost considerable purchasing power. Inflation had inhibited the emergence of a strong middle class consumer group within the Nigerian society" were his words. However, the various economic reform policies of the government and the debt relief provided the country by the Paris Club and other of the country's creditors a few years back have led to massive economic improvements and stability.

An important analysis provided by the Managing Director of Game stores in respect of the economic environment in the markets where they operate is that:

> "we try to understand our international retail activity in the context of the general patterns of international trade. Quite a number of trading blocs exist around the world like the EU, ASEAN group, African Union, ECOWAS, etc. for us, world trading blocs especially those to which we belong, offer an important opportunity for future expansion; so, we first exploit opportunities within our own trading blocs unless there exist particular reasons for doing otherwise. Likewise, we equally try to know the general trend in the global economy in terms of following in the direction and flow of foreign direct investment (FDI)".

This executive also mentioned that

> "the imposition of taxes and tariffs, quota (limiting import to a specific quantity or value) and other non-tariff regulations introduced by the government in some of our foreign operations have negatively impacted on the use of our own facilities in such markets. Some of these came in the form of: inappropriate anti-dumping regulations, foreign exchange controls, product standard regulations, as well as customs and documentation requirements. This was difficult for us especially because of our particular format and distinct product lines".

Some of the other interviewees support this view.

6.7.2.4. Government imposition/inducement policies

The MD of T-Mart supermarket mentioned that "in general terms, the Nigerian government's attitude towards the retail industry can be described as positive. There is no specific legislation that can be said to be inimical either to local or foreign retailers". This, she stated, was because the government's direct intervention in retailing is minimal as a result of the predominantly informal nature of the sector which makes regulation a difficult and expensive task. However, some other interviewees added that policies that affect the supply side have notable effects on the sector. One of the major policies with a direct impact on the retail sector which almost all the interviewees mentioned, is the import ban placed on selected grocery and non-grocery items. The retailers say they have had to source these prohibited items from local suppliers, sometimes with significant cost and quality implications in relation to the good quality items they would have brought in from their home markets. Game's Director for Africa Richard Fuller stated that around 35% of their products in the Nigerian market are currently bought from local Nigerian suppliers, partly because of a ban on the importation of certain products such as furniture, plastics and textiles. Fuller says they do extremely well on furniture bought from local suppliers and that import restrictions have not affected their sales in any way.

This study also revealed that the attempt by the government to boost FDI by the establishment of such free trade zones as the TINAPA project and others like it, has not really succeeded in attracting international retailers to take up floor spaces in these mega shopping facilities. The TINAPA project in Calabar was particularly criticized for its very poor location; the interviewees noted that the site is too far away from the consumers, as such there is very little consumer traffic into the complex. A field visit confirmed this claim because this researcher saw a huge number of retail floor spaces waiting to be occupied. These retailers claim that the major policy of the Nigerian government in respect of the establishment of these free trade zones is quite commendable but they ask for their location to be close to the market. So despite some of the policies of the government aimed at attracting FDI to these locations such as: The liberalisation of exchange control regulations and abolition of all restrictions on the importation of foreign capital, 100% repatriation of dividends, 100% foreign ownership, as well as 100% exemption from all taxes for companies licensed to operate in the free trade zones, the aim has not been achieved so far. Some of the interviewees noted that the Lekki free trade zone in Lagos (a former capital of the country) with a huge population of over fifteen million inhabitants with its nice location and provision of other infrastructural facilities like an airport and seaport will be a site that would greatly attract foreign retail firms. This site is still under development.

Equally important as highlighted by the interviewees is the fact that the establishment of the Nigeria Investment Promotion Commission (NIPC) to serve as a one-step-resource for exploring and planning foreign investment and new businesses in Nigeria, the simplification of the business incorporation procedures such that with the right documentations, a business can be fully registered in Nigeria within a day, all of these the interviewees claim is only on paper. There are very many practical difficulties in getting the right support from such organisations. The bureaucratic process is so long and often there are too many personnel involved with corrupt tendencies.

Some of the interviewees added also that the policy directives by the government in respect of items imported through the nation's ports has been another area of confusion. They mentioned that there are often frequent changes to the government directives on importation and a lot of inconsistencies with respect as to what is allowed and what is not allowed to be imported into the country. Even the government directive that all imports into the country must be cleared from the ports within 24-48hours is far from the case. All the interviewees agree that the various government policies and directives are good, but the only problem has been with the implementation of these guidelines and this has often been the failure in the past by the government to attract FDI and growing the economy.

Figure 6.3   Summary of the effect of Institutional variables on entry modes.

Institutional factors   Influence on entry mode choice

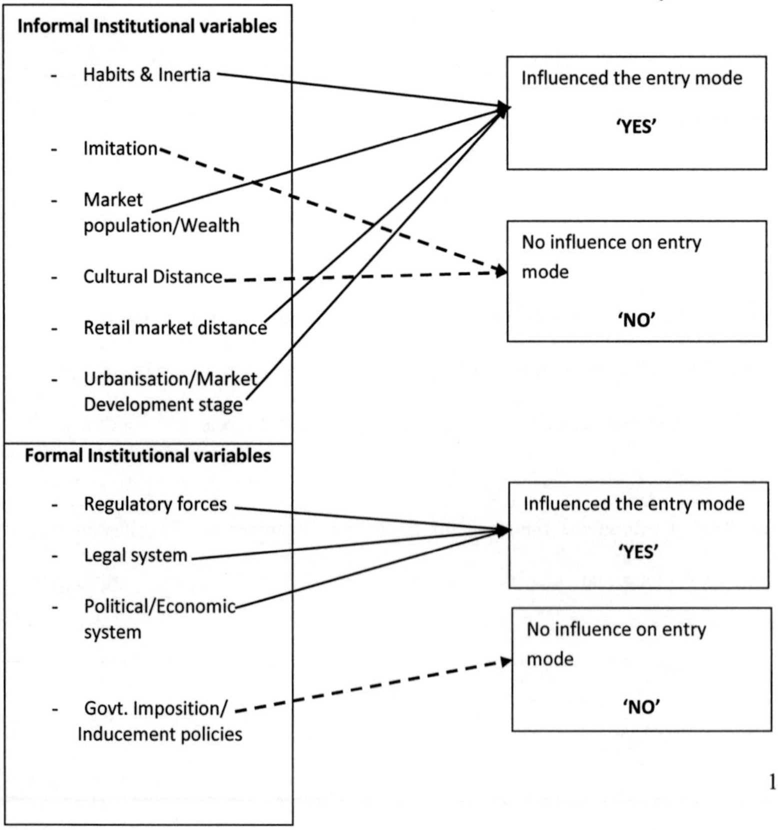

195

Table 6.3   **Summary of the effect of Institutional variables on entry mode choices**

Institutional factors	Outcome/Findings
- Habits & Inertia	Supported by empirical study
- Imitation	Not supported by empirical study
- Market population/Wealth	Supported by empirical study
- Cultural Distance	Not supported by empirical study
- Retail market distance	Supported by empirical study
- Urbanisation/Market Development stage	Supported by empirical study
- Regulatory forces	Supported by empirical study
- Legal system	Supported by empirical study
- Political/Economic system	Supported by empirical study
- Government Imposition/Inducement policies	Not supported by empirical study

Figure 6.3 and Table 6.3 above shows the formal and informal institutional factors that have influenced the entry mode choices of the retail firms from analysis of the empirical data as was done for the firm characteristics factors earlier. Table 6.3 shows the level of support/non support from the analysis.

6.7.3   Effect of other moderating external factors

6.7.3.1.   Collaborative/Hierarchical network relationship management

In a bid to get the views of the interviewees in respect of the above, the interviewees were asked questions concerning the type of arrangement they operate in the Nigerian market. Other questions covered such areas as: the factors they considered in coming into the Nigerian market, the method of partner selection, as well as the market selection process.

The interviewees' responses show that market screening, market attractiveness, and market selection processes are followed by the bulk of the retail firms in Nigeria before ultimately selecting a partner in the market. An executive of Nandos mentioned that "as a result of the experience we have gained from the past, we look at the population, social structure, inflation, and currency fluctuations, in addition to the level of competition, retail structure and types of regulation in deciding the markets to enter". This view is supported by the executives of the other retail firms interviewed; however, the Business Development Manager Africa for Nandos further adds that the amount of similarity in operations and business philosophy between their company and a foreign partner firm in addition to the growth potential of the market are considered by their firm in deciding on markets to enter and entry strategies to use.

Having decided on the market to enter, this study reveals that the financial stability, business know-how, local market knowledge, and similarity in business practice are the major considerations by the retail firms in choosing a partner in the foreign market. The growth plan for the business by the franchisee and the understanding of the brand of the company are other considerations the executives for Nandos, Nu Metro Media stores, KFC, and Metro Cinemas further added influence their choice of partners. It was mentioned by the Area Manager for KFC that they require the franchisee to put up a five year business plan so as to see what growth plans are possible before approving the business relationship. This, he says, must include the understanding and believe of the franchisee on the company brand as well.

It is important to state that these above reasons were also mentioned by the executives of firms like Shoprite, Wal-Mart, and Game stores for their use of the independent entry mode. For example, the favourable retail regulations, huge population, limited competition, nice social structure, local market knowledge, and having established buying agents and procedures etc. are some of the reasons given for the use of this independent entry method.

6.7.3.2.   Cost of establishing and monitoring operations

The interviewees in this study noted that the amount of influence they needed to achieve for their operations in the Nigerian market greatly determined their choice of entry mode; in addition to the associated cost and risks involved. The interviewees for firms like KFC and Nandos mentioned that the contact they were able to establish with their partners in the Nigerian market who have a lot of local knowledge as a result of their many years of operation in the Nigerian market, informed their use of the collaborative mode. One of the managers had stated that "where we can find a local partner who understands the market and shares our business philosophy, we do not hesitate in going into some joint business relationships". Ordinarily, the expansion plans for firms like Nandos and KFC have most often been to enter into foreign markets using such modes as franchising, joint ventures or licensing. Executives from these firms mentioned that depending on the type and level of control they seek in the foreign market and the associated costs and risks they are likely to face, they further decide on whether to use a master franchise or area developer system, or a direct franchise relationship. With their assessment of the Nigerian market, these retail firms have used the indirect franchise relationships in the Nigerian market.

The views of other interviewees for retail firms like Wrangler, Roca, Nu Metro, and T-Mart, can be summed up to show that they have used the collaborative entry mode because they are not prepared to commit a large part of their investment yet into the

Nigerian market. Some of these interviewees mentioned that their present operation in the Nigerian market is a way of testing the waters to see if there is the need to increase investment with a growth in the market. Such a system will limit their losses in the event of a failure in the market.

On the other hand, however, the firms that operate in the market using the independent mode like Shoprite, and Game stores, argue that the need for them to effectively coordinate their actions and to design their strategies for the Nigerian market made them consider such a mode. They equally mentioned that the limited cost of establishing their operations in the market as a result of the development of major retail infrastructures in major urban centres also helped to inform their decision. Lastly, the desire to capture a huge share of the market was also mentioned as one factor for the use of the independent mode. With the absence of other foreign competitors of their type, they have decided to fully exploit the very fertile market on their own before it becomes saturated.

6.7.3.3.   Quality and number of available networks

The retail sector of the Nigerian economy is still just developing as mentioned by most of the interviewees and as shown by available records. The level of infrastructural development is still very low and so also, there is a limited number of qualified persons and organisations that understand modern retail practice. The Shoprite manager said that

> "in as much as we needed to fully take advantage of the untapped Nigerian market, a limitation we would have faced if we wanted a collaborative arrangement is the problem of seeking out qualified partners to work with. By this I mean organisations that would understand our operations as quickly as possible and would not run our image and prestige aground".

The Business Development Manager for KFC expressed this same view as 'free riding risk'. He mentioned that they only would choose partners in foreign markets who will help protect their trade secrets and hold tightly to the terms of their agreement. He stated that they have had situations in the past, where it had been difficult for them to achieve the uniformity in their product and brand offerings because their partners had failed to follow the business practice and philosophy; a situation that led to withdrawals from such markets.

Just as earlier stated, the limited concentration of both local and established foreign retail firms in the Nigerian market has played and is still playing a major impact in the entry mode decision choice of the firms operating in the market and those contemplating entry into this huge market. The General Manager Game stores expressed shock at the government position that even when individuals and corporate organisations are caught for copyright violations, they are not prosecuted unless the party who they have infringed, reports such violations. He mentioned that working in collaboration with others in such a market would heighten this challenge, hence their decision to use a wholly owned subsidiary in the Nigerian market.

Figure 6.4   Summary of other external moderating Factors

External moderating factors

- Network Relationship Management
- Cost of establishing & monitoring relationships
- Quality & Number of available networks

Effect on entry mode decision

- Influenced the entry mode
- No influence on entry mode

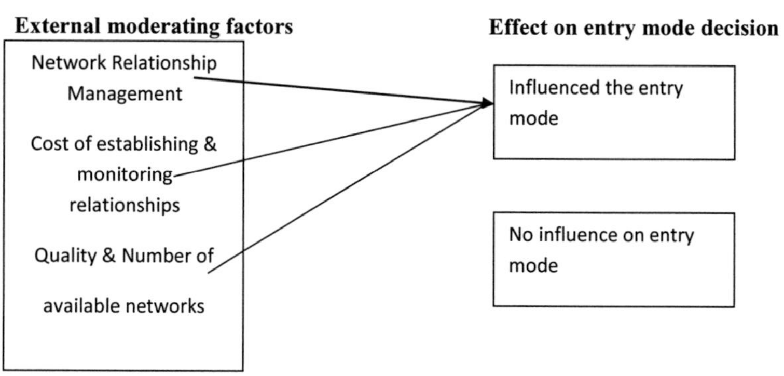

Figure 6.4 above indicate that all of the external moderating factors: network relationship management, cost of establishing and monitoring relationships, and the quality and number of available networks all influenced the entry mode decision choices of the retail firms in Nigeria. Table 6.4 below further summarises the support for these factors from the analysis.

Table 6.4   Summary of external moderating Factors

External moderating factors	Outcome/Findings
- Network Relationship Management	Supported by empirical study
- Cost of establishing and monitoring operations	Supported by empirical study
- Quality & Number of available networks	Supported by empirical study

6.8   Chapter Summary

This chapter has presented the major findings from this present study. The profile of the various retail firms used for this study is first presented, including their location in Nigeria and entry mode used, after which a cross case analysis of the findings from the study is presented.

In line with the major objectives and research questions set out for this study, the findings are presented clearly in a manner that allows for understanding to show to what extent the objectives and research questions have been answered. Findings on the Nigerian market and foreign retail entry which addresses the first two research questions are provided; after which, the retail firms' characteristics in terms of their retail concept, brand, image and reputation, size and market resource commitments, international experience, market orientation, etc are outlined.

The chapter also presents the findings in respect of the institutional environment in Nigeria, as it affects the entry modes used by the retail firms in the market, in addition to the effect of other moderating external variables. This section presents the findings from the informal and formal environmental factors in such areas as: cultural and retail market distance, market population and wealth, legal, political and economic systems in Nigeria.

CHAPTER SEVEN- DISCUSSION OF RESEARCH FINDINGS

The previous section outlined the major findings of this study. In the following section, the research questions set out for this study is first addressed, then the findings are discussed in line with the underpinning theoretical background of the study interpreted so as to be able to draw some meaningful conclusions from the analysis. This section discusses and locates the results within the ex-ante relevant theoretical/conceptual and empirical literature. Importantly, it highlights what is in line with existing literature, what is different (and explanations why), and also, explains aspects of the literature that have been extended or complemented in order to show which of the results are context-specific and which may potentially be generalisable. The essence is to try and provide a better insight into the developments of the international retail practice in the Nigerian market.

7.1   *RQ 1   What entry modes do international retail firms use to internationalize into the developing Nigerian market and why?*

As stated in the previous chapter, the results from this present study have shown that most of the retail firms in the Nigerian market use the collaborative mode of entry in the market - mainly joint venture arrangements, licensing, and franchising. Interestingly also, it is discovered that it is the biggest of the international retail firms in the Nigerian market that used the independent entry mode, by establishing their wholly owned subsidiaries.

Quite a number of reasons and factors have been mentioned as influencing the choice of market entry mode into the Nigerian market. It is quite clear from the evidence gathered from this present research that the collaborative mode of entry seems to be the dominant strategy used by the retail firms because of the prevailing conditions of the firms and the situation in the Nigerian market. Besides problems from the larger institutional environment, the level of involvement sought by the firms, cost of investment in the Nigerian market, knowledge dissemination risks, the need for rapid expansion, as well as return on investment, have all been mentioned as factors influencing the choice of entry mode of the retail firms in the Nigerian market.

Meyer and Estrin (2001) noted that the resources held by local firms in the host market e.g. assets – technology, market power/barriers to entry, resources held by the investor e.g. transferable knowledge, managerial services, financial capital, as well as the resources available on the market like: real estate, labour skills, and access to utilities all affect the final mode of entry.

According to Meyer (2001) and Chen *et al.* (2009) in a developing economy, institutions are volatile and immature, exerting a large environmental uncertainty on foreign investment, particularly when considering the institutional environments. This suggests a low-control entry mode for foreign firms when operating in such uncertain institutional environment. There is often the view that firms seek increased ownership and control as they go into foreign markets, so as to protect their products and assets. This would entail the use of an entry mode like the wholly owned subsidiary (Brown, Dev and Zho 2003). The broad argument is that modes entailing greater commitment of resources face greater risks, and consequently firms favour modes offering more control to compensate for such risk (Anderson and Gatignon, 1986).

Contrary to this position, Erramilli and Rao (1993) noted that there is an increasing recognition that service firms may gain control through non-equity methods, with it being possible for a service firm to exercise a degree of control that is unrelated to its equity participation. In this case, control can be equally well achieved through inter-firm cooperation in non-equity agreements such as franchising or management service contracts such that even without ownership, control over codified strategic assets (brands, technological systems etc.) and tacit expertise (trained personnel, routines, quality control etc.) remains with the multinational firm. This may go to explain the case of the retail firm operating in the Nigerian market

7.2   RQ 2   What characteristics of the available entry modes affect the retailers' entry mode choice?

Although firms typically enter new markets organically through internal development, a common alternative is to acquire a firm or business unit that is already established, Lee and Lieberman (2010). There is no case of acquisition in the retail sector in Nigeria because before now there were no established retail outlets operating in the market. It is only in the last decade that large foreign retail outlets started off in the market. Firms entering foreign markets choose from different entry modes ranging from licensing and franchising, to joint ventures, acquisitions, and wholly-owned new ventures Rasheed (2005). Essentially, a choice of entry mode comprises choice of location and type of control. Thus, resources may be located domestically or in the foreign market and controlled by the firm itself or through a contract arrangement, where Anderson and Gatignon (1986) define "control" as the ability to influence systems, methods, and decisions.

Scholars (Anderson and Gatignon 1986; Erramilli and Rao 1990) have shown the wholly owned entry mode allows for greater involvement/control and returns than does franchise, while franchise is beneficial because it reduces the investment requirements of the franchisor. The entry mode used is dependent also on its ability to help protect the retailers' internalization advantages, which vary in accordance with the characteristics of the ownership assets. Here, it is important to consider the nature of retail ownership assets in light of perceived dependability (defensibility) and transferability (Erramilli and Rao 1990).

From the entry mode perspective, internalization advantages have been conceptualized as contractual risks (Nakos and Bouthers 2002). Contractual risks refer to the risks of disseminating proprietary know-how (Nakos and Brouthers 2002). Scholars investigating the influence of internalization advantages (contractual risks) have found that when firms perceived low advantages from internalizing foreign operations, they tended to use non-equity modes of entry (Brouthers *et al.* 1999). In a similar vein, Nakos and Brouthers's (2002) study provided empirical evidence that firms perceiving higher internalization advantages tended to favour equity modes of entry.

As mentioned by the interviewees, attempts are made by the various retail firms to reduce their cost of operation in the Nigerian market. This view is supported because the wholly-owned entry mode requires significant resource commitments of capital, informational, and managerial resources. Firms having such resources available for a new venture will use the wholly-owned entry mode (like Shoprite). Firms lacking these resources tend to rely on franchising systems. Resources, especially informational and managerial, would not only be very costly to acquire within a firm but also vary from country to country and/or culture to culture (Rasheed 2005). The executives of the retail firms interviewed mentioned their lack of informational and managerial resources needed to serve the Nigerian market.

Experts have also acknowledged the need for business relatedness in seeking foreign market entry for the firms using the collaborative modes. The foreign exploitation of corporate resources is facilitated if business units are related to some degree; business relatedness has accordingly become a central manifestation of international strategy (Palich *et al*. 2000). A business strategy on a foreign market thus reflects the degree of relatedness between the foreign business unit and the core business of the parent company. Relations to the core are crucial here as they are central to gaining and sustaining competitive advantage in the international firm, Clark (2000).

Through business relatedness, the foreign unit may benefit from core competencies in value processes and more precisely, exploit related and relatively homogeneous knowledge on products and markets Pehrsson (2006). The empirical research on business relatedness has shown that industrial managers not only think of product-market relatedness but also intangible resource relatedness Pehrsson (2006). This has been studied by measuring similarities of product-market factors such as technology, design and prices of products, customer types, and customers' requirements for products and information etc. The interviewees in this study mentioned the importance of this characteristic.

7.3   *RQ 3   What major company and environmental factors influence the entry mode choices of the retail firms under the various levels of institutional pressures?*

Firm market entry and performance is influenced by the strategies and resources brought to bear within a particular operating environment (Chan *et al*. 2011). Firm resources are defined as assets, processes and knowledge that allow managers to design and implement efficient and effective strategies (Daft 1982). In the retailing context, the firms need to understand the foreign market selection and expansion management process. They codify their operational know-how and host country market information into routines, decision support systems, and other processes to create a firm level knowledge base (Morgan *et al.*, 2003). Retailers actively learn from their previous foreign market expansion experiences to improve firm performance in subsequent entries (Palmer and Quinn 2005) their amount of international experience affects firm market selection choices (Gripsrud and Benito 2005).

Internally, firms are often forced to make trade-offs between investments in SBU and corporate portfolios (Wrigley 2000a). Expansion into a new market means serving new customers, discovering new ways to produce a product or service, and employing new technologies employed in some circumstances (Killaly 2001). As a result, firms face different country and business risks in new markets, but also are exposed to different kinds of management processes and technologies (Dawson 1994).

After market selection, retail format choice(s) is another critical entry decision. These capabilities represent a retailer's knowledge of business models, systems and processes related to operating one or more retail formats. Retail formats represent a bundling of a retailer's capabilities and retail mix to distribute products to meet the needs of identifiable customer groups (Goldman 2001). Novel formats with international appeal can be the basis of a strategic competitive advantage (Burt 1991). Again, the rate of international expansion is another important aspect of firm capability. Kerin and Varadarajan (1992) describe salient economic advantages of moving first into a market, including erection of barriers to entry, experience effects, scope effects, information asymmetry effects, advertising efficiency effectiveness, and pre-emption of scarce resources. They argue that these advantages create a gap between the first mover and followers that is difficult to overcome. Larger firms with greater internationalization experience are in a position to leverage their accumulated knowledge to enter markets earlier than their competitors, which can widen the gap (Gaba *et al.* 2002).

Last, many scholars have found a positive relationship between a retail chain's size and its international involvement (e.g. Vida *et al.* 2000; Sternquist 1997). In part, larger firms are more likely to have resources to fund their international operations with increased market commitments (Vida *et al.* 2000) and can typically withstand a longer period of low return on investment than smaller organizations (Evans *et al.* 2000).

This present study considered all of the above dimensions and the findings are as discussed in the following sections.

7.4   Discussion of findings and links to previous literature

7.4.1. Firm Characteristics

This present study has tested the various resources that firms possess, especially the retail firms operating in the Nigerian market. This includes tangible and intangible assets such as financial, human, physical, technological and organisational resources. Others are firm specific skills like distinctive competencies - unique or special capabilities which allow a firm to perform better than its competitors and dynamic capabilities, which are the result of the integration *and* combination of a firm's resources (Kerin, Mahajan and Varadarajan 1990; Mahoney 1995; Brush and Artz 1999; Brouthers *et al.* 2008). Sternquist's SIRE model (1997) as discussed in section 2.2.1.4; Vida Readon and Fairhurst IRI model (2000) as explained in section 2.2.1.6; and Blomstermo et al (2006) view as expressed in section 2.5.1 all highlight the importance of firm characteristics on entry mode choice. It is believed that the combination of these resources and skills influences a firm's choice of market entry strategy and eventual success. Ibeh et al (2006) noted from a study of agri-food companies that the firms' product, service and relationship management competencies emerged as an influential explanation for their international market success. The study reported the importance of product and service competencies.

From this present study, quite a number of the firm characteristics and competences examined were seen to have some influences on the entry mode decision choices of the retail firms in the Nigerian market. These characteristics include:

7.4.1.1.   Unique retail concept

Experts (Ghosh 1990; Burt 1993; Doherty 2000; Picot-Coupey 2006) agree that a retail firm would have an edge over rivals if its retail concept is distinct. Sections 2.2.1.5 and 2.2.1.7 earlier provided an explanation of these conditions. Some of these studies have shown the impact of a very distinct and recognisable store format and offering on patronage of retail stores and their method of entry into foreign markets. The findings from this present study show that majority of the interviewees mentioned their possession of some unique retail concept and recognise the importance of possessing these unique retail concepts however, they added that this was not a major consideration looked into in deciding the choice of entry mode used in entering the Nigerian market.

Recognition of the importance of possessing a unique retail concept by the executives of the retail firms in Nigeria is in line with the findings from previous studies (Goldman 1981; Kacker 1985, 1988; Mason & Mayer 1987; Betancourt & Gautschi 1990; Messinger & Narasimhan 1997). However, not considering this in deciding the method of entry into the market contradicts the findings from these earlier studies. For

210

example, (Burt 1993; Nonaka 1994; Inkpen & Dinur 1998; Doherty 2000) in their discussion of retail formats, distinguished between the *offering* and the *know-how* parts of the format. The first includes the *external* elements (e.g., assortment, shopping-environment, service, location and price) delivering the functional, social, psychological, aesthetic and entertainment benefits attracting consumers to stores. The second, the *internal* part, determines a retailer's operational strength and strategic direction. It consists of the *retail technology* dimension containing the systems, methods, procedures and techniques the retail company uses and of the *retail culture that* includes the repertoire of concepts, norms, rules, practices and experiences. They noted this dimension enhances the retailer's ability to evaluate situations, identify trends and opportunities, and deal with problems. Whereas the external elements are visible to consumers, many of the know-how ones are tacit which will call for the use of independent method of entry.

A possible explanation for the above finding could be in the response provided by the interviewees that what they aimed to achieve is to establish a format and retail structure that delivers benefits to their customers and other targets. They mentioned the ease with which the customers enter into the stores, the store layout and ambience; merchandise arrangement and assortment are some of the unique areas they use to stand out. Equally mentioned is the fact that consumers do not always want to be challenged in whatever form, as they patronize any retail store. This may be seen in the form of having some very complex operating procedures.

As reported earlier, it is interesting to observe that some of these retail firms especially the large and well established ones like Shoprite and Wal-Mart and Game stores, all realise the fact that their formats and procedures have some type of history behind it in each market which may not be repeated in any other market. So, in their bid to establish some distinct concept in the foreign market where they operate, they have remembered to allow the market conditions impact on the concept to be introduced so that its distinctiveness will be appreciated by the consumers in the market. This is an important finding that goes a long way to affect the operations of these international retails firms in foreign markets.

The above finding is also in line with the suggestion by Dawson (2000:128), that: "the challenges for large firms are to keep systems simple, to motivate large numbers of store-level staff and really to know what is going on at store level...with increasing size, it becomes difficult to operate only a single format. It also becomes more difficult to determine the extent to which a store's financial performance is due to the store format or the performance of the store management. With large firms, the difficulties and costs of making minor adjustments to marketing implementations increase with the size of the firm".

The retail firms that came into the Nigerian market using the independent entry mode such as Shoprite, Game stores and Wal-Mart acknowledged the importance of their unique retail concept in the decision to use such an entry mode. However, since the bulk of the other firms in the market used the collaborative mode of entry, a possible explanation that can be drawn from the findings is the fact that the foreign retail firms knowing what this entails and how important it is, selected their partners in the Nigerian market using highly established companies with expertise, experience, and capabilities to deliver outstanding retail concepts suitable for the Nigerian market. As a result of the fact that this type of asset comes from the methods by which things are done, unique capability regarded as a transaction-based asset is one many of the retailers mentioned is hard to possess mainly because organisational capability can only be acquired through time, training, and experience within the organisation and thus cannot be copied by competitors because it is tacit in nature – rooted in the firm's routines and processes, Brown *et al.* (2003). The collaborative partnerships are therefore aimed at enabling the local firms develop these much needed characteristics from their understanding of the local Nigerian market.

This is surprising, especially when one considers the fact that a characteristic like this to a large extent determines the success of a retail firm in the foreign market. Park and Sternquist (2008) noted that having unique capabilities – a distinct/different way of producing a new or established concept is important in retail internationalisation. This, they mentioned, could take the form of superior logistics (efficiency in distribution and inventory management) or distinctive management. Effective supply chain management is seen to lead to a low-cost business model primarily attributed to direct sourcing and better inventory management. The ability to take cost out of the supply chain creates the opportunity for gross profit margin improvement and/or pricing advantages. Pricing advantage, along with the appeal of a distinctive brand that is clearly focused on the market, leads to market share gains for the retailer.

7.4.1.2.   Brand concept

This study revealed that the bulk of the retail firms in Nigeria came into the market with some unique brand concept which influenced their method of entry into the market. The development of private brands was said to be a major factor in this regard, especially for the firms that have come into the market using the equity or independent entry mode. The executives of these firms interviewed had claimed that it is in a bid for them to have absolute control of their products and most especially the

213

private brands that have influenced their choice of entry method (use of the independent mode). It is equally important to note that the use of private brands equally influenced the entry mode decisions of the firms that have used the collaborative mode of franchising in the Nigerian market.

The above finding is in line with views of experts (Anderson and Gatignon 1988; Hill *et al.* 1990; Fernie *et al* 1997; Collins & Burt 2003; Picot-Coupey 2006) (*see sections 2.2.1.7; 2.3.1.3; and 4.2)* that the firm's ability to innovate products and processes is a significant predictor of equity mode of entry, especially with firms that evidenced high technological advancement, differentiated products and efficient organisational and administrative processes. Collins and Burt's (2003) study found that retailers' product-related monitoring intensity was positively related to their strategic use of private brands; implying that a retailer having one or more private brands needs to have control of the brand asset to maintain global uniformity of the concept/image across units. The wholly-owned entry mode allows for this. With the exception of T-Mart supermarket, all other retail firms used in this study mentioned their possession of differentiated products and efficient organisational processes. The findings from the Picot-Coupey (2006) study also showed that all the case study firms studied gave priority to creation, to style and to the signature of the brand in determining their operations mode choice; presenting their private brands as their main asset.

Contrary to the above, however, Doherty (2000); Quinn & Doherty (2000) in their study of fashion retailers, observed that despite the huge importance attached to the retail brands by the firms studied, their use of low control entry modes in the international markets they operated, was still dominant. The argument here they

214

mention, is that the use of a low entry mode does not mean that the retailers would not have some form of increased control of their brands in the foreign market. As a follow up to this, Park and Sternquist (2008) noted that denoting the retail concept by overall retail brand image, retail facilities and services offered – (where retailers offer their own brand products), has made it difficult to demarcate between retail brand, store brand, and private labels. Park and Sternquist (2008) considered this important by adding that: "it is important to separate retail concept from private label in measuring the uniqueness of market offering, because a retailer whose concept by itself does not imply uniqueness can develop a unique offer by innovative private label merchandise. In fact, it is becoming more possible for a retailer to develop a unique market offering by a private brand(s) with a unique brand concept(s), even though its retail concept is no longer unique".

The lifestyle, buying habits, high buying power, and familiarity of the average Nigerian consumer to the products offered by the international retail firms is revealed by this study as playing an important role in the entry mode decision choices of the retail firms. Summarising this earlier statement is in saying that the retail firms in Nigeria have not had the problem of adapting their products to fit into the Nigerian market.

The fast food retailers KFC, Nandos, and Big Treat all claim not to have significantly changed their product offerings in the Nigerian market. Other retailers like Game stores, Wrangler, Nu Metro stores, Shoprite, T.M. Lewin, Rocawear, and T-Mart also say they offer the same products in Nigeria as they have in their home markets. Experts believe that where a significant level of product adaptation is needed, international retail firms see this as a measure of risk as such, they would want to use some form of non-equity investment (Dawson 2001; Collins & Burt 2003; Humphrey, 2007; Durand & Wrigley 2009). In addition, requests from international stores for specific products are satisfied if the scheduling and scale of production is feasible. Along this line, Leelapanyalert and Ghauri's (2007) study quoted the Merchandising Manager of M&S Hong Kong as saying "The Company made small adaptations to the local market in sizes, colours and styles of products. We have two inches shorter sleeves shirt for Asian men. We also have unique products for proper climate, e.g., we developed a range of short sleeves T-shirts to fill in the longer summer period in Hong Kong''.

If the retail firms in Nigeria would need to adapt their products and processes to local conditions, they may face any or all of the three distinct market orientation processes that concern different levels within the organization (Elg 2007). He explained the three levels to be (i) The store development process which emphasizes the single retail units and the adaptation to local conditions (ii) The product and category development process which concerns the interaction between local units and corporate strategies concerning the retailer's products and categories and (iii) The store concept and brand development process which emphasizes the long term strategic positioning of the whole retail firm and involves corporate level management.

Scholars agree that the shift into international retail franchising by foreign firms (the entry mode choice used by the majority of the firms in the Nigerian market), however, might conceivably be handled more readily in situations where a company is able to support the move through the strength of a well-known brand name and established international market presence (Segal-Horn & Davison 1992). These retail firms claim to have this hence their decision to use the collaborative entry mode strategy.

7.4.1.3.   Product/company image & reputation

The huge image of the firms and their brands were stated by the interviewees in this study as influencing their entry mode decision choice in the Nigerian market. The views of the interviewees is that as a result of the fact that they want to promote and sustain the positive image of their companies and products, they have decided to come into the Nigerian market with some entry methods that allow them some measure of control over these. Many of the interviewees felt a strong market image and standing and their firm's prestige and esteem were important considerations in their entry mode decisions. For some of them, a strong market image and prestige which has been built over the years is their most "valuable asset". Experts have often referred to this as free riding potential. According to Anderson & Gatignon (1986) *(see section 4.2)* when a brand name is valuable, short-term gains can be had at the expense of the long term. Firms will take control to protect their brand name from degradation by free-riders or to prevent the local operation from using the name in an inconsistent manner, thus diluting or confusing the international positioning of the brand. This is one important dimension of the transaction cost theory.

This finding is supported by the views of Carruthers (2003); Park and Sternquist (2008); and Bianchi (2008) that higher control modes are more efficient where the potential for 'free-riding' is higher. The free-riding risk concerns the probability that a firm's reputation or image overseas is tempered by its local partner's misconduct, unilateral pursuit, or wanton behaviour. Following the analysis by Anderson and Gatignon (1986), examiners of entry mode tend to separate free-riding potential from physical asset specificity. Thus, free-riding potential is not a concept parallel to asset specificity but rather a special indicator of risk property of asset specificity (Carruthers 2003). Barry (1982) noted that positioned retailers compete on image as it was harder to imitate than price.

Company/store image has been variously described. As stated by Burt and Carralero-Encinas (2000), the nine attributes derived by Lindquist (1974) from a review of 19 previous studies is important. These attributes are: merchandise, including factors such as quality, assortment, styling or fashion, guarantees and price; service, encompassing staff service, ease of return, credit and delivery service; clientele, consisting of social class appeal, self-image congruency and store personnel; physical facilities, such as layout and architecture; convenience, primarily location related; promotion, including sales promotions, product displays, advertising programs, symbols and colours; store atmosphere, defined as "atmosphere congeniality" which represents a customer's feeling of warmth, acceptance or ease; institutional factors, such as the conservative or modern projection of store, reputation and reliability; and post-transaction satisfaction, seen as returns and adjustments. These authors further noted that if a retailer's main source of competitive advantage in the domestic market is based upon the intangible dimensions of image, that which takes time to develop, there is the danger of assuming that the customer values and perceptions experienced in the domestic market have transferred automatically to the new market. This, in turn, may then lead to complacency and mistakes in positioning and other marketing related activities both at home and foreign markets. In broad classifications, the intangible dimensions are "Customer service", "Character" and "Reputation" and the tangible dimensions are "Physical characteristics", "Product range" and "Pricing policy".

The views of the executives interviewed concerning the important role played by their price; service, return policy, positive self-image, effective promotion and favourable displays in determining the entry mode used is supported by the above position by Burt and Carralero-Encinas (2000) as well as other scholars as discussed in section 4.2. This is a general finding that retail firms operating in any market (developed/developing) would need to consider in deciding on the entry mode choice to use to serve the market.

7.4.1.4.　　　Company Size & market resource commitment

The results of this study show that for retail firms like Shoprite, Game stores and Wal-Mart their financial strength in terms of the cash available to them played a major role in their choice of entry mode into the Nigerian market (using the wholly-owned subsidiary). This study equally revealed that for these firms mentioned above and the other case study firms studied, the amount they were willing to commit to the market also affected their choice of market entry; the firms were seen to have different resources ranging from tangible to intangible assets.

The views of various researchers support this position. According to Park and Sternquist (2008), larger firms tend to possess greater resources and competencies for effectively competing in foreign markets and, as a result, are in a better position to make the necessary investments enabling them to take advantage of these resources. Similarly, large size reflects not only the firm's ability to absorb the high cost and risks associated with operating in foreign markets, but also enforces patents and contracts in international expansion through sole ownership (Carruthers 2003). Vida, Reardon and Fairhurst IRI model (2000) as discussed in section 2.2.1.6 showed the importance of these factors.

Etgar and Rachman-Moore (2007) added that such resources are not restricted to a firm's tangible assets but to anything available to the firm that has an enabling capacity. Thus, resources can be financial (e.g. cash reserves and access to financial markets), physical (e.g. plant, raw materials, and equipment), legal (e.g. trademarks and licenses), managerial (e.g. the skills and knowledge of management, competencies and controls of organization), informational (e.g. knowledge about consumers, competitors, and technology), and relational (e.g. relationships with competitors, suppliers, and customers) Hunt (1997). Financial strength in the form of cash reserves and access to foreign capital, skilled management and staff, as well as knowledge of competition and customers are some of the assets the retail firms in Nigeria claim to possess which have influenced their choice of entry mode into the market. This is supported by experts that the international retailer's mode choice of entry will be contingent upon the assortment of available resources (Owens & Quinn 2007; Bianchi 2008).

Different entry modes require different resource commitments (Burt 1993). Resource commitment is widely used at the moment to differentiate between shared and wholly-owned entry modes, and research has used the degree of ownership control as a proxy for resource commitment, the greater the degree of ownership in the entry mode, the larger the resource commitment. A number of studies (Delios and Beamish 1999; Erramilli 1991; Luo 2001) have used market knowledge to explain why firms prefer specific entry modes and found that firms having lower market knowledge tended to reduce the strategic risk by entering these markets through licensing agreements rather than wholly-owned entry modes. From the literature, it can be reasoned that the greater the degree of market knowledge (informational resource) a firm has, the more likely the firm is to prefer the wholly-owned entry mode as stated by the executives of Shoprite and Game stores.

Taken collectively, the wholly-owned entry mode requires significant resource commitments of capital, informational, and managerial resources. Firms having such resources available for a new venture will use the wholly-owned entry mode. Firms lacking these resources tend to rely on franchising systems Etgar & Rachman-Moore (2007). Resources, especially informational and managerial, would be not only very costly to acquire within a firm but also vary from country to country and/or culture to culture. A firm entering a foreign market may feel that it has sufficient informational or managerial resources for choosing the wholly-owned entry mode. At the same time, they may feel deficient in these resources with regard to entering another foreign market where significant differences of culture or managerial practices are present Bianchi (2008). For this reason, a firm expanding to a culturally distant market often has to depend on a franchising system for acquiring resources. According to Pedersen and Petersen (1998), resource commitment is something that a company builds gradually, as market knowledge increases. Besides the above findings, the studies by Moore (2000) and Vida and Vodlan (2003) could not clearly establish a link between the financial resources of a firm and its level of commitment in the market in terms of its market entry mode.

7.4.1.5.   International experience

The findings from this present study show that majority of the retail firms in Nigeria have developed established procedures and processes over the years from operating in various international markets which has aided their entry into the Nigerian market. Majority of the interviewees from the firms from South Africa (see list of firms from SA in table 6.1) mentioned that their experience gained from operating in other developing markets in Africa have been extremely useful.

The above findings from this empirical study are in line with the views of experts. Luo and Peng (1999) for example, agree that experience is a prime source of learning in organizations; as firms gain experience in assessing prevailing business practices and consumer preferences in various host markets, the perceived risk of further international expansion is reduced. Tan and Vertinsky (1996); Gielens & Dekimpe (2001), noted that operating in many countries increases the variety of events to which a firm is exposed, which leads to a more extensive and diverse knowledge base. The latter is acquired through operations in a specific target area because such operations cause logistical and more extensive intelligence-gathering advantages in that region. Both forms of experience are believed to increase the size of entry.

Furthermore, the more similar a potential host market is to other markets with which the firm already has experience, the easier is the transfer of knowledge. Following the work of Mitra and Golder (2002) some of the interviewees highlighted the impact of prior experience in both culturally and economically similar markets when they stated that the former, often referred to as near-market cultural knowledge, only reduces potential acculturation problems, whereas its economic counterpart helps replicate the firm's business in countries in which customer income and the cost and quality of resources are similar. Studies by (Vida 2000; Ghemawat 2001; Palmer & Quinn 2005; Bianchi 2008) all support this view. Both forms of market knowledge are believed to impact the speed and size of entry positively.

The knowledge possessed by the employees in this area of international operation as revealed by the interviewees also has played a key role in their entry mode decision choice. Firms like Shoprite and Game stores mentioned this fact that their use of the independent mode is partly due to the huge experience of their skilled employees. Oviatt and McDougall (1994) had observed that new international ventures composed of management teams with extensive experience in dealing with certain foreign markets are likely to prefer equity modes of entry when compared to those which lack this experience. Burt (1993) adds that as experience is gained over time, retailers might be expected to move from lower risk entry methods and markets to those exhibiting higher risk elements.

7.4.1.6.   Market orientation

The findings from this present study indicate that the retail firms in the Nigerian market, apart from introducing some product offerings that can be considered 'local' are not significantly changing their operations and practices in the market as advocates of market orientation would suggest. So market orientation has not been a major influencing factor of their market entry strategy. The product offerings of these retail outlets have been more of standardization. Though market orientation involves a lot of activities, the noticeable aspects from the operations of the retail firms in Nigeria are in their product adaptation strategies. This finding on the market orientation practice of the retail firms in Nigeria falls short of what scholars and researchers have described market orientation to be. For example, Narver and Slater

(1990) explain market orientation as all activities related to obtaining customers' and competitors' information from the target market as well as disseminating it throughout the organisation in order to create value for customers by developing responsive strategies. It has been previously defined as understanding customer orientation, competitor orientation and coordinating information within the organisation (Narver & Slater 1990; Slater & Narver 1994). The views of other experts and the influence of market orientation on entry strategy is discussed in section 2.6.

Kohli and Jaworski (1990) explain the method that companies use to achieve market orientation as the following: companies create intelligence by conducting market research to understand what consumers need; and disseminates this information by communicating it throughout the organisation using information exchange systems between departments. The organisational responsiveness means designing an implementation plan that corresponds to the customer's needs in a particular market. Different studies provide different definitions of market orientation (Kohli & Jaworski 1990; Narver & Slater 1990; Deshpande *et al.* 1993; Clark 2002) however; they generally agree that it includes collection, analysis and communication of market information throughout the organisation and adapting products and strategies accordingly. These studies found that the method of market entry is an outcome of market orientation process (Deshpande *et al.* 1993; Narver & Slater 1990).

Possible explanations for the above finding could be that because the market is just developing, there are still very few of these firms operating in the market; and also, as a result of the warm embrace of the firms and their products by the market (especially the consumers' familiarity with the organisations and their products), the firms have served the host Nigerian market like it were their home market. It is possible that as the market develops with increased competition, regulations from various stakeholders would be introduced and this would force the firms to try and adapt to these conditions. With this, various levels of market orientation may be seen in the market.

7.5. Institutional Environmental Forces

Retailers consider a country's market potential in their country selection. Retail market attractiveness is formed by such factors as the public policy environment, economic development, social conditions, and cultural assumptions (Alexander and Doherty 2009). Since the overall level of economic development also tends to reflect the level of retail market development, the host country retail market characteristics and its growth prospects are important enticements to large retailers seeking growth and profit opportunities. Firms assess the potential of their international investments in terms of the size and growth potential of the host country market (Quinn 1999). Broad-line specialist retailers tend to locate in trade areas with high per capita income and high population density (Karande and Lombard 2005). Countries with larger populations represent interesting targets to explore (Makino *et al.* 2002) because they tend to possess a larger potential demand, even when per capita income levels are not particularly high.

Finnegan and Good (2009) find that foreign retailers capture larger market share in developing economies than in advanced economies. In the 1990s, when dominant international retailers entered newly opened less developed markets, in part due to "low capital requirements and typically smaller, less efficient local competitors compared to their core markets" (Wrigley 2000b: 305). Retailers are attracted to

225

larger economies with lower retail spend per capita (Alexander *et al.* 2007) but yet developed enough to allow the utilization of proprietary logistics systems and enjoy the benefits of economies of scope and scale.

A potential risk to overall profitability is environmental uncertainty, which is manifested in country risk factors that include transparency and stability of the political, legal, financial and regulatory systems. Managers weigh numerous risks in the international business environment (Miller 1992). Economic and political risks associated with foreign entry factor into the location strategies of European manufacturing firms (Tahir and Larimo 2004). In the internationalization process, Dawson (2007) argues that committed retailers make four major transfers to the host country, including transfers of the firm's business culture and business model as well as its operational techniques. Because many operational advantages are transparent in retail operations, each new entry represents a risk that parts of the firm's business model may be replicated by competitors (Coe 2004). As a result, retailer market entry plans are impeded and/or slowed down when considering riskier regulatory environments (Evans *et al.* 2008). As the host country environment becomes more unpredictable, total business costs will likely increase, diminishing gross margins and profitability. Sections 4.2.1.1 and 4.2.1.2 discussed of the above views and more.

As earlier mentioned, the external environmental forces have been classified into: Formal and Informal environmental forces. The findings in this area are as discussed below:

7.5.1 Informal Factors

7.5.1.1.   Habits & Inertia

This study found that a bulk of the retail firms in the Nigerian market came into the market using a particular entry mode strategy based on the experience obtained from the use of such mode in similar markets in the past. This means the habits and inertia of these firms played an important role in their entry mode decision strategy. The view that is not well supported from this empirical study, however, is the effect of imitation of competitors in the entry mode decision choices of these retail firms in Nigeria. There is no evidence to show that the retail firms in the Nigerian market have imitated their competitors in adopting their entry mode.

The views of (North 1990; Porter 1990; Davis et al. 2000; Forest & Mehier 2001; Lu 2002; Yin and Makino, 2002; Quinn and Alexander 2002; Park and Stenquist 2008) support the above findings. It has been acknowledged that 'today and tomorrow's choices are shaped by the past', North (1990:8). Not only is the decision socially determined, it is also historically located. Decisions are not independent they are inseparable from the result or performance linked to previous decision-making, Forest & Mehier (2001). Part of the informal institutional perspective is that organizations possess habits and inertia. As Porter (1990:580) notes: "Firms would rather not change... Past approaches become institutionalized in procedures and management controls...". According to North (1990), organizations tend to use investment modes consistently. For instance, Lu (2002) observed a strong tendency of intra-organizational imitative behaviour among Japanese multinationals as to foreign entry mode choice; this intra-organizational imitative behaviour is called "parent isomorphism" by Davis et al. (2000:243). Treadgold (1988) wrote also, that retail companies with an established domestic franchise base are associated with a globally relevant format and merchandise and the desire to replicate their format in non-domestic markets Treadgold (1988). This is true of firms like KFC and Nandos in Nigeria.

Findings from the studies mentioned above have found that firms tend to follow the mode of entry that was used most frequently in the past (Davis et al, 2000; Lu, 2002; Yin and Makino, 2002). The underpinning reason found in these studies is a firm's internal mimicry behaviour, by which subsidiaries are likely to adopt the same organisational practices: firms repeat what they have done in the past, Park and Stenquist (2008). The proportion of an entry mode a firm used in the past will influence future entry mode decisions because decisions are institutionalised, as a result, decision makers come to favour the entry mode most frequently used. Quinn and Alexander (2002) further added that firms seeking to expand abroad tend to use the method that has worked for them domestically.

The view expressed by the interviewees that the experience gained in the use of an entry method in similar markets affects their decision choice for similar markets in the future is in line with what experts refer to as organizational imprinting; which means that once a practice or decision has been chosen and implemented, the likelihood of alternatives being considered and used in future decisions will be reduced (Lu, 2002). Frequently, organizational habits and inertia preclude rational changes, Grewal & Dharwadkar (2002). Over time, the decisions are institutionalized and become taken for granted Yiu & Makino (2002). Therefore, it is believed that the imprinting influence of the entry mode used by a retailer in its earlier entries will result in the same entry mode in later entries, especially when the situations are similar to the past.

On the other hand also, firms are seen not to exist in isolation but are connected to each other in a network context, Anderson (2002). As such, the decisions of firms are

228

influenced by others' actions. Prior decisions or actions by other firms increase the legitimacy of similar decisions and actions. Uncertainty encourages imitation DiMaggio & Powell (1983). Firms tend to follow similar firms (such as competitors) that they perceive to be more legitimate or successful than themselves to reduce uncertainty Grewal & Dharwadkar (2002). As earlier mentioned, this view is not supported by this study, as no clear indication emerged to show that the retail firms in Nigeria came into the market following a method used by the competitor.

It is most likely that since the level of competition in the market is so low, i.e. the retail firms not having other established firms to compete with; then the case of imitation can be ruled out for the firms to rely solely on their experience from the past. In a very competitive market situation, experts are of the opinion that firms can learn from not only their own experience but also the experience of others and from what is happening in their surroundings, Sengupta (2001). Strategic choice theories suggest that imitation can be a strategic response to competitor activities, whereby late movers take advantage of the fact that the risk and the costs associated with a new situation have been absorbed by the first-movers, Lieberman & Montgomery (1988). A retailer can decide which country to enter by following other retailers. The few retail firms in Nigeria came in at just about the same time. Writing on China, Grub & Lin (1991) note that one motivation for foreign firms investing in China is to follow their competitors' move to China. Meanwhile, ''organizations within the same population facing the same set of environmental constraints will tend to be isomorphic to one another and to their environment because they face similar conditions'' Dacin, (1997:48).

It is in line with the above that the point is made that when considering a totally unknown foreign area in which little similarity to previous practices is found; retailers will naturally avoid or try to postpone the consideration of the market entry first. However, if the retailer decides to expand into this new area and has no past experience to rely on, the retailer may resort to other retailers' experience—that is, the retailer will mimic others' expansion behaviours. For example, Wrigley & Currah (2003) explain Ahold's expansion into Latin America as inspired by "the super-normal 'first mover" returns on the investments of Carrefour in emerging markets such as Brazil and Argentina". Ahold used the same joint venture entry strategy to enter these Latin American markets.

Conclusively therefore, the interviewees in this study agreed that their decision to use a particular entry strategy in the Nigerian market is influenced more by their company habit of what they have done in the past rather than imitating what their competitors are doing. Uncertainty according to Huang and Sternquist (2007) encourages imitation. The executives interviewed for the retail firms in Nigeria believe their knowledge of the market has reduced significantly, some of the uncertainties which have helped them to make more conscious decisions in the market especially in this area of entry strategy decision. The fact that the majority of these firms came into the Nigerian market from other markets in Africa, mostly South Africa and Kenya, is worthy of note. According to the executives interviewed, in as much as they realise no two markets are the same, still a great amount of similarities can be observed in markets within a particular region like that in Africa. A possible explanation for this case may be that since there are only a few of these international retail firms in the market, they are more or less the pioneer firms in the market with no other rival firms existing in the market to look at. This area of research may find some support in the future when the number of firms in the market would have increased for new entrants to look at what the predecessors' have done.

7.5.1.2.   Market population/wealth

This study revealed that the size of the population of Nigeria (almost 150 million inhabitants) serves as one attractive factor for the retail firms operating in the market as reported by the interviewees. Also, the size of the national economy and the potential for growth in the market are mentioned as other variables of interest. The provision of the much needed infrastructure and formulation of favourable policies are some of the potential signs for growth in retailing in Nigeria as indicated by this study. All of these the study revealed have affected the entry mode decision choices of the retail firms in the country.

The views expressed by the interviewees that the population of a market is important in determining its attractiveness; and that a large market with high levels of economic activity and disposable income will be attractive to international retailers, is supported by the literature. The United Nation's world population prospect report (2009) stated that the size of Nigeria's population is a major attraction for international retailers; the country ranks high in the league of world markets with huge population, as shown in the table below which provides population data for selected markets around the world.

Table 7.1. Selected market populations 2009, and projected populations 2050

Population (000,000)

Country	2009	2050	Actual Change	Percentage Change
China	1,331	1,437	106	7.96%
India	1,171	1748	577	49.27%
United States	307	439	132	43.0%
Indonesia	243	343	100	41.15%
Brazil	191	215	24	12.57%
Pakistan	181	335	154	85.08%
Bangladesh	162	222	60	37.03%
Nigeria	**153**	**285**	**132**	**86.27%**
Russia	142	104	-38	-26.76%
Japan	128	109	-19	-14.84%

Source: UN Population Division, World population prospects (2009).

Firms interested in servicing foreign markets are expected to use a selective strategy and favour entry into more attractive markets. The attractiveness of a market has been characterised in terms of its potential and investment risks, Agarwal and Ramaswami, (1992). Market potential size and growth has been found to be an important determinant of overseas investment Brouthers *et al.* (2008). The interviewees for this study indicate that the Nigerian market has a high growth potential. In high market potential countries, investment modes are expected to provide greater long term profitability to a firm, compared to non-investment modes through the opportunity to achieve economies of scale and consequently lower cost of operation, Canabal and White (2008). Even if scale economies are not significant, a firm may still choose investment modes since they provide the firm with the opportunity to establish long term market presence.

Based on the finding of this study, it is not surprising that the retail firms in the market have chosen to use high investment modes even when the market is rated as being risky. Sakarya *et al.* (2007) note that a cursory review of actual firm choices shows that investment mode may be chosen by larger multinational firms even in low potential countries, and by smaller and less multinational firms in high potential countries. Countries that have relatively lower market potential can be expected to have a lower likelihood of attracting foreign firms. However, firms that are larger and that have a regional or worldwide presence may be interested in entering these markets for achieving their growth and profit objectives. Brouthers *et al.* (2008) in their study gave example of developing countries such as Brazil and India, noting that even though not as attractive as the developed countries, still have sufficient potential and strategic importance to warrant consideration. They further added that an additional benefit offered by these target markets, is the opportunity for higher returns (in excess of the risks taken) due to the presence of greater market imperfections. Ecological models predict that only larger organisations have the resources required to bear the risks associated with entering low potential markets (Sakarya *et al.* 2007; Brouthers *et al.* 2008).

In a related study, Canabal and White (2008) noted if firms decide to enter relatively lower potential markets, they may have a higher propensity to choose a sole venture mode to satisfy their strategic need to coordinate activities on a global basis. Research on global strategy has suggested that such firms will or should be more concerned with global strategic position than with the transaction costs associated with a given market (Porter and Fuller, 1986; Doherty, 2000). Though joint venture and licensing may be more appropriate for low potential markets from a risk reduction perspective, they may not allow the strategic control, change, and flexibility that are needed to secure long-term global competitiveness.

The view of the General Manager of Shoprite that they have chosen to use the wholly owned entry strategy in Nigeria as a result of the problem of a shortage of experienced partners to work with is in line with the findings of Sakarya *et al.* (2007), who revealed that the presence of partners can create impediments to strategic coordination. Their motivations are often incongruent with that of the investing firm, which can lead to significant difficulties. On the other hand, firms can gain competitive advantage by exploitation of strategic options provided by integrated operations, Kogut (1989). They can spot opportunities and threats that may be beyond the horizon of individual operations; they can bring the full weight of their resources to bear on selected competitors or markets; they can shift resources across national boundaries very easily; and they can use the experience gained in one country in another, where it may be relevant. The literature holds that markets with high-current demand and high potential for future demand provide a firm with long-term investment potential (Brouthers *et al.* 1996).

7.5.1.3.   Cultural Distance

This study revealed that the majority of the retail firms in the Nigerian market seem to have some close cultural distance with the host Nigerian market. The interviewees mentioned that there are no wide cultural and organisational differences in their operations in the Nigerian market. In the words of experts, this means the psychic distance between their home and host markets is small. As mentioned earlier, the fact that most of these firms are coming into Nigeria from other markets in Africa particularly South Africa, with similar market conditions are some of the reasons accounting for the small psychic distance. The interviewees added that apart from the unregulated nature of the Nigerian market, most other conditions are not remarkably different. This view, however, is in contrast with the position of some other experts

(Evans and Mavondo 2002; Duran and Wrigley, 2009), especially with respect to the bulk of the retailers in the Nigerian market using the collaborative mode like franchising, despite the existence of close cultural distance. These experts believe the existence of such a situation would favour the use of the independent entry mode strategy.

The conclusion that can be drawn from this is that despite the claim of having some close cultural distances between the home countries of the retail firms and the host Nigerian market, the existence of other problem areas in the market like political instability, insecurity, high cost of operations in the market etc. have all overshadowed the need to use the independent entry mode. In some other markets around the world where foreign retail firms experience huge cultural differences, one problem has always been the impact of the foreign retail firm's country of origin effect on the host market. With the majority of these retail firms in the Nigerian market using franchising, they have not suffered the negative perceptions that follow some foreign retail firms in the host markets.

According to Simon (1959) decisions are socially and culturally determined. The cultural distance between the home and host country affects the choice of foreign expansion form Durand & Wrigley (2009). Cultural distance exists where there is significant differences of culture or managerial practice. For this reason, a firm expanding to a culturally distant market often has to depend on a franchising system for acquiring resources. Evans and Mavondo (2002) agree that psychic distance, defined as the distance between the home country and a foreign country as a result of the perception of both cultural and business differences, is particularly significant for retailers when evaluating the viability of foreign markets and determining the most appropriate entry mode.

A great deal of research suggests that the existence of significant cultural similarities between the home and host country will result in high control entry modes (e.g. Gatignon & Anderson 1988; Kim & Hwang 1992). The interviewees in this study say the consumers in the Nigerian market are no different from those in their home markets and other similar markets they serve, so they do not feel the intense pressure deriving from the need to serve customers who differ culturally from those to whom they have become accustomed. This is why retailers may choose to enter countries with cultures that are similar to the home market before entering countries with dissimilar cultures (Vida, 2000; Sternquist 2007) thus, UK retailers have favoured Ireland; French retailers have favoured Spain; and Japanese retailers have favoured Hong Kong and Taiwan. In these cases, the retailers may choose high control modes because a high level of understanding of norms and values already exists; therefore, local partners are less necessary.

In his study, Pinho (2007) writes that it is assumed that the propensity for choosing an equity-entry mode arises out of a low-distance perception in terms of culture and business practices between the home and host-countries. In this, he noted also, that the accumulation of experience may also influence managers' expectations of the likely effects of internationalisation on the growth and development of the firm and could reduce the perceived psychological distance. These incremental approaches, from non-risky modes to wholly controlled modes, however, were not clearly supported in some other studies (Moore, 2000; Vida & Vodlan 2003).

236

7.5.1.4.   Retail Market Distance

This present study revealed that 'the average Nigerian consumer has developed the habit of seeking western styled goods and culture, and have developed the western shopping habits'. These are some of the reasons the interviewees gave that have made it easy for them to serve the market without many difficulties. There has not been the need to adapt their merchandise to suit the consumers or to change their retail formats significantly. The study also reveals that the retail market in Nigeria has no strict restrictions that affect the operations of the retail firms. The summary of this is that the retail firms in Nigeria also see a close retail distance between the Nigerian market and their home markets.

Studies have shown that international retailers are subject to norms from not only the national culture, but also the retail industry in the host country. Thus, in addition to cultural distance, retail market distance acts as one other factor affecting retailers' internationalization decision-making (Gripsrud & Benito 2005). Retail market distance has been described as the difference between the market conditions of the home market and that of the foreign market in the host country. The findings from this study that no noticeable differences exist in the two aspects of retail distance (target customer preference and retail practice) go to explain the use of the independent entry mode by some of the retailers in the market and also the use of some high equity collaborative modes. The retailers have served the Nigerian market with the same product offerings as seen in their home markets. In international markets, the view is that the boundary-spanning role of retailers requires retail offerings be adapted in the new environment served by the retailer (Vida *et al*. 2000).

The above position therefore provides some partial support for the fact that the use of high-control entry modes is favoured when there is a close retail market distance. This is so because, going by the acknowledgement from the interviewees that a close retail market distance exists, one would have expected more than just three of these retail firms to use the independent (high-control) entry modes. The use of the collaborative entry strategy seems to dominate the practice of the retail firms in the Nigerian market.

Many studies have shown the importance of adapting the product offerings to suit the consumers' preferences. Salmon and Tordjman (1989) wrote that retailers introducing "global" concepts to the market always encounter problems. As reported by Home Depot and Wal-Mart in Brazil, opening stores in South America is not very difficult; the bigger challenge is translating the brand's culture to the local market (Alexander and Marcelo de Lira e Silva 2000). This study showed the Brazilian consumer and retail culture has proved notably resistant to wholesale introductions of concepts that have worked elsewhere, raising the issue of corporate responsiveness to local conditions. In this same market, it was reported to have taken McDonalds a decade to educate the market, needing a generation of consumers to grow up with the product before it became a recognised part of consumer culture.

The retail management practice also represents another kind of norm to which experts believe retailers must conform. Ignoring the norm may result in failures. Section 4.2.1.2 for example, explained the problem faced by Sephora in Japan that led to its failure in that market. The important point is that organisations need to be responsive to the needs of the market rather than try to impose their system on the market like Sephora tried to do.

As contained in the literature, retailers expanding into a foreign market that has a high level of retail market distance compared to its home market may have to consider product adaptation as a way of mitigating against the normative pressures it will face so as to "legitimately fit" into the new environment (Evans & Mavondo 2002; Pinho 2007). However, adaptation they state is a long term and accumulative process. The retailers may seek local partners to accelerate the process; hence, low control entry modes may be preferred. With the help of local partners, the foreign retailer gains isomorphism legitimacy through adaptation. On the contrary, a high level of retail market similarity requires less adaptation (a fact revealed by this study).

So, apart from the close proximity between the home countries and the host Nigerian market of most of the retail firms, equally important is the fact that no retail format is new in the Nigerian market. The consumers are aware of all the available retail concepts in supermarkets, department stores, etc.; this is why one of the interviewees stated that it is in a bid for them not to transfer their knowledge and experience gained over the years (tacit asset) to some local partners in the market that has made them use the independent market entry mode because the consumers are familiar with their retail concept.

7.5.1.5.   Urbanisation/Market Development stage

As indicated by the interviewees, it is clear that the levels of urbanization are an important factor for retailers considering moving into new markets. Isolated rural communities are known not to benefit from the same retail facilities as urban agglomerations. A United Nations report (2007) shows Nigeria has an urban/rural distribution of the population in 2005 of 48.2% and 51.8% respectively. In the contemporary environment also, retailers consider the young/old market composition.

The UN report (2007) mentioned above indicates that Nigeria has about 44% of its population as at 2007 under 15 years of age with only 10% over 60years. This has important implications for retailers; a market with proportionately small population under 15 years might suggest limited demand for products by and for the younger population. The study by Henderson *et al.* (1995) showed that in respect of urban specialization and product cycles: new industries prosper in large, diverse metropolitan areas, but with maturity, production de-centralizes to smaller, more specialized cities. For mature industries, there is also a high degree of persistence in individual employment patterns across cities, and persistence in regional comparative advantage.

A Euromonitor International report (2010) shows that the new developments of improved retail infrastructures like mega shopping malls in Nigeria have attracted international brands into the Nigerian market as well as make shopping more attractive to other segments of the population. Men, children, teenagers and young adults who were not very much disposed to shopping in the open markets have been attracted by the convenience of free and safe parking, and the availability of banking services, cinemas, and restaurants. The modern facilities, security and location within working class neighbourhoods have also attracted top retailers into the Nigerian market. The popularity of these malls has increased footfall in retail outlets in the major cities and consequently increased overall sales volume in the entire market.

The findings from this study is in line with the view expressed by Moriarty *et al.* (2007) that one of the key drivers of growth in markets such as India is the increased westernisation of culture via modern media. In Nigeria, the major growth of modern retailing occurring in the major cities and towns helps shape daily life and offers a glimpse into modern retail enticements- a vast selection of products and the ability to shop in well-structured and laid out locations.

Again, Pellegrini (1994) identified one location issue relevant to retailing to include competitor's moves. Park and Sternquist (2008:290) support this view and noted that for the global retailer, "pioneering advantages may be lost if competitors pre-empt a foreign market. In other words, being the pioneer of a certain type of retailer to a specific segment of customers is more relevant to the global retailer's location advantages". The recent massive developments, expansion and modernisations in the retail sector in Nigeria, meant that the few firms now in the market see themselves more as pioneers, a possible explanation for firms like Shoprite and Game stores using the wholly owned entry method so as to reap pioneering advantages. Therefore, innovation perceived by a global retailer is a base for pioneering opportunities. For innovative retailers, giving away their innovation through contractual arrangements without being the first to exploit is not a rational strategy. It is thus critical for the innovative retailer to expand rapidly to obtain pioneering advantages over potential imitators. This reason also explains the use of an entry method like franchising in the Nigerian market.

7.6   Formal Factors

As previously explained, the regulatory forces in the host markets in which foreign firms operate, act as an influencing formal institutional variable. Organizations are embedded in their political environment (North 1990). Foreign entry-mode choice reflects the extent to which the foreign subsidiary conforms to the regulatory domain of the host-country environment. The elements of the regulatory domain include laws and rules that construct and constitute the grounds of organizational and industry action as well as ensure stability and order in societies (North 1990, Scott and Meyer 1994; Williamson 1991). Compared to indigenous organizations, foreign subsidiaries in the host countries are under different institutional pressure from the native governments. Multinational enterprises' organizational forms and their capacities to operate as networks of affiliates are also affected by cross-national variations in political institutions. Hence, the foremost concern of a multinational enterprise when entering a foreign market is to gain market legitimacy: to establish the right to do business in the new market (North 1990). The political and economic conditions in the host market as well as the various policies and regulations of the government also form part of the formal institutional forces.

Available records show that the present efforts of the government in Nigeria are aimed at improving on its various institutions. The interviewees in this study mentioned that they sought to partner with firms in the Nigerian market that have experience and knowledge of the local market conditions. It is clear from this position that the retail firms seek to acquire some intangible assets from the market, which according to several scholars (Williamson 1985; Buckley and Casson 1998; Kogut and Zander 1993; Alexander and Doherty 2009) are potentially subject to information asymmetries, asset specificity, or costly transfer of tacit knowledge. Though there are no cases of acquisition in the retail sector in Nigeria, joint venture arrangements are used by some of the retail firms. The collaborative mode is therefore preferred because of this need to gain some intangible resources.

7.6.1.1.   The Legal System in the Nigerian market

The General Manager of Shoprite mentioned that "It was only after the change from military rule in 1999 that we started contemplating our entry into Nigeria...besides operating in many other countries in Africa". This study reveals the importance of a sound political and legal system in the operations of foreign retail firms in Nigeria. From available records, all the foreign retail firms operating in Nigeria, especially those chosen for this study, have all come into the Nigerian market only after the return of the country to a democratic political system. Before this time, the country had been under a military system of government which is believed not to have regard for the rule of law.

The independent entry mode of wholly owned subsidiaries and the collaborative mode of franchising have been used by the retail firms in the Nigerian market. The political system in Nigeria is still developing and so is the rule of law. In the recent past, the government has introduced a lot of reforms to strengthen the court system and improve the rule of law. The interviewees mentioned the efforts of government in stabilising the political system and the court system as influencing their entry mode choice in the Nigerian market. The positive efforts of the government they say have given them the motivation to seek increased commitment in the market. Equally important is the absence of stringent regulations concerning retail practice such as: restrictions on land planning, store opening, pricing, store size, etc. All of these the study reveals are the reason why the retail firms are seeking increased control of their operation in the Nigerian market.

The findings from this study is consistent with the views expressed by researchers; as earlier stated, Globerman & Shapiro (2003) highlighted the importance of a strong rule of law in governance decisions (*see section 4.2.1.1*). The important point made is that where a country has weak governance structure, its protection function is undermined resulting in political and economic instability (Hoskisson, Eden, Lau, & Wright 2000). This makes it difficult to attract FDI and where foreign investment exists, low investment modes tend to be used Tse *et al.* (1997). The effect of some government regulations concerning retailing have also been shown in previous studies as outlined in section 4.2.1.1.

From the above, therefore, the empirical evidence from this present study shows that the retail firms in Nigeria agree that their level of resource commitment in the Nigerian market is directly related to the strength of the rule of law, political, and court system.

7.6.1.2.   Political/Economic System

Once the political characteristics of a market have been determined and considered and the market meets fundamental levels of regulatory openness required by the retailer, economic factors will then become an important determinant of market selection decisions. An executive of the (NIPC) stated that "the Nigerian economy is certainly in a better state now than it has been for many years. The economy has been growing rapidly, due in part to gains from rising prices of oil and economic reforms of the government, part of which is government's success in tackling Nigeria's massive external debt which must rank as one of its biggest achievements to date, as the $30bn debt deal was the largest financial agreement in the history of sub-Saharan Africa".

In the last decade, the pace of economic liberalization and financial sector reforms in Nigeria has accelerated. With the liberalization of the telecom sector, the country has one of the fastest growing cellular telecommunication sectors in the world; and financial sector reforms have increased bank capitalization ten-fold in two years. While Nigeria successfully concluded a debt forgiveness agreement with the Paris Club, the country has also been rated highly by leading credit rating agencies. In 2005, the International Monetary Fund (IMF) also approved a two-year Policy Support Instrument (PSI) for Nigeria under the IMF's newly created PSI framework, which is intended to support the nation's economic reform efforts (IMF 2005). The satisfactory review of the benchmarks for the PSI has paved the way for the clearance of the debt to the Paris Club in April 2006 (IMF 2006a).

The general improvements in infrastructures and systems like the good capitalisation of the stock exchange and efforts aimed at reducing the high inflation in the economy are some of the improvements in the economic situation in Nigeria as stated by the interviewees. The average Nigerian consumer now has more buying power unlike before. These developments in the Nigerian market would appear to support Godley and Fletcher's (2000:399) contention that market entrants are particularly responsive to demand that is "relatively income, as opposed to price, elastic". This manifests itself within the retail structure through "new and novel retail formats and products". Furthermore, the policies of government which may be either imposition or inducement in nature have been seen to affect retail entry strategies as well.

Economic development may also be used to classify markets. The GNP or GDP per capita are common measures. In markets where there is a high GDP per capita figure, service industries make a far more significant contribution to GDP calculations than in markets with a low GDP per capita, where agriculture will contribute a higher share of economic activity. International retailers, as part of the service sector, will tend to enter more developed markets. Specific local conditions or cultural/political associations may encourage some international retail expansion, but international activity is primarily focused on developed markets with relatively high levels of GDP per capita and a well-established service sector that encourages expansion. Other important economic measures such as productivity, inflation, balance of payments, reserves, savings, interest rates, money supply, and the purchasing power parity (PPP) within a market must also be considered before international expansion is considered. The World Bank figures on the GDP per capita for selected nations are as shown in the table below.

Table 7.2:   Per capita GDP US$ (2010)

Ranking	Country	GDP per capita
1	Monaco	186, 175
2	Liechtenstein	134, 392
3	Luxembourg	108, 747
4	Norway	84, 880
5	Switzerland	67, 236
6	Denmark	55, 778
7	Sweden	48, 754
8	Netherlands	47, 130
9	United States	47, 084
10	Canada	40, 060
20	United Kingdom	35,165
21	Italy	33, 866
40	Brazil	10, 710
57	South Africa	7, 280
78	China	4, 393
92	Indonesia	3, 039
113	India	1, 477
120	**Nigeria**	**1, 224**
129	Pakistan	1, 008
140	Bangladesh	609

Source: World Bank Report 2009.

International retail development is clearly a product of international political stability. In its absence, international retailers are very vulnerable (Alexander and Doherty 2009). Onah (2002) writing on Marketing and Nigeria's economic development noted that it is pertinent to look at Nigeria's economic performance since the level of marketing development depends on the country's economic development. For example, with the return of the country to democratic governance in 1999, the government set up a committee to provide a vision for the country; this led to the vision 2010 committee that had the following terms of reference:

- To constructively analyse why, after more than thirty-six years of political independence, our development as a nation in many spheres has been relatively unimpressive, in relation to our potential,
- To envision where we would like to be at the time the nation will be marking fifty years of independence as a nation and
- To develop the blueprint and action plans for translating this shared vision into reality

(Vision 2010 Main Report 1997).

Many Nigerians believe that Nigeria's economic problems arose from poor implementation of policies, the Nigeria's Vision 2010 Committee identifies that Nigerian public policies suffer from both poor formulation and implementation for the following reasons:

(1) Policies are made without consulting the institutions directly affected, such that inconsistencies often exist in their interpretation.
(2) Poor coordination of government policies; use of parallel structures to implement government policies of education and health.
(3) Rapid turnover of people in positions of authority has often led to policy inconsistencies and lack of clear direction. Associated with this is the frequent change in governments at all levels.
(4) Frequently changing policies which often cause confusion, and corruption, embezzlement and diversion of funds. (Vision 2010 1997:66).

The above is clearly evident going by the abandonment of the Vision 2010 by a subsequent democratic government and the creation of another vision for the country 'Vision 2020'. The government claims this is a comprehensive framework designed to stimulate economic growth in the country. The framework offers a blueprint for sustainable political development in the country and is aligned with the goals of the National Development Plan (NDP). One objective of this Vision 2020 is to place Nigeria in the top 20 leading economies of the world by the year 2020. To be able to achieve this, the government set out what it called- The Seven Point Agenda[10]. As is typical of the country, with the demise of the President (Musa Yar'Adua) in office in 2010, it is not surprising that not much is said now about this Vision 2020 even when his successor (the then Vice President Goodluck Jonathan) was a part of the government in the formulation of this Vision.

In all, as noted by Hadjikhani and Ghauri (2001:264) "foreign enterprises are dependent on the actors in their political environment, and these actors are also dependent on foreign enterprises, as firms make investments that affect groups like the media or others on which politicians are dependent". Business actors in their interactions with political actors, gain experience and information about values and activities of others in the network – like some other interested parties and therefore, behave accordingly.

The exchange relationship requires the adjudication of conflicting interests and provides the condition for exploring options and sharing common values; as such, the firms require rules and supportive measures distributed by governments, and governments gain legitimacy as these firms satisfy the people and others to whom they are responsible. As earlier mentioned, the behavioural options for the political actors are either coercive or supportive, and can contain general or specific influence. On the part of the firms, they have the option of adaptation and influence. Adaptation means aligning their behaviour to the rules, while influence means negotiation and co-operation (Boddewyn and Brewer, 1994).

---

[10] Government attempt at addressing the main sectors of the economy namely: Politics, macro-economy, infrastructure, education, health, agriculture, and manufacturing.

7.6.1.3.   Government imposition/inducement policies

The retail industry is a very important sector of the economy as such; it is often the object of government regulations. Governments use regulations to limit imported merchandise, reduce excessive price competition, and protect small businesses (Sternquist, 1998). Government activities are seen to affect the operations of business and the economy at large hence the explanation of State as Strategist in Retailing (SSR) model by Sternquist (1998)[11]. Mihn's (1988) framework for considering government's role in industrial policy identified four levels of intervention: general, sector specific, industry-specific, and firm-specific[12]. The Nigerian government unlike other foreign governments like those of India, Vietnam and some others does not have any stringent imposition policies affecting retail practice in the country outside the import prohibition list.

When a retailer considers expanding into a certain country, it first takes into account this country's regulations on foreign investment if there are any. There are two primary types of this regulatory force: imposition and inducement policies (Grewal & Dharwadkar 2002). Imposition is coercive, which means that retailers have to follow the law. For example, retailers in Germany have to follow at least four major strands of regulation: mandated union representation, restricted store hours, constrained pricing and limits on big box retail construction (Badillo, Naro, & Spiwak 2005). India currently bans foreign retail direct investment, preventing foreign retailers such

---

[11] This was developed from Lenway and Murtha's (1994) State as Strategist Dimension and Mihn's (1998) Hierarchy of Government Involvement.

[12] The general level refers to a government policy that affects the entire economy like promoting investment, research, resource allocation, etc. Sector-specific policies target an economic sector like manufacturing through export promotion or import substitution. Industry-specific policies target specific industries like steel or chemical, while firm-specific policies target individuals, firms or group.

as Wal-Mart, Carrefour, and Tesco from investing in and operating their own stores. If a retailer perceives the regulations of the host country as unfavourable, the host country market becomes less attractive to the retailer, and therefore, low control entry modes that involve relatively low resource commitments are often adopted (Kim & Hwang 1992)

On the other hand, a host country may provide strong inducements in order to attract firms (Hollander, 1970; Meyer & Scott, 1992). For example, Hollander (1970) reports that the Argentine government once issued a decree providing tax and import benefits for supermarkets, sparking the entry of the US firms into the Argentine supermarket industry. In China, many special economic zones (SEZs) along the coast provide tax incentives and lower foreign exchange restrictions for potential overseas investors, attracting foreign firms who are motivated to reap the benefits of investment in China (Grewal & Dharwadkar 2002; Ma & Delios 2007). In such a case, a retailer choosing low-control entry modes may be limited in its gains or may have to share benefits with other parties. To avoid these situations, the retailer may choose high control entry modes whenever possible. Using a longitudinal sample of 2998 foreign business activities in China between 1979 and 1993, Tse *et al.* (1997) conclude that foreign firms operating in China prefer WOS or JV to licensing.

This is an area that is not well supported in this study of foreign retail firms in Nigeria. Attempts by the government aimed at attracting foreign investment have led the government into improving the necessary infrastructure that would boost business practice as well as formulating favourable regulations in this direction. The TINAPA project estimated at N26 Billion (US$184 million) is a good example. It is a 65,000 sq

250

m^2 complex having warehousing, wholesaling as well as retail floor spaces. Several others of such projects are presently under development in various parts of the country like: Olokola free trade zone, Kano free trade zone, Maigatari Border free trade zone, Banki Border free trade zone, as well as the Lekki free trade zone. As part of the inducement policy, the Federal Government of Nigeria established the Nigeria Investment Promotion Commission (NIPC) as a one-step-resource for exploring and planning foreign investment and new business in Nigeria and also set up the Nigerian Export Processing Zone Authority (NEPZA) in 1992. To encourage further inflow of direct investment, the government has also streamlined investment regulations for foreign firms seeking to invest in Nigeria providing some other concessions like:

- Liberalisation of exchange control regulations and abolishment of all restrictions on the importation of foreign capital.
- 100% repatriation of dividends
- 100% foreign ownership
- 100% exemption from all taxes and levies such as import licenses for the companies,
- Additional incentives for (pioneer status) for applicable industries etc.
- 100% permission to sell manufactured imported and assembled goods to the Nigerian domestic market.
- 100% restriction free to hire foreign employees, waiver on all expatriate quotas for companies operating in the zone.
- 100% hassle free business environment

These are some of the attractive inducement policies of the government directed mainly at the companies licensed to operate in the free trade zones established across the country. The interviewees for retail firms like Wal-Mart and T-Mart supermarkets the firms operating at the TINAPA site claimed that the above incentives motivated them to come into the Nigerian market. In general terms, the Nigerian government's attitude towards the retail industry can be described as positive. There is no specific legislation that can be said to have adverse effects on retail practice of foreign retailers in the country. The Nigerian government's direct intervention in retailing is minimal. This may not be unconnected with the predominantly informal nature of the sector which makes regulation a bit difficult and an expensive task. However, the interviewees have criticized the government policies in respect of the supply side which is the import ban placed on selected grocery and non-grocery items. Retailers claimed they have had to source these prohibited items from local suppliers, sometimes with significant cost and quality implications in relation to imported products.

This present study was therefore designed to consider the entry strategies of these retail firms within the Nigerian market. Since these firms come from different parts of the world, no attempt was made to investigate the policies in each of the home markets of the international retail firms to see what impact this has on their entry decision into the Nigerian market.

On the other hand also, evidence from this present study reveals that the government ban on importation of certain grocery and non-grocery products is an imposition policy the retailers feel negatively affects their operations, thereby making them favour entry modes with low-resource commitments. However, with many of the firms not influenced greatly by the various inducement policies of the government, the expectation that such attempts by the government would encourage the use of entry modes that involve high-resource commitments is not supported by empirical evidence from this present study, since a larger number of the firms in Nigeria favour the collaborative mode of entry (franchising/joint venture) with a relatively lesser resource commitment.

7.7. Other moderating external forces

7.7.1 Hierarchical/Collaborative Network relationships

It has been explained that the network approach views a market as a web of connected relationships between firms. The firms interact with important actors and establish relationships by investing time and resources (Johanson and Kao 2010). Learning and mutual adaption are the consequences of these interactions and result in relationship building. Relationships and networks have been considered to be resources and intangible assets of the firm as they enable firms to access market information and knowledge that is not available to those outside the network (Forsgren 2008; Williams, McDonald, Tuselmann, and Turner 2008), which the firm acquires through first-hand experience and gradual market commitment.

The importance of networks in internationalisation is widely recognised (Ibeh 2000; Chetty and Wilson 2003; Chetty and Campbell-Hunt 2004; Blomstermo *et al.* 2004; Ibeh and Kasem 2010). Section 2.2.2 highlighted that networks are extensively used when formal institutions are weak Peng (2000). Its strength lies in explaining the internationalisation process and illuminating how the resources, activities and actors within the network affect the various dimensions thereof and also help provide the context for international activity (Sharma and Blomstermo 2003; Jones and Coviello 2005).

This study reveals that most of the retail firms in the Nigerian market do not really have reliable network relationships as a result of a limited number of local partners to work with. Even where qualified local networks exist, the benefits have not been enjoyed because of the limited scope allowed the subsidiary. The tight hold on the subsidiary in decision making and operations make network relationships difficult in the Nigerian market.

7.7.2. Cost of establishing and monitoring operations

A firm seeking to perform a business function outside its domestic market must choose the best "mode of entry" for the foreign market. The would-be entrant faces a large array of choices, including: a wholly-owned subsidiary, a joint venture, or a non-equity arrangement such as licensing or a contractual joint venture, Meyer (2001). The entry modes into foreign markets have been seen to have significant and far-reaching consequences on a firm's performance and survival, Gatignon and Anderson (1988).

A large part of the literature on entry modes is structured in terms of the degree of control each mode affords the entrant, Ekeledo and Sivakumar (2004). Also, control (the ability to influence systems, methods, and decisions) has been identified as having a critical impact on the future of a foreign enterprise. Without control, a firm finds it more difficult to coordinate actions, carry out strategies, revise strategies, and resolve the disputes that invariably arise when two parties to a contract pursue their own interests, Ekeledo and Sivakumar (2004). It can also be used by an entrant to obtain a larger share of the foreign enterprise's profits; it is a way to obtain higher returns. However, the amount of control has been seen to be directly related to the cost of the particular entry mode as well (Erramili and Rao 1993).

Developing markets like Nigeria with weak institutional frameworks have been described as having a very huge cost implication for firms looking to invest in such markets and have control of the market (Bianchi and Ostale 2006; Bianchi 2008). Control, while desirable, carries a high price (Vernon 1983). To take control, the entrant must assume responsibility for decision-making. Control entails commitment of resources, including high overheads which in turn create switching costs, reducing the firm's ability to change its institutional arrangement should its choice turn out to be suboptimal. Resource commitment also increases the firm's exposure, thus, to assume control, is also to assume some forms of risk.

Control, then, is the focus of the entry mode literature because it is the single most important determinant of both risk and return. High-control modes can increase return and risk. Low-control modes minimize resource commitment but often at the expense of returns. Anderson and Gatignon (1986) write that international entry mode choices are most usefully and tractably viewed as a trade-off between control and the cost of resource commitments, often under conditions of considerable risk and uncertainty. Preserving flexibility should be a major consideration of most firms in making the trade-off. Flexibility, the ability to change systems and methods quickly and at a low cost, is always an important consideration, particularly in lesser-known foreign markets where the entrant is likely to change systems and methods as it learns the new environment. Apart from the effect of other variables earlier discussed (firm characteristics and external environmental pressures) one very important factor that equally influences a firm's entry mode strategy into a foreign market is the firm's networks and relationship in that foreign market.

This study revealed that the most common entry mode methods used by the international retail firms in Nigeria are mainly: Organic growth (WOS), joint venture arrangements, and franchising. Each of these as explained earlier, besides control, also has different cost and risk implications for the international retailer. Alexander and Doherty (2009) write that organic growth is particularly appropriate where control may be exercised across comparatively small geographical distance. For example, a retailer operating in the Netherlands may consider expansion into Belgium through organic growth, an issue that requires very little thought or consideration. In such instances that may be the case, where markets are governed by similar regulatory structures, language does not pose a problem, and the retail competitive landscape is such that the retailer may relatively easily replicate its offerings in a geographically close market. Organic growth need to be given sufficient management time, and significant market research is required before a retailer commits the huge financial outlay organic growth requires.

For joint ventures, they equally noted that this method provides the incoming retailer with an opportunity to learn about operations in a new market, while at the same time giving indigenous retailers the opportunity to learn from an international player. International retailers use joint ventures in a bid to gain access to new geographical markets, gaining access to entrepreneurial skills and site locations, recruiting new executives, and establishing a store image and retail brand in a new market. They further added that some retailers may consider joint ventures preferably in markets where they feel they have fewer cultural reference points. A major problem they said is associated with joint ventures is the incompatibility of trading partners.

Again, franchising was described as an approach designed to maintain uniformity of the brand. It can take the form of master franchising, or area development franchising.

This method has low risk, limited financial outlay, rapid expansion across markets, and the presence of local market knowledge. It is further stated that franchising involves complex legal agreements that may lead to problems of definition, control, and rights. The choice of a local franchise partner is determined by a good local knowledge, financial security, with good business know-how, and chemistry between both parties.

This last view is the situation that describes the case of the international retail firms used in this present study. It was revealed that the retail firms that used some form of collaborative entry mode like franchising/licensing in the Nigerian market avoided the direct method (direct franchising), but used the indirect franchise system - appointing a master franchise/area development partner in the Nigerian market. The interviewees stated most of the above reasons for this choice of entry mode namely: the low risk associated with it, limited financial outlay on the part of the foreign firm, ease of rapid expansion across markets, and the presence of local market knowledge by the partner firm in the host market. On the whole, going by the unregulated nature of the market in Nigeria in terms of formulation of polices and directives to guide market operations in addition to the difficulty and huge cost implications in working with local networks, one would have expected the retail firm in the market to favour the use of the independent mode of entry.

Yip et al (2000) stated that international firms can choose between various market entry modes for foreign markets depending on the amount of resource commitment available, extent of risk, potential for returns and degree of control required. The retail executives interviewed for this present study had also mentioned that the huge risk faced in terms of political instability, corruption, insecurity, infrastructural development, inconsistent government policies and regulations, limited number of experienced network partners and so on, meant there was a very high cost of operating in the Nigerian market so to limit this risk, they needed to come down on their financial commitments in the market hence the use of the collaborative modes of entry. Even for such firms like Game stores and Shoprite that are operating their own outlets, their level of financial commitment is equally low because they have not incurred huge cost in building their own outlets but have taken up floor spaces in major shopping malls.

According to transaction cost theory, *(see sections 2.3; 2.3.1; and 4.2)* foreign enterprises should choose the entry mode that minimizes the transaction costs. Several factors affect the transaction costs, including opportunism, the costs of monitoring and enforcing the contract, the existence of transaction-specific assets (Williamson 1996). The transactions costs are higher when (1) the opportunistic behaviours of the partner can cause more damage (Williamson 1993), (2) when it is more difficult to enforce the contracts, and (3) when the degree of asset specificity is higher. If the transaction costs associated with finding, negotiating and monitoring potential partner firms are low, foreign enterprises tend to rely on the market arrangement to deliver products and services. But if these transaction costs are high, foreign enterprises tend to switch to hierarchical modes (Erramilli & Rao, 1993; Makino & Neupert 2000). On the other hand, asset specificity increases the costs of switching from one transaction partner to another, leading to contract hazards (Hill, *et al.* 1990). Asset specificity therefore encourages hierarchical control.

7.7.3. Quality and Number of available Networks

When asked about the effect the networks in the Nigerian market had on their entry mode strategy, a larger number of the interviewees stated they have chosen to enter the Nigerian market because of the absence of strong competition; the relatively cheap cost of acquiring and developing their retail sites; as well as the absence of experienced agents to partner with. As one of the top executives interviewed put it: "our internationalisation efforts into most markets in Africa the Nigerian market inclusive, have called for a lot of careful political, operational, and cultural management... most often, we have been forced to use our own networks which has forced us to internalise our operations but we have not allowed these challenges to deter us because we have found these challenges to be offset by a higher store margin than that enjoyed in the domestic market".

The networks established by the firms with various stakeholders constitute a basis to develop a capacity of opportunism. This echoes the proposal of Dawson (2001) who underlines the importance of opportunism in the strategy of retail firms, and also the argument of Elg *et al.* (2004) who discuss the role of networks in retail firms' internationalisation process. It was suggested that retailers cultivate this opportunism capacity by developing networks of relationships with government authorities, real estate experts, logistics experts, marketing consultants, competitors, and journalists. KFC in Nigeria is one firm that claims to have come into the country exploring an opportunistic proposal presented to it.

The above findings are in line with Coe and Hess's (2005) study which revealed that licences were relatively easy to obtain in under-developed markets, the costs of site acquisition and development low, and the existing competitor set often proved unsophisticated and lacked the necessary scale to provide strong competition making firms seek increased control of their operations. Building dependable and high-quality supply networks has been seen to be a major challenge the international retailer faces, Coe and Hess (2005). In doing a study on the internationalisation efforts of firms in Europe, Cavusgil *et al.* (2002) emphasized that building, developing and managing business relationships are crucial issues for western companies investing in emerging markets. The findings of this study have gone to show that this challenge is not only for western retailers that are investing in developing markets but an obstacle for all retailers going into developing markets.

To this present time, the number of international retail firms operating in the Nigerian market is still very few compared to some other developing markets in Africa and other parts of the world. The fact that there were no rivals (other established retailers) to compete with the present retail firms in the Nigerian market was the reason given by retail firms like Game stores and Shoprite for using the independent mode of entry in the Nigerian market. Apart from the established foreign retail firms, this study revealed there were no local rivals that could compete with the foreign firms entering into the market; and the retail firms that used the collaborative entry modes in the market sought to do this using well established firms with many years of local market knowledge and huge financial capacity (UAC Nigeria Plc. and Chellarams).

Studies have shown that in some developing markets where there are local rivals that are quick to emulate the practices of the foreign firms coming into the market; this has greatly influenced the method of entry used by the foreign retail firms. In such developing markets, the local retail chains have been seen to rapidly and successfully emulate some of the organisational innovations and best practices of the international firms, particularly where the international retailers faced significant institutional, regulatory and operational/logistical barriers, or where they failed to invest sufficiently in the necessary territorial embeddedness – i.e. to localise the operations and achieve organisational legitimacy in the host economy (Bianchi and Ostale 2006).

The conclusion drawn by Bianchi and Ostale (2006) is that some international retailers failed in Chile because of a combination of: the indigenous chains being able to anticipate and respond to the international retailers' sources of competitive advantage; the international retailers being unable to gain sustainable advantage in the local supply chain network; and because these international firms failed to embed themselves in the institutional environment and social networks of the host economy. This conclusion cannot be drawn in the case of the retailers in the Nigerian market because there is just about no competition for the few firms in operation in the market. In this case of Chile, Ahold, Carrefour and Home Depot failed to establish themselves in the market against consistent and fierce defence by the largest indigenous chains (D&S and Cencosud in grocery retailing, and Sodimac in home improvement retailing).

The finding from this study indicates that retail competition in the Nigerian market is low, mainly due to the limited number of the foreign firms in the market. Dunning *et al.* (2007) argued that any reduction in strategic flexibility may be unwise when competition is volatile, which requires quick responses from the firm. In such markets, firms tend to be less profitable and therefore do not justify a permanent organization which involves heavy resource commitments. Because resource commitments limit a firm's ability to adapt to changing market circumstances without incurring substantial sunk costs, a firm can be theorized to favour entry modes involving low resource commitments when competitive pressures in the host market are intense (Park & Sternquist 2008).

It is also important to note the views of Humphrey (2007) who argues that even in emerging markets where international retailers rely on their own supply systems; this does not exclude the use of very small suppliers in the host markets because it is a way for the international retailers to invest in territorial embeddedness. Shoprite is using a wholly-owned method in the Nigerian market; its General Manager mentioned that they have about 300 local Nigerian suppliers and 41 local farmers supplying their store. As reported by Humphrey (2007) Tesco's partnership in East Asia- with CP Group in Thailand, Samsung in South Korea, Sime Darby in Malaysia and Ting Hsin in China, have proved a vital mechanism for territorially embedding its operations and achieving organisational legitimacy in the host economies. In particular, Tesco cites: knowledge gained of local business conditions, the regulatory environment and local consumer culture; retention of the market specific retail skills of the management of the operations acquired; political and/or business network influence obtained; and the ability in some cases to maintain the 'local' nature of the acquired chain's customer face Coe and Lee (2006). In contrast, Tesco's inability to identify a suitable local partner for its entry into Taiwan is widely believed to be at the heart of its subsequent exit (2005) from the market.

In terms of market selection, Doherty (2000) contends that the process occurs in three stages: screening, identification, and selection. The findings from this study do acknowledge a three-stage process of international market selection for retail firms — market screening, market attractiveness and market selection culmination; however, this is only in the case of strategic market selection. In the area of the partner selection literature, both Ulas (2005) and Tatoglu (2000) identify a partner's knowledge of the local market as the major criterion for firms choosing a joint venture partner, a factor that this current research also identifies. This adds weight to the earlier arguments of Doherty (1999) and Doherty and Quinn (1999) on the importance of information asymmetry in international retail franchising. Current findings also support those of Al-Khalifa and Peterson (1999), Salavrakos and Stewart (2006), and Ulas (2005) on joint venture partnerships, with financial status, similar goals and aspirations, serving as major considerations. These findings also have strong resonance with Dawson's (2001) work on the role of opportunism in international retailing. By examining five cases of retailers entering and establishing retail networks in Poland, he concludes that developments in international retailing have a "strong opportunistic streak" (Dawson, 2001:264).

Cavusgil, *et al.* (2002) emphasised that building, developing and managing business relationships are crucial issues for companies investing in emerging markets. It is believed that international retailers go through the process of search, entry, and establishment (Elg *et al.* 2004). At the first stage, the emphasis is on gathering information about the market; a difficult phase in an emerging market since the information and market research infrastructure is often not fully developed. The firm therefore needs to develop trust and relationships with the market as a whole after which it analyses the operating conditions and opportunities to build up a contact network and relationship with other actors in the market. Legitimacy, commitment and trust are suggested as the basic elements of the relationship (Hadjikhani and Ghauri 2005). The respondents expressed these views as problems they faced going into the Nigerian market.

It is therefore not surprising to see that as a way of helping its investors, the U.S. government established the U.S. Commercial Service in Nigeria (CS Nigeria) which maintains a reliable client management system known as NUSA (Networking with United States of America). NUSA offers a unique service and a database of over 3000 verified local companies to U.S. firms wishing to access the Nigerian market. The integrity of the system provides the confidence U.S. exporters and other investors need to engage potential agents, distributor and partners. They advise that using an agent or distributor is advisable for U.S. companies wishing to penetrate the Nigerian market.

Building, developing and managing network relationships are therefore important considerations for these foreign retail firms their size notwithstanding. Writing on this, Dawson (2000:127) noted that: "A challenge of size is to establish to what extent, for what purpose and how the channel power should be used in relationships with suppliers. Managing these power relationships requires a level of managerial sophistication which sometimes takes time to evolve. A second area of managerial challenge in respect of large retailers and their position in the channel is the extent to which channel integration policies, both formal and informal, should be pursued. The larger the retailer, the greater is the extent to which integration becomes feasible".

7.8. Summary of Discussions

The in-depth interviews revealed that the whole nature of the process of entry mode decision is driven by each company's characteristics, marketing strategy and foreign market characteristics, and the degree of influence of these elements are affected by the set of relationship networks built by the firm and its motive for internationalisation. The findings from this study supports the view of Ibeh and Young (2001) that considerable evidence has accumulated from previous research, suggesting the importance of managerial, physical and intangible resources in facilitating international marketing success of foreign firms.

A summary of the above discussions from the perspective of studies in the literature pertaining to retail firms in respect of the degree of consensus is as shown in the figure below. The positive sign (+) shows support from the literature for the factor under investigation and a negative sign (-) shows some disagreement between the findings from this study and available evidence from previous literature. The sign (n.c) shows non-conclusive evidence from previous literature in respect of the factor under consideration. It can therefore be seen from Table 7.3 below that in respect of an internal company variable like brand strength/use of private brands, the view of experts like Gatignon & Anderson (1988); Burt (1993); Fernie et al (1997); Collins & Burt (2003) support the use of this type of strategy. Other scholars and researchers like Doherty (2000); Quinn & Doherty (2000); and Picot-Coupey (2006) hold opposing views whilst the studies by Moore (2000); and Hill et al (1990) have inconclusive evidence in respect of this factor.

Table 7.3   Degree of literature support in respect of variables affecting entry mode decisions of Retail firms

Internal Variables	Degree of literature support
Brand strength/private brands	+Gatignon & Anderson (1988); +Burt(1993); +Fernie et al(1997); +Collins & Burt(2003) n.c: Moore(2000); +Hill et al(1990) -Doherty(2000); -Quinn & Doherty(2000); +Picot-Coupey(2006)
Concept shop strength	+Burt(1993); -Doherty(2000); n.c: Moore(2000); +Picot-Coupey(2006)
Local knowledge Experience	+Burt(1993); +Burt et al(2008); +Davies & Fergusson(1995); +Bianchi(2008); +Bianchi & Ostale,(2006)
International Experience	+Burt(1993); +Owens & Quinn(2007); +Bianchi(2008); n.c: Vida(2000); Moore(2000); Vida & Vodlan(2003); +Palmer & Quinn,(2005)
Size/Company resources	+Burt(1993); +Sternquist(1997); +Park & Sternquist(2008); +Carruthers(2003); +Etgar & Rachman-Moore(2007); +Burt et al(2008); +Bianchi(2008); +Owens & Quinn(2007) Finance n.c: Moore(2000); Vida & Vodlan(2003)
External Variables	**Degree of Research Consensus**
Competition	n.c: Moore(1996); +Dunning et al(2007); +Vodlan & Vida(2009); +Bianchi & Ostale,(2006); +Doherty(2009); +Park & Sternquist(2008); +Evans & Mavondo(2008)
Geographical/ Socio-cultural distance	+Anderson & Gatignon(1988); +Kim & Hwang(1992); -Burt(1993); n.c. Vida & Vodlan(2003); n.c. Moore(2000); +Durand & Wrigley(2009); +Dunning et al(2007); +Gripsrud & Benito(2005); +Vida et al(2000); Alexander & Silva(2000); +Jose-Carlos(2007); +Sato(2004); +Evans & Mavondo(2002); +Vida(2000); +Sternquist(2007)
Networks of relationship	+Burt(1993); +Doherty(2000); +Elg et al(2004); +Vida & Vodlan(2003); +Sparks(1995); +Etgar & Rachman-Moore(2007); +Bianchi(2008); +Doherty(1999); +Tatoglu(2000); +Doherty & Quinn(1999); +Al-Khalifa & Peterson (1999), +Salavrakos & Stewart (2006); +Dawson(2001); +Ulas(2005)
Market potential	n.c: Gielens & Dekimpe(2001), +Doherty(2000), +Dawson(2001)

Key: +: Positive association; -: negative association; n.c: both types of association observed by authors, no conclusion possible.

CHAPTER EIGHT: CONCLUSIONS, RECOMMENDATIONS, AND FUTURE RESEARCH DIRECTIONS

This study has explored retail internationalisation in the developing Nigerian market. The aim of this chapter is to synthesize the findings from this present research, outline the implications for the retail firms and managers, and make appropriate recommendations. The final sections of this chapter highlight some of the major limitations of the study and sets out avenues for future research.

8.1 Headline findings

The main findings of this thesis can be summarised as follows:

(i) This study revealed that most of the retail firms operating in the Nigerian market used the collaborative mode mainly: franchising/licensing and joint ventures. An interesting finding from this present research, however, is that even for the international retail firms that strategically in all foreign markets where they operate use the same entry strategy like franchising, their operations in the Nigerian market comes with some modifications. Their franchising operations is the Nigerian market is carried out not as direct franchising, but indirect franchising which uses other operation modes. The use of this collaborative mode was identified as a way of addressing the agency problem, specifically, the issue of monitoring managers and to allow for the additional learning required in order to acquire local market knowledge and experience.

(ii) The analysis from this study reveal that much as other factors were considered by the retail firms in Nigeria in their choice of the collaborative mode of entry, an important consideration was the benefits they derived from such entry strategies which is the defining characteristics of these modes. This present research revealed for example, that franchising allowed the firms in Nigeria greater direction over the development of their retail operations compared to the use of independent retail outlets. These foreign retail firms have been able to use this as a way of accelerating retail expansion without having to become involved in day-to-day operations, while reducing the financial demands and risks associated with growth.

(iii) This present study revealed that important firm characteristics such as: the possession of some unique brand concept mainly in wide product assortments and the introduction of private brands, the need to protect the product and company image and reputation, the level of market commitment sought, size of the firm notwithstanding, and experience gained from operating in other similar markets like Nigeria, all impacted on the decision of the retail firms to use more of the collaborative mode of entry

(iv) Also, the company habits & inertia in respect of the entry mode strategy used in the past, the huge size of the Nigerian market and high levels of disposable income and good exposure to western style shopping, proximity in the retail market distance between their home country markets and the market in Nigeria, and the provision of infrastructures like mega shopping malls, all influenced their market entry strategy.

(v) This present study revealed the importance of the legal system in the host market in the entry mode decision choices of the foreign retail firms in the Nigerian market particularly the effect of the legal system of the country, strength of the rule of law, structure of the court system, and regulations of the government in relation to ownership structure and system of conflict resolution.

(vi) This study equally revealed that: the level of political stability, past political behaviour, the form of government, political, social, and ethnic conflicts in the market, as well as the strength of the government, all played a significant part in the decision to use the collaborative mode of entry by the international retail firms in Nigeria.

(vii) This present study also showed that the limited number of experienced and qualified local network of partners in the Nigerian market and the level of control sought by the foreign retail firms in the market, all equally impacted on the entry mode choice of the retail firms.

(viii) Lastly, and quite interestingly, the findings from this study show that some important dimensions of international retailing as explained in previous studies such as: the possession of some unique retail concept; existence of close cultural distance between the home market of the retail firms and the host Nigerian market, in addition to the various inducement policies of the Nigeria government have not been major influences in the entry mode decision choices of the retail firms in Nigeria.

8.2 Contributions

As earlier stated in section 1.3, this present study contributes both theoretically and empirically, and equally makes some important managerial contributions. This section revisits the research gaps from the extant literature that were identified during the literature review as detailed in the literature review and conceptual chapters. The major contributions from this study are outlined below:

8.2.1. Theoretical Contribution

Quite significantly, this present study contributes to the theoretical developments in the area of International business strategy and particularly retail internationalisation into developing markets. The combined consideration of both the transaction cost theory and the new institutional theory in this study under the context of a developing market is a notable contribution to the existing theoretical frameworks. Previous studies on retail internationalisation have looked at the effect of either of these theoretical frameworks with some considering just certain aspects of these theories; none (*except for some few studies conducted in markets in Asia*) has looked at the effect of both theories on the entry mode strategies of international retail firms into developing markets in Africa and particularly the Nigerian market.

This combined use of the transaction cost theory and the institutional theory has broadened the framework used for the evaluation of entry mode decision choices of international retail firms into foreign market especially the developing/emerging markets. Critical influencing variables important for such strategic decisions have been identified from this study most of which are again highlighted in the sections below.

8.2.1.1 Implications for Transaction Cost Theory

The findings from this study are very significant especially with respect to transaction-cost-related factors in determining the entry mode choices of firms an area that has witnessed so many mixed findings. The research studies have been proliferated to explore how entry mode is selected, and the factors that determine this selection. The assessment of TCA determinants remains important, as the alignment between entry mode and transaction properties has subsequent performance consequences (Woodcock et al., 1994; Li, 1995).

As earlier explained, the transaction cost perspective views the entry mode choice as a critical decision of governance. Resting on the interplay of two key assumptions of bounded rationality and opportunism and the three key dimensions of transaction (i.e., asset specificity, uncertainty, and frequency), advocating a governance form that can minimize the costs associated with governing and monitoring transactions (Williamson, 1985, 1996). As rightly mentioned by Zhao et al. (2004: 525) "TCA has served as the over-riding perspective for theorizing entry mode choice and, accordingly, transaction-cost-related covariates have been recognized as major determinants of entry mode decision". This present study focused on transaction-cost-related determinants of entry mode choices of international retailers, so as to verify the overall significance of TCA-based factors in determining entry mode strategies along with other intervening external variables.

The view was expressed that in a perfectly competitive market, market specialists will perform efficiently, and thus keeps transaction costs low (Peng, 2006). Therefore, the firm is better off using a market governance structure for its transactions. In reality, however, and especially in a developing market context like Nigeria, the market is often imperfect. The fear from bounded rationality and opportunism lead to increased transaction costs, making an internal governance structure more attractive to the firms. This present study has discussed the major categories of TCA (Free-riding potential, Asset specificity, External uncertainty, internal uncertainty) and some of its major variables derived from these categories (Physical asset specificity, Country risk, Cultural distance, International experience, Research & Development intensity, etc.) A number of limitations can be observed about the explanatory power of this perspective which motivated the researcher to follow the view of experts that due to some shortcomings, the limitations of the TCA perspective should be complementarily addressed (Goodnow, 1985; Zhao et 2004) some of these shortcomings of TCA have been listed as: its over-determination (Kogut and Zander, 1995), exaggerated threat of opportunism (Hill, 1990), ad hoc theorizing (Simon, 1991), 'bad practice' implications as sole reliance on rational control that deteriorates trust and trustworthiness (Ghoshal and Moran, 1996), and an under-socialized view of human motivation and an over-socialized view of institutional control (Granovetter, 1985). The implications of some of these shortcomings are discussed below.

There is the issue of the ability of the TCA to detect intervening effects of moderators such as study-setting variables (location of sample firms, country of origin of parent firms, and industry type). Overall, the moderating effects of location, country of origin, and industry type raise concern about the generalizability of TCA determinants across national settings. The TCE effects of cultural distance, and international experience for example on entry mode choice vary significantly, depending on the country of origin of parent firms (see Erramilli, 1991; Arora and Fosfuri, 2000; Shrader et al 2000; Chang and Rosenzweig, 2001; Herrmann and Datta, 2002; Kim et al 2002). Table 6.1 shows the country of origin of the firms used for this study but no empirical evidence support the effect of the country of origin on their entry mode decision.

Location significantly moderates the effects of cultural distance which influences entry mode choices differently depending on where the firms studied in the sample were located. To the extent that firms opt for entry strategy in response to the location-specific disadvantages (Anand and Delios, 1997; Zhao et al 2004). The big questions is, given the moderating effects of location and country of origin, is environmental uncertainty postulated by TCA theory virtually country- or location specific? If strategic roles of foreign subsidiaries differ (Bartlett and Ghoshal, 1989; Dunning, 1993; Birkinshaw et al., 1998), then does site specificity, play a role in entry choice?

Another important area is the moderating effect of industry type. Quite a number of studies of manufacturing firms tended to report a larger effect size of asset specificity, and R&D intensity for example than those focused on service or other industries (see Davidson and McFetridge, 1985; Anderson and Coughlan, 1987; Gatignon and Anderson, 1988; Delios and Henisz, 2000; Makino and Newport 2000; Brouthers, 2002). These results suggest that TCA determinants are industry specific, and that caution should be taken when generalizing TCE effects on entry modes across industries. Specifically, the skewed results towards the manufacturing sector point to the need to continue to treat different industries separately when analyzing the entry mode determinants. The above situation therefore raises some serious questions:

- Insofar as service industry tends to be location bound (Carman and Langeard, 1980), and service and manufacturing firms respond differently to transaction-cost-based uncertainties (Brouthers and Brouthers, 2003), is industry type simply a moderating variable in TCE and entry mode relationships, or does it interact with location specifics to intervene in the TCE effects?

- Should industry-specific attributes (e.g., the nature and degree of competition, entry barriers, industrial policy of governments, supportiveness of related industries etc) be conceptually and methodologically captured and incorporated, as many of the industry attributes themselves constitute dimensions of external uncertainty? This present study is able to capture the above dimensions from the institutional perspective of this study rather than the TCA view because these variables are not clearly defined and incorporated within the TCA framework.

- Can we find such cross-sectional answers that can hold across different national settings? How, and in which aspects of TCE variables, are national settings related to industry specifics?

8.2.1.2   Implications for Institutional theory

The findings from this study go to support the view of Williamson (2000) that not much is known yet about the new institutional theory because institutions are very complex. This present study has focused on the institutional theory which suggests that a country's institutional environment affects firm boundary choices because the environment reflects the "rules of the game" by which firms participate in a given market. An important aspect of the use of this theory in this present research is the introduction of the new institutional theory perspective. This new perspective suggests that a country's institutional environment is made up of a set of three dimensions: regulatory, cognitive, and normative (Scott, 2001). These three dimensions vary by country and have an influence on the decisions managers make because they influence the way business is conducted in a particular country. Because these influences are relatively uniform in a given host environment, isomorphic pressures tend to bring conformity in the way business is conducted and the structures that are acceptable. Firms that attempt to defy these institutional norms risk losing legitimacy and, hence, get selected out of the marketplace (Brouthers, 2007).

As figure 6.1 shows, scholars have now classified the three dimensions of regulatory, cognitive, and normative broadly into two namely: Formal and Informal institutional environments. The former is the level of embeddedness and includes such variables as: customs, taboos, traditions, norms, etc. while the latter introduces formal rules: constitution, laws, property rights, etc North, (1991). *Its use in this present study on entry mode choice of international retailers has been very beneficial because it has helped to increase our understanding on how to explore the institutional environmental factors that should be considered in entry mode research. Brouthers (2007) noted that before its use, available research lacked a theoretical basis on which to select the risk factors to be included in each study such that each study used those risk factors that are deemed appropriate (or available) by the authors.*

Therefore in this area of market entry mode choices some very clear variables have been identified as influencing the organisations' decision from both the formal and informal dimensions. This is an added insight into the understanding of the application of the institutional theory. Available evidence for example shows that researchers have now extended this theory in various ways from the aspects of its dimensions. Uhlenbruck, Rodriguez, Doh, and Eden (2006) examined the impact of host country corruption, finding that corruption had a significant influence on entry mode choice. (Kirkman, Lowe, & Gibson, 2006; Tihanyi, Griffith, & Russell, 2005) have looked the cultural distance concept, others focused on lists of host country risks or uncertainties that might influence mode choice (Okoroafo, 1989; Delios & Beamish, 1999; Brouthers, Brouthers, & Werner, 2000, 2002; Ahmed, Mohamad, Tan, & Johnson, 2002). Equally investigated is host country industry structure as a barrier affecting entry mode choice, providing mixed results (Chen & Hennart, 2002; Elango & Sambharya, 2004; Somlev & Hoshino, 2005).

Another important implication of the institutional theory to this study of retail entry strategy is that variables and explanations from this perspective have come in to

275

better complement the other variables from the transaction cost analysis perspective.
For example, the institutional theory framework provides detail explanations of the
effects of cultural and retail market distance on market entry choices; an area the
transaction cost theory explanations is not clear about.

Worthy of note also, is that the findings from this study shows there are some other important aspects of this theory that needs to be further investigated. This has raised some important questions such as:

- How do we examine the interactive effects of institutional factors on other decision-making criteria? For example, which component of the institutional environment moderates the influence of which transaction cost dimension on entry mode choice?
- Also, how do institutional dimensions influence the ability of firms to exploit specific resource-based advantages?

Furthermore, the use of this theory for this present study again has again gone on to highlight Hoskisson et al.'s (2000) view of the institutional theory as one of the three most significant theories when probing into emerging economies (the other two are transaction cost economics/agency theory and the resource-based view). Its adoption in a developing market context like Nigeria equally supports the views of scholars (Nwankwo 2000; Hoskisson *et al.* 2000; Burgess and Steenkamp 2006) that contextual international business studies have concentrated on studies of developed markets and the extant theories are not necessarily applicable to emerging and developing markets. These scholars call for more studies of business in Africa. The existing studies on foreign firms in Africa are mainly cross-sectional surveys or FDI studies based on macroeconomic data (see, e.g., Asiedu 2005; Malgwi, Owhoso,

Gleason, & Mathur 2006; Bartels *et al.* 2009). This present research therefore responds to the above call and provides some added theoretical understanding to firm internationalisation into the developing African market.

8.2.2. Empirical Contribution

A major empirical contribution from this present study is the context in which the study was based; the use of the developing Nigerian market (second largest economy in Africa with a huge growth potential and an early exposure to international retail practice) for this present study represents an appropriate and under-studied setting. Much of the studies in retail internationalisation have been done in the developed economies of the west (Europe and America) and in other developing markets in Asia and some in Latin America. Only a handful of studies have looked at international retail practice generally in the developing African market.

This present study is about the first to consider entry mode entry choices of international retail firms into the developing African market and that of the Nigeria market particularly. This present study has therefore added to the understanding of retail internationalisation from this developing African market context thereby improving on the existing literature on this subject. Scholars and practitioners generally believe and agree that developing markets have their peculiarities and difficulties in international retail practice, but no study has been directed at identifying the specific factors needed to be considered in entry mode decision choices of the international retail firms going into a developing market like the Nigerian market.

Therefore, given that this study is one of the first systematic attempts to empirically investigate retail internationalisation into the developing African market, this study has empirically explored some of the conceptual discussions in the extant literature by finding support for some of the dimensions of the arguments and also providing possible reasons for major areas of disagreement. The findings from this research therefore contributes conceptually towards theory building by the empirical support for concepts so far not sufficiently researched in a context like that used in this study which further adds to the extant literature on retail internationalisation.

Also, this present study contributes to the research on international expansion moves of retail firms by combining the firms' economic rationale for entry into distant markets with influencing factors in the social context to show that these perspectives point to different characteristics of the same decision. While the former looks at economic rationale of risky foreign market entry, the latter refers to ways of reducing this risk.

8.2.3. Managerial contribution

This present research has made an influential impact on the international business and strategy fields especially from the context of developing markets as used in this study. This present research has provided much more understanding and answers to the very many questions asked in conducting international business (particularly retailing) in developing countries. Its focus on internal and external variables that either directly or indirectly affect this process has been particularly useful.

This present study sets out the foundation for an understanding of the entry mode choices to be used by international retail firms in entering the Nigerian market. The findings of this study will greatly assist the management of international retail firms in the formulation of strategies relating particularly to entry mode into the Nigerian market and other developing markets. The findings from this study provide them an understanding of how to gain legitimacy and acceptance in the host market; how and why this is important is an added dimension this study provides. Besides strategy formulation for international retail firms, this study also sheds significant light on the most fundamental questions confronting international retailers especially those operating in developing markets such as "what drives the firms' strategy in deciding on the entry mode to use in such developing markets?

8.3   Implications and Recommendations for companies and managers

This research has some important implications and recommendations for entry into the developing Nigerian market that the management of foreign retail firms operating in the market or thinking of coming into the market should consider; they are as discussed below:

(i) The mode of entry has been identified as a fundamental decision a firm makes when it takes its operation outside of national boundaries because the choice of entry automatically constrains the various strategies of the firm, and affects how the firm faces the challenges of operating in this new environment and how it deploys its resources and skills to successfully market its products (Gillespie, Jeannet and Hennessy 2007). A key attribute that distinguishes the different modes of entry is the degree of control it gives a firm over its key marketing resources (Anderson & Gatignon 1986). With the institutional pressures existing in the Nigerian market and the relative cost of operation in the market, management of foreign retail firms should properly consider how they intend to reap the benefits of control (safeguarding key resources from leakage and allowing internal operational control) and manage the cost of operation as well. High control in entry strategies entails high commitment such that the higher the resource commitment and desired control of an entry mode, the higher the cost. These higher costs imply higher levels of investments needed to break-even and make a profit.

(ii) The management of the retail firms should also noted that in as much as the collaborative mode of franchising/licensing/JV seem to be the most dominant entry mode because of the need to enjoy such benefits as: gaining access to new geographical markets; gaining access to entrepreneurial skills and site locations; in addition to establishing a store image and retail brand in the Nigerian market. With a gradual stability of the political and economic conditions in the country; the situation now favours the use of the independent entry mode strategy because there are little or no major regulatory structures, and the retail competitive landscape is such that the retailers can easily replicate their offering in a geographically close market.

(iii) Also, the dominant use of the collaborative entry mode strategy call for the retail firms to be able to address the critical issues pertaining to this method of entry. Palmer and Owens (2006) classified these as: business policy factors, decision making factors, and knowledge exchange factors namely – understanding the regulatory environment, knowing the ethical background of the potential partners, human resource management issues, e.g. as management capability, deciding on operating autonomy, extent, direction, and role of governance mechanisms, as well as knowing how to handle trust and conflict resolution issues that arise.

(iv) Again, stemming from the collaborative entry mode used in the Nigerian market, the management of international retail firms in Nigeria should equally be mindful of some major problems associated with this form of market entry one of which is the incompatibility of trading partners (Alexander & Doherty, 2009). The differences that different partners bring to the relationship – may undermine its long-term survival. A good partner must have good local knowledge, be financially secure, have good business know-how, and above all have some 'chemistry' with the foreign retailer. Also, an entry strategy like franchising involves complex legal agreements that may lead to problems of definition, control, and rights. The nature of the agreement may involve franchisors tied into agreements that they would prefer to terminate but are unable to do so. All of these conditions must be properly understood.

(v) The foreign retail firms in Nigeria equally need to ascertain the type of assets they possess; transaction specific assets are the main construct through which transaction cost theory explains the choice of governance structure. Transaction-specific assets are those which are tailored to the user. When they are present in a transaction, they eliminate competitive market pressures and therefore the superiority of the market over integrated governance structures (Chan and Makino, 2007). This present study identified the importance of possession of such assets as: unique retail concept, brand concept, image and reputation, and international experience. The foreign retail firms need to know which of these to direct to the end users because transaction specific assets when used in conjunction with uncertainty (which introduces bounded rationality, or cognitive limitations, in the form of lack of information) and opportunism (or self interest seeking with guile-Williamson 1996), make it more likely that firms will integrate rather than use market mechanism for their transactions (Chan and Makino, 2007).

(vi) Lastly, though this present study only noted the importance of cultural distance in entry mode decisions retail firms looking to enter the Nigerian market need to be able to ascertain the effect of the cultural distance between their home country and the host Nigerian market on its entry mode strategy especially as the market develops. The fact that most of the retail firms used in this study come from other markets in Africa like (South Africa and Kenya) partly explains the reason for the present finding. Management of retail firms need to decide which of the following positions affect their entry mode strategy the most.

Firstly, from a transaction cost perspective, cultural distance increases information asymmetry and consequently leads to increased monitoring costs accordingly; internalized foreign activities would be more efficient (Padmanabhan and Cho, 1996; Zhao et al. 2004). Also, large cultural distance might lead to the desire to exert greater control over foreign activities (Tihanyi et al. 2005). It is equally argued that cooperation with local partners would involve "double-layered" acculturation whereby the company expanding abroad would have to cope with the foreign culture of customers and corporate culture of a cooperative partner thus enhancing complexity (Barkema et al 1996; Brouthers and Hennart, 2007). This suggests that wholly owned subsidiaries could be used to avoid this complexity.

Secondly, there is the argument that the propensity to use a cooperative mode of entry increases with the degree of cultural distance. In this case, the capabilities and competence of a company are seen as being strongly rooted in the home country (Kogut, 1988); therefore transferring a company's capabilities to a culturally dissimilar host country is difficult and it is linked to high learning costs in the unfamiliar environment consequently, the use of a cooperative strategy is in order to access a partner's capabilities and cultural knowledge (Madhok, 1998). High cultural distance increases the risk of operating in a certain market and of the loss of company resources. Using a cooperative entry serves as a risk-reduction strategy (Tihanyi et al. 2005).

International retail firms therefore need to understand the above situations to know the effect of the cultural distance between their home country and the host foreign market and the entry strategy to adopt. This is crucial for their eventual survival and profitability.

8.4   Limitations of the study

Some limitations were encountered in the course of conducting this empirical research in the light of which, its findings and conclusions should be considered. The following are the major limitations:

1. This study uses Hofstede's cultural index as a measure of uncertainty. Scholars are beginning to acknowledge that this index seems ineffective to capture the diversity and subtlety of cultural influences. Hofstede's cultural index comprises cultural groupings defined by national or geographic boundaries. However, cultures and nations are not equivalent, as scholars have discovered (Erez and Earley, 1993; Shenkar, 2001). Using broad national cultural groupings to measure the uncertainty surrounding a decision choice of foreign entry mode at firm level is at best a crude measure to capture the broad national cultural differences, and may obscure regional-level (location-type)

and industry (industry-type) cultural differences within a host country (Zhao et al. 2004). To address this issue, they suggested using more rigorous analyses using more culturally diverse samples is studies.

2. This present study has not focused on uncovering the effects of sub-cultural variances exhibited at the level of managers involved in making entry strategies since, in the spirit of microanalysis of TCE, uncertainty is also apparent at behavioural level. As is theorized in the TCE literature, behaviour uncertainty stems from difficulties in monitoring the contractual performance of exchange partners (Williamson, 1985). The varying behaviour of individuals may be due to the different sub-cultural traits that may induce uncertainty. Operationalizing behaviour uncertainty by collecting subculture data is thus a viable alternative to the current measurement, as individual perceptions of country distance tend to differ from aggregated national cultural distances (Stottinger and Schlegelmilch, 1998; Lenartowicz and Roth, 2001).

3. Again, in investigating the effect of international experience on the entry mode decision of the retail firms, this present study relied primarily on firm-level information. The diverse set of measures includes firms' host country experience, trans-nationality index, number of years in international business, and percentage of foreign assets. These added dimensions were not investigated because of the unwillingness of the management of these firms to provide evidence in support of these dimensions. Zhao et al (2004) study show for example that international experience effects varied significantly depending on host country experience and percentage of international assets. So the use of firm-level measures as done in this study may be inadequate to capture the complete effects of behavioural uncertainty, as international

experience can be personal (Padmanabhan and Cho, 1999). Personal international experience of decision-makers can serve as an important factor mitigating potential hazards associated with a given entry decision. For instance, prior business experiences (e.g., negotiation, contractual experience) in a foreign market may develop skills and knowledge that assist in identifying trustworthy partners, and hence may increase the chance of entering a partnership-based entry. Thus this omission of personal-level measure, relying instead on the convenient measure at firm-level international experience, may leave out the potentially important effect of behavioural uncertainty, because entry decisions are, after all, made by persons with preferences due to different prior foreign experiences (Zhao et al 2004).

4. This study investigated the effect of the implementation of formal and informal rules on the entry mode choices of international retailers. The institutional theory mentions two other important dimensions: enforcement indeterminacy (the degree of not fully and strictly enforcing formal institutions (Amsden et al., 1994) and dysfunctional competitive behaviour (an environmental scenario of violating 'the rules of the game in a society' (North, 1990: 3). Each of these is explained to vary across countries and industries, and each is said to have direct influences on the entry decision of firms. An inclusion of these dimensions may have better enriched our understanding of the relationship between external uncertainty and entry mode choice, along with other TCA determinants.

5. Williamson (1985: 526; 1996: 58-60) specifically identified six types of asset specificity: site specificity, physical asset specificity, dedicated assets, human asset specificity, brand name capital, and temporal specificity. Transaction

specificities of human asset, site, and temporal specificity, have not been captured in this present study. It is likely that this could have significant differential impacts on the choice of entry modes adopted by the foreign retail firms in Nigeria if investigated.

6. Lastly, the relatively small number of international retail firms taken for this study is another limitation. As explained in the earlier sections of this thesis, due to the various conditions that existed in the Nigerian economy in the past in terms of the state of the economy, the political system in use, government directives and regulations (e.g. indigenisation decree, import prohibition, etc.) most foreign businesses including retail firms divested from the Nigerian market. It is only in the last decade that government efforts at trying to attract FDI into the country being successful; the various reforms, institutional and infrastructural changes introduced by the government has resulted in the re-emergence of foreign retailers in the Nigerian market. As a result of this therefore, having identified about nineteen foreign retail firms operating in the market and contacting them, only twelve agreed to be part of this present research.

8.5 Avenues for future research

Several interesting avenues for future research emerge from this present study.

Firstly, results from available studies show the country of origin affects a foreign firm's market entry mode decision. It is important therefore to consider not only the host market environmental variables but also the home market forces. This raises a number of questions that needs to be addressed in future.

- As entry decisions are made at the level of top management teams, is the moderating effect of country of origin in essence indicative of managerial preferences arising from different cultural traits of decision-makers, or is it a mere reflection of country-specific knowledge and decision-specific experience of the top management team?

- Through what possible paths does country of origin actually influence transaction cost determinants of entry mode choice? Is it through cultural distance, environment familiarity, liabilities of foreignness, or a combination of all three?

- Can individual firms overpower such country of origin effects through their enhanced experience and learning? Because the international experience effect is significantly moderated by the parent firm's location and industry type, it implies some interaction effects between experience- and setting-sensitive variables of country of origin and industry type. This intertwining effect requires some investigation.

Also, some very important questions that must be answered arise in the area of the extent to which foreign firms respond in relation to location-specific disadvantages (Anand and Delios, 1997). Some of the areas that may be looked at include:

- In what ways do location-specific disadvantages (or advantages) constrain (or delimit) the transferability of firms' proprietary assets, the nature of which influences the choice of entry mode?

- Which aspects of location specificity attenuate or strengthen the entry mode strategy effects of a variable like cultural distance? How does cultural distance interact with location characteristics?

-   What is the interplay of local culture within a foreign market, as cultural distance is mostly measured by national culture?

Additional research considering a wider number of international retail firms in Nigeria would be particularly helpful in enhancing the conceptualisation and understanding of the main factors influencing the entry mode decision choices of these foreign retail firms in the country. Additional research may also go further to consider the effect of the entry mode choice on the operations of the retail firms and their eventual profitability. A study like this would be particularly interesting knowing that some foreign firms operate different entry mode strategies for different foreign markets mostly based on institutional pressures from the host foreign markets.

Also, despite the fact now that the retail sector of the Nigerian economy is just developing with a limited number of foreign retail firms, the rate of increase of the firms in the market is phenomenal. As the market expands, quite a number of changes would begin to occur in the host market. Future research could consider the effect of these institutional changes on the entry strategies of the retail firms and also, look into any changes in the internal characteristics of these retail firms as a result of the external environmental changes.

Again, the institutional framework of retail internationalisation provides a theoretical insight about the optimal alignment of the international retail strategy in incorporating elements from the home market as well as the host market. The main issue for these foreign retail firms is that they must adapt their retail practice to fit the needs and expectations of the host market. Evidence from this present study shows that the internationalising firms (especially those using their wholly owned subsidiaries) usually send their managers that have been successful in the home market as managers of their foreign operations. Although these managers have generally strong knowledge of the firm's source of competitive advantage because of their position, they often do not belong to the host country and have very little knowledge of institutional pressures. It would be interesting to try and ascertain the effect of a practice like this on the overall operations and profitability of such retail firms.

Again, applying these same frameworks to other markets in Africa will also be useful in the determination of the influencing factors on the entry mode strategies of the retail firms in these developing African markets. The results from such studies would be particularly helpful when compared with the results from this study to try and build a theory on entry mode strategies for foreign retail internationalisation in Africa. The findings from such studies will help determine any significant variations and effect of the context in which the frameworks can be applied. The findings will go a long way to better enlighten the management of these firms on this all important decision area.

Lastly, future research may consider supplementing the frameworks used in this present study with the Real Options theory as suggested by Brouthers *et al.* (2008); the argument is that despite producing encouraging results, the transaction cost theory's focus on cost minimization instead of value creation is problematic in that it does not consider opportunity costs associated with timing of entry, it fails to acknowledge the potential for growth generated by making investments when uncertainty is high, it ignores the notion of strategic flexibility (Brouthers *et al.* 2008). It will be interesting to see the level of theoretical and empirical support will provide for a better predictive and normative model especially in trying to explain firm strategy based on the value of potential future actions and a consideration of the impact of past investment decisions.

References

Adamgbe, E.T. (2006), 'Exchange Rate Management under the Wholesale DAS in Nigeria: Policy Implications' *West African Journal of Monetary and Economic Integration*, Vol. 6(1): 58-83

Adegbite, E. and Nakajima, C. (2009) 'Institutional determinants of good corporate governance: Insights from Nigeria' Paper presented at the *Academy of Management Annual Meeting*, Chicago, Illinois, USA, August 7th -11th , 2009.

Agarwal, S., & Ramaswami, S. N. (1992), Choice of foreign market entry mode: Impact of ownership, location and internationalization factors. *Journal of International Business Studies*, 23(1):1–27.

Aharoni, Y. (1971) 'On the definition of a multinational corporation', *Quarterly Review of Economics and Business*, 11(Autumn): 27–37.

Aharoni, Y. (1966), The Foreign Investment Decision Process, Boston.

Ahmed, Z. U., Mohamad, O., Tan, B., & Johnson, J. P. (2002), International risk perceptions and mode of entry: A case study of Malaysian multinational firms. *Journal of Business Research*, 55: 805-813.

Ahunwan, B. (1998) *Contextualising Company Law: A Comparison of the Canadian and Nigerian Shareholder's Remedies* in Ahunwan, B. (2002), 'Corporate governance in Nigeria' *Journal of Business Ethics,* 37: 269-287.

Akehurst, G and Alexander, N (1996) (eds.) *The internationalisation of retailing*, Frank Cass, London.

Aker, J.C., Klein, M.W., O'Connell, S.A., and Yang, M. (2010), 'Borders, Ethnicity and Trade', National Bureau of Economic Research (NBER) Working Paper series 15960 available at http://www.nber.org/papers/w15960. Accessed 5th March, 2011.

Akerlof K. (1970), The market for 'lemons': qualitative uncertainty and the market mechanism. *Quarterly Journal of Economics* 74: 448–500.

Akinsanya, A. A. (1983), 'State strategies towards Nigerian and foreign businesses' in Ahunwan, B. (2002), 'Corporate governance in Nigeria' *Journal of Business Ethics,* 37: 269-287.

Alexander, N. (1990a), Retailers and International Markets: Motives for Expansion, International Marketing Review, Vol. 7(4): 75-85.

Alexander, N., Rhodes, M., Myers, H. (2007), "International market selection: measuring actions instead of intentions", *Journal of Services Marketing*, Vol. 21(6): 424-34.

Alexander, N., and Marcelo de Lira e Silva (2002) "Emerging markets and the internationalisation of retailing," *International Journal of Retail & Distribution Management,* 30(6): 300-314.

Alexander, N. (1995), "Expansion within the single European market: a motivational structure" *The International Review of Retail, Distribution and Consumer Research,* Vol. 5(4): 472-87.

Alexander, N. (1997), International Retailing, Oxford: Blackwell Business.

Alexander, N., and Doherty, A.M. (2009), International Retailing Oxford University Press

Alexander, N. and Myers, H. (2000), 'The retail Internationalisation process' *International Marketing Review* 17, 4/5 333-353.

Al-Khalifa A.K, and Peterson S.E. (1999), "The partner selection process in international joint ventures", *European Journal of Marketing,* 33(11/12):1064–81.

Alon, I., and D. I. McKee (1999), "Towards a Macro-Environmental Model of International Franchising," *Multinational Business Review* 7(1): 76–82.

Alon, I. and Welsh, D. eds. (2003), "International Franchising in Industrialized Markets: Western and Northern Europe," Chicago IL: CCH Inc.

Amine, A. and Lazzaoui, N. (2011), 'Shoppers' reactions to modern food retailing systems in an emerging country the case of Morocco', *International Journal of Retail & Distribution Management* Vol. 39(8): 562-581

Amsden, A, Kochanowicz, J and Taylor, L (1994), The Market Meets its Match: Restructuring the Economies of Eastern Europe, Harvard University Press: Cambridge, MA.

Anand, J. and Delios, A. (1997), "Location specificity and the transferability of downstream assets to foreign subsidiaries", *Journal of International Business Studies,* Vol. 28(3): 579-603.

Andersen, O. (1997), "Internationalisation and market entry mode: a review of theories and conceptual frameworks", *Management International Review,* vol. 37(2): 1-27.

Andersen, E. and Coughlan, A.T. (1987), "International Market Entry and Expansion Via Independent or Integrated Channels of Distribution," *Journal of Marketing,* 5(1) (January), 71-82.

Anderson, E. and Gatignon, H. (1986), 'Modes of foreign entry: a transaction cost analysis and propositions', *Journal of International Business Studies* 17(4): 1–26.

Anderson, P. (2002), 'Connected internationalisation processes: The case of internationalising channel intermediaries', *International Business Review*, 11, 365–383.

Anderson, J. C., Hakansson, H., & Johanson, J. (1994), 'Dyadic business relationships within a business network context', *Journal of Marketing, 58*, 1–15.

Antal-Mokos Z. (1998), '*Privatisation, Politics, and Economic Performance in Hungary',* Cambridge University Press: Cambridge, UK.

Arnold, S.J., Handelman, J. and Tigert, D.J. (1996), ``Organisational legitimacy and retail store patronage'', *Journal of Business Research,* Vol. 35: 229-39.

Arora, A and Fosfuri, A (2000) 'Wholly owned subsidiary vs technology licensing in the worldwide chemical industry', *Journal of International Business Studies* 31: 555-572.

Arrow K.J. (1971), Essays *in the Theory of Risk Bearing.* Markham: Chicago, IL.

Asiedu, E. (2005), 'Foreign direct investment in Africa, The role of natural resources, market size, government policy, institutions and political instability' (WIDER Research Paper No. 2005=24). United Nations University, World Institute for Development Economics Research (WIDER), Helsinki, Finland.

A.T. Kearney Global Retail Development Index Report (2010), 'Expanding opportunities for Global Retailers', available at http://www.atkearney.com/images/global/pdf/2010_Global_Retail_Development_Ind ex.pdf

Badillo, F., & Kidder, A. (2007), Top 200 retailers worldwide, 2005. Retrieved March 28, 2007, from retail forward website: /http://www.retailforward.com/membercontent/naris/content/SR/ci0710/ci0710.pdfS

Barkema H.G, Vermeulen F. (1998), International expansion through start-up or through acquisition: a learning perspective. *Academy of Management Journal* 41(1): 7–26.

Barkema, H.G., Bell, J.H.J., and Pennings, J.M. (1996), "Foreign entry, cultural barriers, and learning", *Strategic Management Journal,* Vol. 17(2): 151-66.

Barney J.B. (1991), Firm resources and sustained competitive advantage. *Journal of Management* 17: 99–120.

Barney, J.B. (2001), 'Is the Resource-Based "View" a Useful Perspective for Strategic Management Research? Yes', *The Academy of Management Review,* Vol. 26(1): 41-56

Barry, L.(1982), "Retail Positioning Strategies for the 1980s", Business Horizons, Vol. 25, November-December: 45-50.

Bartels, F. L., Alladina, S. N., & Lederer, S. (2009), Foreign direct investment in Sub-Saharan Africa: Motivating factors and policy issues, *Journal of African Business*, 10, 141–162.

Bartlett, CA and Ghoshal, S (1989), Managing Across Borders, Harvard Business School Press: Boston, MA.

BBC News (2004), 'Corrupt' Nigerian judges held', BBC News Chanel April 2004 available at http://news.bbc.co.uk/1/hi/world/africa/3648895.stm accessed 20th July, 2011.

Bearden, W.O. (1977), Determinant Attributes of Store Patronage: Downtown versus Outlying Shopping Centres, *Journal of Retailing*, 53(2): 15-22, 92, 96.

Bell, J., Crick, D., and Young, S. (1998), Resource Dependency Theory and Small Firm Internationalisation: An Exploratory Approach.

Bengoa M, and Sanchez-Robles B. (2003), Foreign direct investment, economic freedom and growth: new evidence from Latin America. *European Journal of Political Economy* 19: 529–545.

Benito, G. and Gripsrud, G. (1992), "The expansion of foreign direct investment: discrete rational location choices or a cultural learning process?", Journal of International Business Studies, Vol. 23(3): 461-76.

Benito, G.R.G. and Welch, L.S. (1994), ``Foreign market servicing: beyond choice of entry mode", Journal of International Marketing, Vol. 2 (2): 7-28.

Betancourt R.R, and Gautschi, D.A. (1990), Demand complementarities, household production, and retail assortments, *Marketing Science* 9: 146–61.

Bevan A, Estrin S, and Meyer K.E. (2004), Institution building and the integration of Eastern Europe in international production, *International Business Review* 13: 43–64.

Bianchi, C. and Arnold, S. J. (2004), 'An Institutional Perspective on Retail Internationalization Success: Home Depot in Chile'. *International Review of Retail, Distribution, and Consumer Research* 14(2): 149-169.

Bianchi, C.C. and Ostale, E. (2006), "Lessons learned from unsuccessful internationalization attempts: examples of multinational retailers in Chile", Journal of Business Research, Vol. 59: 140-7.

Bianchi, C. (2008), 'Inward Internationalisation of Consumer Services: Lessons from Australian Educational Firms', In *Proceedings 37th EMAC Conference: Marketing landscapes - a pause for thought*, Brighton.

Bianchi, C. (2009), Retail internationalisation from emerging markets: case study evidence from Chile, *International Marketing Review* Vol. 26(2): 221-243

Bilkey, W.J. and Tesar, G. (1977), 'The export behaviour of smaller-sized Wisconsin manufacturing firms', *Journal of International Business Studies* 8 (1): 93-98.

Birkinshaw, J., Hood, N. and Young, S. (2004), 'Subsidiary entrepreneurship, internal and external competitive forces, and subsidiary performance', *International Business Review* 14: 227-248.

Birkinshaw, J, Hood, N and Jonsson, S (1998) 'Building firm specific advantages in multinational corporations: the role of subsidiary initiative', *Strategic Management Journal* 19: 221-241.

Blomstermo, A., Eriksson, K., Lindstrand, A. and Sharma, D.D. (2004), "The usefulness of network knowledge in the international firm", *Journal of International Management*, Vol. 10(3): 355-73.

Blomstermo, A., Sharma, D. D., & Sallis, J. (2006), Choice of foreign market entry mode in service firms, *International Marketing Review,* 23(2): 211–229.

Boddewyn, J.J. and Brewer, T.L. (1994), 'International business political behaviour: new theoretical directions', *Academy of Management Review*, 19(1):119-43.

Bockem, S. and Tuschke, A. (2008), A Tale of Two Theories: Market Entry Decisions from the Perspectives of Industrial Economics and Institutional Theory - Why do Firms Enter Eastern European Markets?

Boeije, H. (2010) Analysis in qualitative research. Los Angeles, Sage.

Brouthers, K. D., Brouthers, L. E., & Werner, S. (1996), 'Dunning's eclectic theory and the smaller firm: The impact of ownership and locational advantages on the choice of entry-modes in the computer software industry', *International Business Review*, 5(4): 377–394.

Brouthers, KD (2002) 'Institutional, cultural and transaction cost influences on entry mode choice and performance', *Journal of International Business Studies* 33(2): 203-221.

Brouthers, L; Brouthers, K; and Werner, S. (2008), "Real Options, international entry mode choice and performance" *Journal of Management Studies*, 45(5): 936-960.

Brouthers, K.D, and Hennart J.F. (2007), Boundaries of the firm: insights from international entry mode research. *Journal of Management,* 33: 395–425.

Brown, J.R., Dev, C.S., and Zhou, Z. (2003), "Broadening the foreign market entry mode decision: separating ownership and control", *Journal of International Business Studies,* Vol. 30 (4): 473-88.

Brush, Thomas H. and Artz, Kendall W. (1999), "Toward a Contingent Resource-Based Theory: The Impact of Information Asymmetry on the Value of Capabilities in Veterinary Medicine", *Strategic Management Journal.* 20 (March), 223-250.

Bruton G.D., Dess G.G., Janney J.J. (2007), Knowledge management in technology-focused firms in emerging economies: caveats on capabilities, networks, and real options. *Asia Pacific Journal of Management* 24: 115–130.

Bryman, A. (1988), *Quantity and quality in social research*. London: Routledge.

Bryman A. (2006) Integrating quantitative and qualitative research: how is it done? *Qualitative Research* 6: 97–113.

Buckley P.J, and Casson M.C. (1976), *The Future of the Multinational Enterprise*. Macmillan: London, UK.

Buckley, P. J., Clegg, J., Wang, C., & Cross, A. R. (2002), 'FDI regional differences and economic growth: Panel data evidence from China'. *Transnational Corporation*, *11*, 1–23.

Buckley, P.J. and Casson, M.C. (1998), "Analyzing foreign market entry strategies: extending the internalization process", *Journal of International Business Studies,* Vol. 29: 539-62.

Buckley, P. J. & Ghauri, P.N. (1999), The internationalization of the firm 2nd. Ed. London: Dryden Press.

Burgess, S. M., & Steenkamp, J.-B. (2006), 'Marketing renaissance: How research in emerging markets advances marketing science and practice', *International Journal of Research in Marketing,* 23: 337–356.

Burns, T. and Stalker, G.M. (1961), The Management of Innovation, London, Tavistock.

Burt, S. (1991), 'Trends in the internationalization of grocery retailing', *International Review of Retail, Distribution and Consumer Research,* 1: 487–515.

Burt, S. (1993), "Temporal trends in the internationalisation of British retailing", The International Review of Retail, Distribution, and Consumer Research, Vol. 3(4): 391-410.

Burt, R. (1997), "The contingent value of social capital", *Administrative Science Quarterly*, Vol. 42: 339–365.

Burt, S. and Carralero-Encinas, J. (2000), "The role of store image in retail internationalisation", *International Marketing Review* Vol. 17, (4/5): 433-455.

Burt, S., Davies, K., Dawson, J., and Sparks, L. (2008): Categorizing Patterns and Processes in Retail Grocery Internationalisation, in: *Journal of Retailing and Consumer Services*, Vol. 15(2): 78–92.

Carman, J.M. and Langeard, E. (1980), 'Growth strategies for service firms', *Strategic Management Journal* 1: 7-12.

Canabal, A. and White, O.G. (2008), Entry mode Research: Past and Future, *International Business Review*, 17(3): 267-284.

Capron, L, Mitchell, W. & Swaminathan, A. (2001), 'Asset Divestiture Following Horizontal Acquisitions: A Dynamic View', *Strategic Management Journal*, Vol. 22(9): 817-844.

Carley, K. 1990. Group stability: A socio-cognitive approach. In Lawler E., Markovsky B., Ridgeway C., and Walker H. (Eds.) *Advances in group processes: Theory & research.* Vol. VII. (pp. 1-44). Greenwhich, CN:JAI Press.

Carruthers, R. (2003), "Rapid response retail", Marketing, April, pp. 20-1.

Casson M.C. (1997), *Information and Organization: A New Perspective on the Theory of the Firm.* Clarendon: Oxford, UK.

Caves, R. E. (1971), International corporations: The industrial economics of foreign investment. Economica, February: 1-27.

Cavusgil, T; Ghauri, P; Agarwal, M. (2002), 'Doing Business in emerging markets: Entry and negotiation strategies', Thousand Oaks, CA: Sage.

Cavusgil, T.S. (1980) 'On the internationalisation process of firms' European Research 8 (6): 273-281.

Cavusgil, T.S. (1984) 'Organisational characteristics associated with export activity' *Journal of Management Studies* 21(1): 3-50.

Chan, P., Finnegan, C., and Sternquist, B. (2011) "Country and firm level factors in international retail expansion", *European Journal of Marketing*, Vol. 45 (6): 1005 – 1022.

Chan, M.C. and Makino, S. (2007),'Legitimacy and multi-level institutional environments', *Journal of International Business Studies* 38: 621–638.

Chain Store Age (2000), Speaking the Language of the Consumer, Dec., 119-128.

Chang S.J, and Rosenzweig P.M. (2001), The choice of entry mode in sequential foreign direct investment. *Strategic Management Journal* 22(8): 747–776.

Chen, S. S., & Hennart, J. F. (2002), Japanese investors' choice of joint ventures versus wholly-owned subsidiaries in the US: The role of market barriers and firm capabilities. *Journal of International Business Studies*, 33(1): 1-18.

Chen, Y., Chyan C., Hsu, S., and Wang, Y. (2009), 'Entry mode choice in China's regional distribution markets: Institution vs. transaction costs perspectives, *Industrial Marketing Management* 38: 702–713

Chetty, S. and Campbell-Hunt, C. (2004), "A strategic approach to internationalization: a traditional versus a 'born-global' approach", *Journal of International Marketing*, Vol. 12(1): 57-81.

Chetty, S.K. and Wilson, H.I.M. (2003), "Collaborating with competitors to acquire resources", *International Business Review*, Vol. 12(1): 61-81.

Childers, T. L. and Rao, A. R. (1992), The Influence of Family and Peer-based Reference groups on Consumer Decisions, *Journal of Consumer Research,* Vol. 19: 198-212.

Clark, D.N. (2000), 'Implementation issues in core competence strategy making', *Strategic Change* 9(2): 115–127.

Common, J. R. (1931), 'Institutional economics' *The American Economic Review*, 21, 648–657.

Coase, R.H. (1937), 'The nature of the firm', Economica, 4: 386-405.

Coe, N.M. (2004), "The internationalisation/globalization of retailing: towards an economic – geographical research agenda", *Environment and Planning A*, Vol. 36: 1571-94.

Coe, N.M., and Wrigley, N. (2009), *The Globalization of Retailing. Volumes I and II.* Cheltenham: Edward Elgar Publishing Ltd

Coe, N. and Hess, M. (2005), The Internationalisation of retailing: Implications for supply network restructuring in East Asia and Eastern Europe. *Journal of Economic Geography,* 5: 449-473.

Collins, A. and Burt, S. (2003), "Market sanctions, monitoring and vertical coordination within retailer-manufacturing relationships: the case of retail brand suppliers", *European Journal of Marketing,* 37(5/6): 668-83.

Coviello, N. and Munro, H. (1997), Network Relationships and the Internationalisation Process of small Software Firms, International Business Review, Vol. 6 (4): 361-86.

Creswell, J. (1998), Qualitative inquiry and research design. Thousand Oaks, CA: Sage.

Cyert, R. M., & March, J. G. (1963), A behavioural theory of the firm. Englewood Cliffs, NJ: Prentice-Hall.

Czinkota, M. R., and I. A. Ronkainen (1997), "International Business and Trade in the Next Decade: Report from a Delphi Study," *Journal of International Business Studies* 28(4): 827–844.

Czinkota, M. R. (1982). *Export development strategies: US promotion policies.* New York: Praeger.

Dacin, M. T. (1997), Isomorphism is context: The power and prescription of institutional norms, *Academy of Management Journal,* 40: 46–81.

Daft, R.L. (1982), "Bureaucratic versus non-bureaucratic structure and the process of innovation and change", in Bacharach, S.B. (Eds), *Research in the Sociology of Organizations: Theory and Research,* JAI Press, Greenwich, CT, .

Datta, D.K, Herrmann, P. and Rasheed A.A. (2002), Choice of foreign market entry modes: critical review and future directions, *Advances in International Management,* 14: 85– 153.

Davidson, WH and McFetridge, DG (1985) 'Key characteristics in the choice of international technology transfer mode', Journal of International Business Studies 15(2): 5-21.

Davis, P. S., Desai, A. B., & Francis, J. D. (2000), 'Mode of international entry: An isomorphism perspective', *Journal of International Business Studies,* 31(2): 239–258.

Davies, K., and Ferguson, F. (1996), 'The international activities of Japanese retailers', *Service Industries Journal,* 15(4): 97–117.

Davis, L., K. Meyer (2004), Subsidiary research and development, and the local environment, *International Business Review,* 13(3): 359-382.

Dawson, J.A. (1994), "Internationalisation of retailing operations", *Journal of Marketing Management,* Vol. 10: 267-282.

Dawson, J. (2000), "Retailing at century end: some challenges for management and research", *International Review of Retail Distribution and Consumer Research,* Vol. 10(2): 19-48.

Dawson J. (2001), Strategy and opportunism in European retail internationalization. *British Journal of Management,* 12: 253–366.

Dawson, J. (2007), "Scoping and conceptualizing retailer internationalisation", *Journal of Economic Geography,* Vol. 7: 373-97.

Delios, A. and Beamish, P. (1999), "Ownership strategy of Japanese firms: transactional, institutional, and experience influences", *Strategic Management Journal,* (20): 915-33.

Delois, A and Henisz, WJ (2000) "Japanese firms' investment strategies in emerging economies', *Academy of Management Journal* 43(3): 305-323.

Deluca, F. (2002), The Subway story: Making North American history. In *International franchising in industrialized markets: North America, the Pacific Rim, and other countries,* edited by DianneWelsh and Ilan Alon, 209-22. Chicago: CCH Publishing.

Demirbag, M., Apaydin, M., and Tatoglu, E. (2010), Survival of Japanese subsidiaries in the Middle East and North Africa', *Journal of World Business* 463: 1-15

Deshpande, R., Frederick, E., and Webster (1993), Corporate cultures, Customer Orientation, and Innovation in Japanese Firms: A Quadrad Analysis, Journal of Marketing 57:23-37.

Doherty A.M. (1999), Explaining international retailers' market entry mode strategy: internalisation theory, agency theory and the importance of information asymmetry. *International Review of Retail, Distribution, and Consumer Research,* 9(4):379–402.

Doherty, A.M. and Alexander, N. (2004), "Relationship development in international retail franchising", *European Journal of Marketing,* Vol. 38(9/10): 1215-35.

Doherty A. M. and Quinn B. (1999), International retail franchising: an agency theory perspective, *International Journal of Retail and Distribution Management;* 27(6):224–66.

Doherty, A.M. (2000), "Factors influencing international retailers market entry mode", *Journal of Marketing Management*, Vol. 16:223-45.

Doherty, A.M. (2009), "Market and partner selection processes in international retail franchising", *Journal of Business Research*, Vol. 62(5): 528-34.

Douglas, M. (1986), 'How Institutions Think', Syracuse University Press, Syracuse, NY.

DiMaggio, P., & Powell, W. W. (1983), "The iron cage revisited: Institutional isomorphism and collective rationality in organizational fields", *American Sociological Review*, 48, 147–160.

Dimgba, N. (2010), 'Anti-competitive Business Practices by dominant firms in Nigeria and the Securities and Exchange Commission's company break-up powers under the Investments and Securities Act 2007' Paper delivered at the Nigerian Bar Association, 5th Section on Business Law Conference, Abuja, April 7th, 2010.

Dimitratos, P., Lioukas, S., & Carter, S. (2004), 'The relationship between entrepreneurship and international performance: The importance of domestic environment. *International Business Review*, 13: 19-41.

Driscoll, A.M. (1995), ``Foreign market entry methods'', in Paliwoda, S.J. and Ryans, J.K. Jr (Eds), International Marketing Reader, Routledge, London.

Driscoll, A.M. and Paliwoda, S.J. (1997) 'Dimensionalizing international market entry mode choice', *Journal of Marketing Management*, 13(2–4): 57–87.

Dunning, J.H. (1977), Trade, Location of Economic Activity and the Multinational Enterprise: A search for an Eclectic Approach, in Ohlin, B., Hesselborn, P.O. and Wijkman, P.M. (1977), The International Allocation of Economic Activity, London, Macmillan.

Dunning, J.H. (1979) 'Explaining changing patterns of international production: in defence of eclectic theory', *Oxford Bulletin of Economics and Statistics*, 41(Nov): 269–95.

Dunning, J.H. (1983), Market power of the firm and international transfer of technology, *International Journal of Industrial Organisation* 1 :333-351

Dunning, J. H. (1988), "The eclectic paradigm of international production: a restatement and some possible extensions", *Journal of International Business Studies,* Vol. 19(1):1-31.

Dunning, J. H. (1989), Multinational enterprises and the growth of services: Some conceptual and theoretical issues, *Service Industries Journal,* 9(1): 5-39.

Dunning, J.H. (1993), Multinational Enterprise and the Global Economy, Addison-Wesley Publishers, Reading, MA.

Dunning, J. H. (1995), "Reappraising the eclectic paradigm in an age of alliance capitalism", *Journal of International Business*, vol. 25(3): 461-91.

Dunning, J.H. (2000), "The eclectic paradigm as an envelope for economic and business theories of MNE activity", *International Business Review,* vol. 19:257-77.

Dunning J.H, Rugman, A.M. (1985), The influence of Hymer's dissertation on the theory of foreign direct investment. *American Economic Review* 75: 228-232.

Dupuis, M. and Prime, N. (1996), Business Distance and Global Retailing: A Model for Analysis of key Success/Failure Factors, *International Journal of Retail & Distribution Management,* Vol. 24(11): 30-38.

Durand, C. and Wrigley, N. (2009), Institutional and economic determinants of transnational retailer expansion and performance: a comparative analysis of Wal-Mart and Carrefour, *Environment and Planning*, vol.41:1534 - 1555

Draucker; C.B; Martsolf; D.S; Ross; R; Rusk, B.T. (2007), 'Theoretical Sampling and Category Development in Grounded Theory', *Qualitative Health Research* Volume 17 (8) 1137-1148.

Easter-by Smith, M., Thorpe, R., and Lowe, A. (1991), Management Research: An Introduction, London, Sage Publication.

Easterby-Smith, M., Thorpe, R., & Lowe, A. (2002), Management research: An introduction, 2nd ed. London: Sage Publications.

Edvardsson, B. (1988), "Service quality in customer relationships: a case study of critical incidents in mechanical engineering companies", *The service Industries Journal,* Vol. 8(4): 427-45.

Ekanola, A. B. (2006) 'National integration and the survival of Nigeria in the 21st century' *Journal of Social, Political and Economic Studies*, 31(3): 279-293.

Eisenhardt, K.M. (1989), Building Theories from Case Study research, Academy of Management Review, Vol. 14(4): 532-50.

Elango B, Sambharya R.B. (2004) The influence of industry structure on the entry mode choice of overseas entrants in manufacturing industries. *Journal of International Management* 10: 107–124.

Elg, U, Ghauri, P. and Sinkovics, R.P. (2004), A market and network based model for retailers' foreign entry strategies Lund Institute of Economic Research Working Paper Series 2004/3

Elg, U. (2007) "Market orientation processes in retailing: a cross-national study", *European Journal of Marketing*, Vol. 41(5/6): 568 – 589

Ekeledo, I. and Sivakumar, K. (1998), "Foreign market entry mode choice of service firms: a contingency perspective", *Journal of the Academy of Marketing Science*, Vol. 26 (4): 274-92.

Ekeledo, I., & Sivakumar, K. (2004), International market entry mode strategies of manufacturing firms and service firms: A resource-based perspective. *International Marketing Review*, 21(1): 68–101.

Engwall, L., & Wallenstal, M. (1988), Tit for tat in small steps: The internationalization of Swedish Banks, *Scandinavian Journal of Management*, 4(3–4), 147–155.

Erez, M. and Earley, P.C. (1993), Culture, Self-Identity and Work, Oxford University Press: New York.

Erramilli, M.K. (1990), "Entry mode choice in service industries", *International Marketing Review*, Vol. 7(5): 50-62.

Erramilli, M.K. (1991), "The experience factor in foreign market entry behaviour of service firms", *Journal of International Business Studies*, Vol. 22: 479-501.

Erramilli, M.K. and Rao, C.P. (1990), "Choice of foreign market entry modes by service firms: role of market knowledge", *Management International Review*, Vol. 30 (2):135-50.

Erramilli, M.K. and Rao, C.P. (1993), "Service firms' international entry-mode choice: a modified transaction-cost analysis approach", *Journal of Marketing*, Vol. 57, July, pp. 19-38.

Estrin S. (2002), Competition and corporate governance in transition. *Journal of Economic Perspectives* 16:101–124.

Etgar, Michael and Rachman-Moore, Dalia (2007), 'Determinant factors of failures of international retailers in foreign markets', *The International Review of Retail, Distribution and Consumer Research,* 17: 1:79 — 100.

Evans, J., Treadgold, A. and Mavondo, F.T. (2000), "Psychic distance and the performance of international retailers: a suggested theoretical framework", *International Marketing Review,* Vol. 4(5): 373-91.

Evans, J., & Mavondo, F. T. (2002), Psychic distance and organizational performance: An empirical examination of international retailing operation. *Journal of International Business Studies,* 33(3), 515–532.

Evans, J., Bridson, K., Byrom, J., Medway, D. (2008), "Revisiting retail internationalisation", *International Journal of Retail & Distribution Management,* Vol. 36(4): 260-80.

Ewah, S.O.E, Ewa, U. and Ekeng, A.B. (2010), "Managing Dissafisfied Customers in Retailing in Nigeria", Available at SSRN: http://ssrn.com/abstract=1612290 Accessed 14th May, 2010.

Fagbadebo, O. (2007), Corruption, Governance and Political Instability in Nigeria' African Journal of Political Science and International Relations Vol. 1 (2): 28-37.

Faust, D. (1982), A needed component in prescriptions for science: Empirical knowledge of human cognitive limitations. Knowledge: creation, Diffusion, Utilisation, 3, 555-570 as quoted in Miles and Huberman (1994:11)

Fernie, J., Moore, C., Lawrie, A. and Hallsworth, A. (1997), "The internationalisation of the high fashion brand: the case of central London", Journal of Product & Brand Management, Vol. 6(3): 151-62.

Finnegan, C.A. and Good, L. (2009), "Within-country retail format diversification: does country context matter?" Proceedings of the AMA Winter Conference, Tampa, FL.

Fladmoe-Lindquist, K., and L. L. Jacque (1995), "Control Modes in International Service Operations: The Propensity to Franchise," *Management Science* 41(7), 1238–1249.

Fontana A. and Frey J. (1994), The interview: From structured questions to negotiated text, In Denzin N. and Lincoln Y.S., (Eds) Handbook of Qualitative Research, London: Sage 645-672.
Forest, J., & Mehier, C. (2001), In: J. R. Commons, & A. Herbert (Eds.), Simon on the concept of rationality. *Journal of Economic Issues,* 35 (3): 591–605.

Ford, D. (Ed.) (2002), *Understanding Business Marketing and Purchasing: An Interaction Approach,* 3rd ed., Thomson Learning, London.

Forsgren, M. (1989), Managing the Internationalization Process: The Swedish Case, Routledge: London.

Forsgren, M. (2008), Theories of the multinational firm: A multidimensional creature in the global economy Cheltenham: Edward Elgar.

Gaba, V., Pan, Y., Ungson, G. (2002), "Timing of entry in international market: an empirical study of US Fortune 500 firms in China", *Journal of International Business Studies*, Vol. 33 No.1, pp.39-55.

Gatignon, H., & Anderson, E. (1988), The multinational corporation's degree of control over foreign subsidiaries: An empirical test of a transaction cost explanation. Journal of Law, Economics and Organization, 4, 305–336.

Gelbuda M, Meyer K.E, Delios A. (2008), International business and institutional development in Central and Eastern Europe. *Journal of International Management* 14(1): 1–11.

Ghauri, P.N. and Cateora, P.R. (2006), International Marketing, 2nd ed., McGraw-Hill Publishing, London.

Ghauri, P.N. and Gronhaug, K. (2002), Research Methods in Business Studies: A Practical Guide, 2nd ed., Financial Times Prentice-Hall, London.

Ghosh, A. (1990). *Retail Management,* Orlando, FL: The Dryden Press.

Ghoshal, S and Moran, P (1996) 'Bad for practice: a critique of the transaction cost theory', *Academy of Management Review* 21: 13-47.

Ghemawat, P. (2001), Distance still matters, Harvard Business Review, Vol. 78(8): 137-147.

Gielens, K., & Dekimpe, M. G. (2001), 'Does international entry decisions of retail chains matter in the long run'? *International Journal of Research in Marketing,* 18(3), 235–259.

Gielens, K. and Dekimpe, M.G. (2007), The Entry Strategy of Retail Firms into Transition Economies", *Journal of Marketing,* 71(2):196-212.

Gillespie K., Jeannet, J., and Hennessy, H.D. (2007), "Global Marketing," 2nd Edition, Houghton Mifflin Company, Boston, MA 02116-3764.

Godley and Fletcher (2000) "Foreign entry into British retailing, 1850-1994", *International Marketing Review,* 17:4/5:392-401

Goodnow, J.D. and Hansz, J.E. (1972), ``Environmental determinants of overseas market entry strategies", *Journal of International Business Studies,* Spring,: 33-50.

Golafshani, N. (2003), 'Understanding Reliability and Validity in Qualitative Research', *The Qualitative Report* Volume 8 (4): 597-607

Goldman, A. (1981), Transfer of a Retailing Technology into The Less Developed Countries: The Supermarket Case, *Journal of Retailing, 57*(Summer), 5–29.

Goldman, A. (2001), "The transfer of retail formats into developing economies: the example of China", *Journal of Retailing*, Vol. 77: 221-42.

Gomes-Casseres, B. (1989), "Ownership structures of foreign subsidiaries: theory and evidence", *Journal of Economic Behaviour and Organization,* Vol. 11: 1-25.

Gomes-Casseres B. (1990) Firm ownership preferences and host government restrictions: an integrated approach. *Journal of International Business Studies* 21: 1–22.

Glaser, B., (1978), Theoretical Sensitivity. Sociology Press, Mill Valley, CA.

Globerman S, Shapiro D. (1999), The impact of government policy on foreign direct investment: the Canadian experience. *Journal of International Business Studies* 30: 513–532.

Globerman, S., & Shapiro, D. (2003), 'Governance infrastructure and US foreign direct investment', *Journal of International Business Studies* 34:19–39.

Granovetter, M.S. (1973), "The strength of weak ties", *American Journal of Sociology*, Vol. 78(6):1360–1380.

Granovetter, M (1985) 'Economic action and social structure: the problem of embeddedness', *American Journal of Sociology* 91: 481-510.

Grewal, R., & Dharwadkar, R. (2002), 'The role of the institutional environment in marketing channels', *Journal of Marketing* 66: 82–97.

Gripsrud, G., & Benito, R. G. (2005), 'International Retailing: Modelling the pattern of foreign market entry', *Journal of Business Research,* 58, 1672–1680.

Grub, P. D., & Lin, J. H. (1991), 'Foreign direct investment in China'. New York: Quorum.

Grùnhaug, K. and Kvitastein, O. (1993), ``Distributional involvement in international strategic business units", *International Business Review,* Vol. 2 (1):1-14.

Guba, and Lincoln (1994), Competing paradigms in Qualitative Research, In N.K. Denzin and Y.S. Lincoln (eds.) Handbook of Qualitative Research (Thousand Oaks, CA Sage).

Habib, M., & Zurawicki, L. (2002), 'Corruption and foreign direct investment'. *Journal of International Business Studies*, 33(2): 291–308.

Hadjikhani, A. and Ghauri, P.N. (2001), 'The behaviour of international firms in socio-political environments in the European Union', *Journal of Business Research* 52: 263-275.

Hadjikhani, A. and Ghauri, P.N. (2005), "Socio-political behaviour of MNCs: a network perspective", unpublished working paper.

Hakansson, H. and Snehota, I. (1995) Developing Relationships in Business Networks, Routledge: London.

Halverson, R. (1997), The Chain that Mr. Sam Built, Discount Store News, March 3, Vol. 36(5): 45-46.

Handelman, J.M. and Arnold, S.J. (1999), The role of Marketing Actions with a Social Dimension: Appeals to the Institutional Environment, *Journal of Marketing*, 63(3): 33-48.

Hartland-Peel, C. (1996), *African Equities: A Guide to Markets and Companies* (Euromoney Publications, London, U.K.).

Haunschild, P. R., & Miner, A. S. (1997), 'Modes of inter-organizational imitation: The effects of outcome salience and uncertainty', *Administrative Science Quarterly*, 42, 472–500.

Haspeslagh, P.C., and Jemison, D.B. (1991), Managing Acquisitions: Creating value through Corporate Renewal. The Free Press, N.Y.

Herbiz, P.A. (1998), Handbook of Cross-Cultural Marketing, The International Business Press, N.Y.

Harzing, A.W.K. (2002) 'Acquisitions versus Greenfield investments: international strategy and management of entry modes', *Strategic Management Journal* 23: 211–227.

Heide, J. and A. Miner (1992), 'The shadow of the future: Effects of anticipated interaction and frequency of contact on buyer–seller cooperation', *Academy of Management Journal,* 35: 265–291.

Henderson, V., Kuncoro, A., and Turner, M. (1995), Industrial Development in Cities, *Journal of Political Economy* 103(5): 1067-1090.

Henisz W.J. (2000), The institutional environment for multinational investment, *Journal of Law, Economics and Organization,* 16: 334–364.

Hennart, J. (1982), A theory of multinational enterprise. Ann Arbor, Mich.: University of Michigan Press.

Hennart, J.F. (1977), 'A theory of foreign direct investment' PhD. Dissertation University of Maryland.

Hennart J.F, and Park Y.R. (1993), Greenfield vs. acquisition: the strategy of Japanese investors in the United States. *Management Science* 39: 1054–1070.

Heron, J. (1996), Co-operative Inquiry: Research into the Human condition, London, Sage Publication.

Herrmann, P and Datta, D (2002) 'CEO successor characteristics and the choice of foreign market entry mode: an empirical study', Journal of International Business Studies 33(3): 551-569.

Hill, C.W.L, Hwang P, Kim W.C. (1990), 'An eclectic theory of international market entry mode', *Strategic Management Journal* 11(2): 117–128.

Hill, C.W.L. and Kim W.C. (1988), 'Searching for a dynamic theory of the multinational enterprise: a transaction cost model', *Strategic Management Journal*, 9: 93–104.

Helpman, E. (1984), `A simple theory of international trade with multinational corporations', *Journal of Political Economy* 2(3): 451-471.

Hofstede, G. (1980), Culture's Consequences: International Differences in work Related Values, Beverly Hills, CA: Sage.

Hofstede, G., Hofstede, G.J. and Minkov, M. (2010), Cultures and Organizations: Software of the Mind, 3rd ed., McGraw-Hill, New York, NY.

Hollander, S. C. (1970), 'Multinational retailing' MSU International Business and Economic studies.

Hollensen, S. (2007), Global Marketing Prentice Hall.

Hopkins, A. G. (1973), An Economic History of West Africa, London: Longman

Hoskisson, R. E., Eden, L., Lau, C. M., & Wright, M. (2000), 'Strategy in emerging economics', *Academy of Management Journal,* 43: 249–267.

Hua N, and Templeton, A. (2010), 'Forces driving the growth of the restaurant industry in the USA', *International Journal of Contemporary Hospitality Management* 22(1): 56–68.

Huang, Y. and Sternquist, B. (2007), Retailers' foreign market entry decisions: An institutional perspective, *International Business Review* 16: 613-629.

Humphrey J, 2007, ``The supermarket revolution in developing countries: tidal wave or tough competitive struggle" *Journal of Economic Geography* 7: 433 – 450.

Hunt, S. (1997), "Resource-advantage theory: an evolutionary theory of competitive firm behaviour?" *Journal of Economic Issues,* 31(1): 59-77.

Hymer, S. H. 1976 (1960), International operations of national firms - A study of direct foreign investment. Cambridge, Mass.: MIT Press.

Ibeh, K.I.N. (2000), "Internationalisation and the small firm", in Carter, S. and Evans, D. (Eds), Enterprise and Small Business: Principles, Practice and Policy, Financial Times and Prentice-Hall, London, pp. 434-52.

Ibeh, K.I.N. and Young, S. (2001), "Exporting as an entrepreneurial act: an empirical study of Nigerian firms", *European Journal of Marketing*, Vol. 35(5/6): 566-86.

Ibeh, K.I.N., Ibrahim, E., and Panayides, P.M. (2006), 'International market success among smaller agri-food companies some case study evidence', *International Journal of Entrepreneurial Behaviour & Research* Vol. 12 (2): 85-104

Ibeh, K. and Kasem, L. (2010), "The network perspective and the internationalization of small and medium sized software firms from Syria," *Industrial Marketing Management*, Vol. 40(3): 358–67.

IMF Report (2005), 'Nigeria: Poverty Reduction Strategy Paper— National Economic Empowerment and Development Strategy', International Monetary Fund Country Report No. 05/433. Available at http://www.imf.org/external/pubs/ft/scr/2005/cr05433.pdf. Accessed 4th June, 2011.

Ingram P, and Silverman B. (2002), Introduction. In *The New Institutionalism in Strategic Management (Advances in Strategic Management) (Vol. 19)*, Ingram P, Silverman BS (eds). JAI Press: Greenwich, CT; 1–30.

Inkpen, A.C. and Dinur, A. (1998), Knowledge Management and International Joint Ventures, *Organizational Science, 9*(July-August),: 454–468.

Johnson, B. R. (1997), 'Examining the validity structure of qualitative research', *Education, 118*(3): 282-292.

Johanson, M., and Kao, P.T. (2010), 'Networks in Internationalisation' in José Pla-Barber, Joaquín Alegre (ed.) Reshaping the Boundaries of the Firm in an Era of Global Interdependence *Progress in International Business Research*, Volume 5: 119–142

Johanson, J. and Mattson, L. (1988), Internationalisation in Industrial Systems- A Network Approach, in Strategies in Global Competition, Neil Hood and Jan-Erik Vahlne, eds. New York: Croom Helm, 287-314.

Johanson, J. and Vahlne, J.E. (1977) "The internationalisation process of the firm – a model of knowledge development and increasing foreign market commitment", *Journal of International Business Studies,* Vol. 8(1): 22-32.

Johanson, J. and Vahlne, J.E. (1990) 'The mechanism of internationalisation' *International Marketing Review*, 7(4):11-24.

Johanson, J. and Wiedersheim-Paul, F. (1975), "The internationalisation of the firm four Swedish case studies", *Journal of Management Studies,* Vol. 12: 305-22.

Jones, M.V. and Coviello, N.E. (2005), "Internationalisation: conceptualising an entrepreneurial process of behaviour in time", *Journal of International Business Studies*, Vol. 36(3): 284-303.

Kacker, M. (1988), International Flow of Retailing Know-How: Bridging the Technology Gap in Distribution, Journal of Retailing, Vol. 64(1): 41-67.

Kacker, M. (1985) Transatlantic Trends in Retailing. Westport, CT: Greenwood Press.

Karande, K., Lombard, J. (2005), "Location strategies of broad-line retailers: an empirical investigation", *Journal of Business Research*, Vol. 58(5): 687.

Kelman, S. (2005), Public Management needs help!, Academy of Management Journal, Vol. 48(6): 967-969.

Kerin, R.A., Vijay, M., and Rajan, V.P. (1990), *Contemporary Perspectives on Strategic Market Planning*. Boston: Allyn & Bacon.

Kerin, R.A., Varadarajan, P.R. (1992), "First-mover advantage: a synthesis, conceptual framework, and research propositions", *The Journal of Marketing*, Vol. 56 No.4, pp.33-52.

Khoury, S.J. (1979), "International banking: a special look at foreign banks in the US", *Journal of International Business Studies*, Vol. 10(3): 36-52.

Kibazo, J. (1995), A New Scramble for Africa, Financial Times 30th November.

Killaly, B.L. (2001), *Firm Performance, Expansion Experience and Current Expansion Forms: The United States International Telecommunications Service Industry, 1985-1998*, University of Michigan, Ann Arbor, MI, .

Kindleberger, C. P., (1970), ed., The international corporation (MIT Press, Cambridge, Mass.).

Kim, W. C., & Hwang, P. (1992), Global strategy and multinationals' entry mode choice, *Journal of International Business Studies,* 23(1): 29–53.

Kim, B, Kim, H and Lee, Y (2002), 'Modes of foreign market entry by Korean SI firms', *Asia Pacific Journal of Marketing and Logistics* 14(4): 13-35.

Kindleberger, C. P. (1969), American business abroad. New Haven, CT: Yale University Press.

Kirkman, B. L., Lowe, K. B., & Gibson, C. B. (2006), A quarter century of culture's consequences: A review of empirical research incorporating Hofstede's cultural values framework. *Journal of International Business Studies*, 37(3): 285-320.

Klein, S., Frazier, G., & Roth, V. J. (1990), A transaction cost analysis model of channel integration in international markets. *Journal of Marketing Research, 27,* 196–208.

Klein, H., & Myers, M., (1999), "A Set of Principals for Conducting and Evaluating Interpretive Field Studies in Information Systems", MIS Quarterly, Vol. 23(1): 67-94.

Kobrin, S. J.(1988), Trends in Ownerships of American Manufacturing Subsidiaries in Developing Countries: An Inter-Industry Analysis, *Management International Review,* Special Issue,: 73-84.

Koch, A.J. (2001), Selecting overseas markets and entry modes: two decision processes or one? *Marketing Intelligence & Planning* 19(1): 65-75

Kogut B, and Singh, H. (1988), The effect of national culture on the choice of entry mode. *Journal of International Business Studies* 19: 411–432.

Kogut, B. (1988), A study of the life cycle of joint ventures, *Management International Review* 28, 39-52 Special Issue.

Kogut B. (1989), 'A note on global strategies', *Strategic Management Journal* 10(4): 383–9.

Kogut B., and Zander I. (1993), Knowledge of the firm and the evolutionary theory of the multinational corporation. *Journal of International Business Studies* 24: 625–645.

Kogut, B., & Zander, U. (2003), A memoir and reflection: knowledge and an evolutionary theory of the multinational firm 10 years later. *Journal of International Business Studies, 34*(6), 505-515.

Kohli, A.K. and Jaworski, B. (1990), "Market Orientation: The Construct, Research Propositions, and Managerial Implications," *Journal of Marketing,* 54, (April), 1-18.

Knickerbocker, F.T. (1973), Oligopolistic Reaction and Multinational Enterprise. Boston.

Kshetri, N. (2008), The Rapidly Transforming Chinese High Technology Industry and Market: Institutions, Ingredients, Mechanisms and Modus Operandi, Chandos Publishing, Oxford.

Kumar, V., & Subramaniam, V. (1997), A contingency framework for the mode of entry decision, *Journal of World Business,* 32(1): 53–72.

Kvale, S. (2008), 'Interviews: Learning the craft of qualitative research interviewing' Sage Publications, Inc.

Lacey, A. & Luff, D. (2001) Trent Focus for Research and Development in Primary Health Care: Qualitative Data Analysis. Trent Focus.

Langer, A., Mustapha, A.R. and Stewart, F. (2009), Diversity and discord: Ethnicity, horizontal inequalities and conflict in Ghana and Nigeria', Journal of International Development Vol. 21(4): 477-482.

Lee, G.K. and Lieberman, M.B. (2010), 'Acquisition vs. Internal development as modes of market entry', *Strategic Management Journal* 31: 140–158.

Leelapanyalert, K. and Ghauri, P. (2007), 'Managing International market entry strategy: The case of retailing firms' *Advances in International marketing* 17: 193-215.

Legrain, P. (2003). Cultural globalization is not Americanization. *The Chronicle of Higher Education, 49*(35): 2-9.

Lenartowicz, T and Roth, K (2001), 'Does subculture within a country matter? A cross-cultural study of motivational domains and business performance in Brazil', *Journal of International Business Studies* 32(2): 305-325.

Leontief, W.W. (1953), 'Domestic production and foreign trade: The American capital position re-examined', Proceedings of the American Philosophical Society 97: 331-349.

Li, J (1995), 'Foreign entry and survival: effects of strategic choices on performance in international markets', *Strategic Management Journal* 16: 333-351.

Lieberman, M., & Montgomery, D. (1988), 'First-mover-advantages' *Strategic Management Journal,* 9: 41–58.

Lin, W., Liu, Y., and Cheng, K. (2011), 'The internationalization and performance of a firm: Moderating effect of a firm's behaviour' *Journal of International Management* Volume 17(1): 83-95

Lincoln, Y. S., & Guba, E. (1985), *Naturalistic enquiry*. Beverly Hills, CA: Sage.

Linder, S. (1961), An essay on Trade and Transformation, Wiley, new York, NY.

Lindquist, Jay D. (1974), Meaning of image. *Journal of Retailing, 50*(Winter), 29–38.

Linton, R. (1970), The Family, Ediciones Peninsula, Barcelona: 31-65.

Lofland, J., and Lofland, L.H. (1984), Analysing social settings: A guide to qualitative observation and analysis Wadsworth Pub. Co. (Belmont, Calif.)

Lu, J. W. (2002), 'Intra- and inter-organizational imitative behaviour: Institutional influences on Japanese firms' entry mode choice', *Journal of International Business Studies*, 33(1): 19–37.

Lubman, S. (1999), Bird in a cage: Legal reform in China after Mao. Stanford, CA: Stanford University Press

Luo, Y. (2001), "Determinants of entry in an emerging economy: a multilevel approach", *Journal of Management Studies,* 38(3): 443-72.

Luo, Y. and Peng, M.W. (1999), "Learning to Compete in a Transition Economy: Experience, Environment, and Performance," *Journal of International Business Studies,* 30 (2): 269–95.

Luostarinen R.K. (1979), The internationalization of the firm. Helsinki School of Economics.

Ma, X., & Delios, A. (2007), A new tale of two cities: Japanese FDIs in Shanghai and Beijing, 1979–2003. *International Business Review,* 16: 207-228.

Mabogunje, A. (1964), "Evolution and Analysis of Retail Structure of Lagos, Nigeria", *Economic Geography,* Vol. 40, 4(304-323).

Madhok, A. (1998), 'The nature of multinational firm boundaries: transaction costs, firm capabilities and foreign market entry mode', *International Business Review* 7, 259-290.

Mahoney, J.T. (1995), "The Management of Resources and the Resource of Management", *Journal of Business Research.* 33 (June): 91-101.

Makino, S., & Neupert, K. E. (2000), 'National culture, transaction costs, and the choice between joint venture and wholly owned subsidiary', *Journal of International Business Studies,* 31(4): 705−713.

Malgwi, C. A., Owhoso, V., Gleason, K. C., & Mathur, I. (2006). Who invests in the least developed countries? An examination of U.S. multinationals in Africa. *Journal of African Business,* 7(1/2): 201–227.

Malone, T. W. (1987), Modeling Coordination in Organization and Markets, *Management Science,* 33(10): 1317—1372.

Makino, S., Lau, C.M., Yeh, R.S. (2002), "Asset-exploitation versus asset-seeking: implications for location choice of foreign direct investment from newly industrialized economies", *Journal of International Business Studies,* Vol. 33(3): 403-21.

Markusen, J.R. & Venables, A.J. (2000), `The theory of endowment, intra-industry and multi-national trade', *Journal of International Economics,* 52(2): 209-234.

Mason, J.B. and Mayer, M.L. (1987), Modern Retailing, 4th edition. Plano, TX: Business Publications.

McDonald, F., Tuselmann, H.J., Voronkova, S., and Golesorkhi, S. (2011), 'The strategic development of subsidiaries in regional trade blocs', *The Multinational Business Review* Vol. 19(3): 256-271

McFelipe, S.W. and Burnett, J.J. (1990), Consumer Religiosity and Retail Store Evaluation Criteria, Journal of the Academy of Marketing Science, Vol. 18(2): 101-112.

McGoldrick, P.G. and Blair, D. (1995), International Market appraisal and positioning, in McGolrick, P.G. and Davies, G. (eds.), International Retailing: Trends and Strategies, Pitman Publishing, London, 168-190.

McIvor, R. (2009), 'How the transaction cost and resource-based theories of the firm inform outsourcing evaluation', *Journal of Operations Management* 27: 45–63

McPhail, J. C. (1995), Phenomenology as philosophy and method. *Remedial and Special Education, 16:* 159-167.

MacMillan, J. (2007) 'Market institutions', in L. Blume and S. Durlauf (eds.), *The New Palgrave Dictionary of Economics*, 2nd ed. Palgrave: London.

MacMillan J. (2008), Market institutions. In *The New Palgrave Dictionary of Economics* (2nd edn). Durlauf S, Blume L (eds). Palgrave Macmillan: London, UK; Vol. 3.

Messinger, P. and C. Narasimhan (1997), "A Model of Retail Formats based on Consumers Economizing on Shopping Time," *Marketing Science*, 16 (1), 1–23.

Meyer, K. E. (2001), Institutions, transaction costs, and entry mode choice in Eastern Europe, *Journal of International Business Studies,* 32(2): 357–367.

Meyer K.E. (2006), Asian management research needs more self-confidence. *Asia Pacific Journal of Management* 23: 119–137.

Meyer K.E. (2007), Asian contexts and the search for general theory in management research: a rejoinder. *Asia Pacific Journal of Management* 24: 527–534.

Meyer KE, and Peng M.W. (2005), Probing theoretically into Central and Eastern Europe: transactions, resources, and institutions. *Journal of International Business Studies* 36(6): 600–621.

Meyer, K.E., & Estrin, S. (2001), 'Brownfield Entry in Emerging Markets', *Journal of International Business Studies,* Vol. 32(3): 575-584.

Meyer, K.E., Estrin, S., Bhaumik, S.K., and Peng, M.W. (2009), 'Institutions, Resources, and Entry strategies in Emerging Economies', *Strategic Management Journal* 30: 61-80.

Meyer, J., & Scott, R. (1992), Organizational environments: Ritual and rationality. Beverly Hills, CA: Sage.

Meyer K.E, and Tran, Y.T. (2006), Market penetration and acquisition strategies for emerging economies. *Long Range Planning* 39(2): 177–197.

Mihn, K.H. (1988), "Industrial policy industrialisation of Koea", KIET Occasional Papers, 8803, KIET, Seoul.

Miles, M.B., and Huberman, A.M. (1994), Qualitative Data Analysis, Thousand Oaks, CA: Sage.

Miller, K.D. (1992), "A framework for integrated risk management in international business", *Journal of International Business Studies*, Vol. 23 No.2, pp.311-31

Minkov M; and Hofstede, G. (2011) 'The evolution of Hofstede's doctrine', *Cross Cultural Management: An International Journal* Vol. 18(1): 10-20

Mitra, D., & Golder, P. (2002), 'Whose culture matters Near-market knowledge and its impact on foreign market entry timing' *Journal of Marketing Research,* XXXIX, 350–365.

Moore, C. (2000), "The internationalisation", unpublished PhD thesis, University of Stirling, Stirling.

Moran, D. & Mooney, T. (2002), The phenomenology reader. London: Routledge.

Morgan, N.A., Zou, S., Vorhies, D.W., Katsikeas, C.S. (2003), "Experiential and informational knowledge, architectural marketing capabilities, and the adaptive performance of export ventures: a cross-national study", *Decision Sciences*, Vol. 34(2): 287-321.

Moriarty, M., Ben-Shabat, H., Gurski, L., Padmanabham, V., Kuppuswamy, R., Prasad, P., Groeber, M., (2007), Growth Opportunities for Global Retailers— The A.T.Kearney2007GlobalRetailDevelopmentIndex.ATKearneyInc., Chicago, IL.

Mudambi R, and Navarra P. (2004), Is knowledge power? Knowledge flows, subsidiary power and rent-seeking within MNCs', *Journal of International Business Studies* 35(5): 385–406.

Musteen, M., Datta, D., & Herrmann, P. 2009. Ownership structure and CEO compensation: Implications for the choice of foreign market entry modes. *Journal of International Business Studies,* 40: 321–338.

Nakata, C., & Sivakumar, K. (1996), 'National culture and new product development: An integrative review', *Journal of Marketing, 60*, 61-72.

Nakos, G., & Brouthers, K. D. (2002), Entry mode choice of SMEs in Central and Eastern Europe, *Entrepreneurship Theory and Practice, 27*: 47–64

Narayanan, V. K., & Fahey, L. (2005), 'The relevance of the institutional underpinnings of Porter's five forces framework to emerging economies: An epistemological analysis'. *Journal of Management Studies, 42*(1), 207–223.

Naro, K. K. (2005), Top 200 retailers worldwide, 2004. Available at: /http://www.retailforward.com/membercontent/naris/content/CI/ci0510/ci0510.pdfS. Accessed 20th July, 2010.

Narver, J., and Slater, S.F. (1990), 'The effect of market orientation on Business profitability', *Journal of Marketing*, 54: 20-35.

Neven, D., Odera, M., Reardon, T., & Wang, H. (2009), 'Kenyan supermarkets and emerging middle-class horticultural farmers, and employment impacts on rural poor', *World Development*, 37(11): 86–96.

Nicita, A., and Vatiero, M. (2007), "The Contract and the Market: Towards a Broader Notion of Transaction?" *Studi e Note di Economia* 1: 1–20.

Nigeria. National Population Commission, *National Census Result 2006*. (Abuja: National Population Commission, 2007).

Nnolim, D.A. (1979), 'marketing as a tool for economic development with special reference to Nigeria' in Julius O. Onah (ed.) *Marketing in Nigeria*. London: Cassell, Ltd.

Nnona, G. (2006), 'The Nigerian Investment and Securities Act: Delineating Its Boundaries in Relation to the Registration of Securities', 50 J. AFR. L. 24 (2006); George Nnona, Choice of Law in International Contracts for the Transfer of Technology: A Critique of the Nigerian Approach, 44 J. AFR. L. 38 (2000).

Nordstrom, K. (1990), 'The internationalization process of the firm: Searching for new patterns and explanations' Ph.D. dissertation. Stockholm: Institute of International Business Stockholm School of Economics.

Noordewier, T. G., George J. and Nevin, J.R. (1990), "Performance Outcomes of Purchasing Arrangements in Industrial Buyer-Vendor Relationships," *Journal of Marketing*, 54 (October): 80–93.

North, D. C. (1990), Institutions, institutional change and economic performance. Cambridge, UK: Cambridge University Press.

Nwokoye, N. G. (1981), Modern Marketing for Nigeria, London: Macmillan

Nwankwo, S. (2000), 'Assessing the marketing environment in sub-Saharan Africa: opportunities and threats analysis', *Marketing Intelligence & Planning*, 18(3):144–153.

Okoroafo, S. C. (1989), Effects of repatriations risk on the choice of entry modes used by US manufacturing forms in LDCs. *Journal of Global Marketing*, 3(2): 25-41.

Olarinmoye, O. O. (2008). 'Godfathers, political parties and electoral corruption in Nigeria', *African Journal of Political Science and International Relations*, 2(4): 66-73.

Olebune, C. (2006) 'Social entrepreneurship, the Nigerian perspective' *In: Social Entrepreneurship* African Events.

Onah, J.O. (2002), Marketing and Nigeria's Economic Development' in Sonny Nwankwo and Joseph F. Aiyeku (ed.) Dynamics of Marketing in African nations' Greenwood Publishing Group Inc. USA.

Onokerhoraye, A.G. (1977), "The changing patterns of Retail Outlets in West African Urban Areas: The case of Benin, Nigeria", Human Geography, Vol. 59, 1(28-42).

Ovia, J. (2008), Blossoming the Nigerian economy: Real sector financing' – Lecture delivered at CBN's National Seminar on 'Banks and the Nigerian economy' at Sheraton Hotel & Towers, Abuja Tuesday February 12, 2008.

Oviatt, M.B. and McDougall, P.P. (1994) Challenges for Internationalisation Process Theory: The case for International new ventures, Management International Review, Special Issue, Vol. 37.

Oxley, J.E. (1999) 'Institutional Environment and the mechanisms of Governance: The impact of Intellectual Property Protection on the structure of inter-firm Alliances' Journal of Economic Behaviour and Organisation, 24: 283-310.

Owen, M. and Quinn, B. (2007), "Problems encountered within international retail joint ventures: UK retailer case study evidence", International Journal of Retail and Distribution Management 35(10): 758-780.

Oyefusi, A. (2007), "Oil-dependence and Civil conflict in Nigeria", WPS/2007-09. http://www.csae.ox.ac.uk/workingpapers/wps-list.html.

Oyesola, B. (2010), 'The economic meltdown and Nigeria', NBF News Monday, April 19, 2010. Available at http://www.nigerianbestforum.com/blog/?p=44659 accessed 14 July, 2011.

Ozughalu, U.M. (2007), 'An econometric analysis of the performance of the Nigerian economy', Economic and Policy Review, Vol. 13(3): 24-30.

Padmanabhan, P. and Cho, K. (1996), 'Ownership strategy for a foreign affiliate: an empirical investigation of Japanese firms', Management International Review 36(1), 45-65.

Padmanabhan, P. and Cho, K. (2005), Revisiting the role of cultural distance in MNC's foreign ownership mode choice: the moderating effect of experience attributes, International Business Review 14 (2005) 307–324.

Palich, L. Cardinal, L., and Miller, C. (2000), 'Curvlinearity in the diversification-performance linkage: an examination of over three decades of research' Strategic Management Journal, 21: 155–174.

Palmer, M. (2005), Retail multinational learning: a case study of Tesco, International Journal of Retail and Distribution Management 33(1): 23–48.

Paliwoda, S. (1993), International Marketing, 2nd ed., Butterworth-Heinemann, Oxford.

Paliwoda, S. and Slater, S., (2009), "Globalisation through the kaleidoscope", *International Marketing Review*, Vol. 26 (4/5): 373 – 383

Palmer, M. and Owens, M. (2006), "New directions for international retail joint venture research", *The International Review of Retail, Distribution & Consumer Research,* Vol. 16 (2): 159-79.

Palmer, M. and Quinn, B. (2003), The strategic role of investment banks in the retailer internationalisation process. Is the venture marketing? *European Journal of Marketing,* 37: 1391-1408.

Palmer, M., Quinn, B. (2005), "Stakeholder relationships in an international retailing context: an investment bank perspective", *European Journal of Marketing*, Vol. 39(9/10)1096-117.

Pan, Y. & Tse, D. (2000), The hierarchical model of market entry modes. *Journal of International Business Studies*, 31: 535–554.

Park, Y. and Sternquist, B. (2008), The global retailer's strategic proposition and choice of entry mode, *International Journal of Retail and Distribution Management,* 36(4): 281-299.

Paton, R. (2003), *Managing and Measuring Social Enterprises* (Sage, London).

Patton, M.Q. (2002), Qualitative research and evaluation methods, Thousand Oaks, CA: Sage.

Parkhe, A. (1993), Strategic Alliance Structuring: A game theory and transaction cost examination of inter-firm cooperation, *Academy of Management Journal* 36: 794-829.

Pavlos D.P., Lioukas, S., and Carter, S. (2004), The relationship between entrepreneurship and international performance: the importance of domestic environment, *International Business Review* 13 (2004) 19–41

Pedler, F. (1974), The Lion and the Unicorn in Africa: A History of the Origins of the United Africa Company 1787-1931, London: Heinemann.

Pehrsson, A. (2006), 'Business relatedness and performance: a study of managerial perceptions' *Strategic Management Journal,* 27(3): 265–282.

Pellegrini, L. (1991), The internationalization of retailing and 1992 Europe, *Journal of Marketing Channels,* 1(2):3–27.

Pedersen, T., & Petersen, B. (1998), 'Explaining gradual increasing resource commitment to a foreign market', *International Business Review*, 7(5): 483–501.

Pellegrini, L. (1994), "Alternatives for growth and internationalisation of retailing" The International Review of Retail, Distribution, and Consumer Research, Vol. 4(2): 121-148.

Peng, M.W. (2000) Business Strategies in Transition Economies, Thousand Oaks, CA: Sage.

Peng MW. (2001), The resource-based view and international business. *Journal of Management* 27: 803–829.

Peng, M.W. (2003), 'Institutional transitions and strategic choices', *Academy of Management Review* 28: 275–296.

Peng M.W. (2006), Making M&A fly in China. *Harvard Business Review* 84(3): 26–27.

Peng M.W. (2008), *Global Business*. South-Western College Publishing: Cincinnati, OH.

Peng, M. W., Wang, D., & Jiang, Y. (2008), An institution based view of international business strategy: A focus on emerging economies. *Journal of International Business Studies, 39*(5), 920–936.

Peng M.W, and Heath, P. (1996), The growth of the firm in planned economies in transition: institutions, organizations, and strategic choices. *Academy of Management Review* 21: 492–528.

Peng, M.W. Li Sun, S., Pinkham, B. And Chen, H. (2009), 'The institution-based view as a third leg for a strategy tripod', *Academy of Management Perspectives*, Vol. 23(3): 63-81.

Penrose, E. (1966), The theory of the growth of the firm. Oxford.

Petersen, B., and Welch, L.S. (2000), International retailing operations: downstream entry and expansion via franchising, *International Business Review 9: 479–496*

Picot-Coupey, K., (2006), "Determinants of international retail operation mode choice: towards a conceptual framework based on evidence from French specialised retail chains", *International Review of Retail Distribution and Consumer Research* 16 (2), 215–237.

Pinho, J. (2007), The Impact of Ownership Location-Specific Advantages and Managerial Characteristics on SME Foreign Entry Mode Choices, International Marketing Review, 24(6): 715-734.

Pine, R., Hanqin Qiu Zhang, and Pingshu Qi. (2000), The challenges and opportunities of franchising in China's hotel industry. *International Journal of Contemporary Hospitality Management* 12 (5): 300-7.

Popkowski, L., Peter, T.L., Sinha, A., and Timmermans (2000), Consumer Store Choice Dynamics: An Analysis of the Competitive Market Structure for Grocery Stores, *Journal of Retailing,* Vol. 76(3): 323-345.

318

Porter, M.E., (1985), Competitive Advantage, The Free Press, New York, NY,

Porter, G., Lyon, F., and Potts, D. (2007), 'Market institutions and urban food supply in West and Southern Africa: a review', *Progress in Development Studies* 7(2): 115–34

Porter, E.M, and Fuller, B.M. (1986), Coalitions and Global strategy in Competition in Global Industries by Porter, E.M. pp. 315-343.

Prahalad, C. and Hamel, G. (1990), "The core competence of the corporation", Harvard Business Review, vol. 68: 79-91.

Priem, R.L, and Butler J.E. (2001), Is the resource-based 'view' a useful perspective for strategic management research? *Academy of Management Review* 26(1): 22–40.

Proudfoot, M.J. (1937), "City Retail Structure", *Economic Geography*, Vol. 13, (425-428).

PRS Group. (1996), International Country risk guide, New York: Political Risk Services, IBC USA (Publications) Inc.

Punch News Editorial (2009), 'Still on Siemens' bribery scandal' Punch Newspapers Monday 5th January, available at http://www.punchng.com/Articl.aspx?theartic=Art20090105221659. Accessed 14 June, 2011.

Quinn, B. and Alexander, N. (2002), "International Retail franchising: a conceptual framework", *International Journal of Retail and Distribution management*, 30(5): 264-76.

Quinn, B. and Doherty, A.M. (2000), "Power and control in international retail franchising – evidence from theory and practice", *International Marketing Review*, 17(4/5): 354-72.

Quinn B. (1999), The temporal context of UK retailers' motives for international expansion. *Services Industries Journal* 19(2): 101– 16.

Rajan, K. S., & Pangarkar, N. (2000), Mode of entry choice: An empirical study of Singaporean multinationals. *Asia Pacific Journal of Management*, 17: 49-66.

Ran, J. Voon, Jan P., Li, Guangzhong, (2007), 'How does FDI Affect China? Evidence from industries and provinces', *Journal of Comparative Economics* 35: 744–799.

Rasheed, H.S. (2005), 'Foreign entry mode and performance: the moderating effects of environment' *Journal of Small Business Management,* 43(1): 41–54.

Reardon, T; Spencer Henson, S, and Julio Berdegue´, J (2007), 'Proactive fast-tracking' diffusion of supermarkets in developing countries: implications for market institutions and trade' *Journal of Economic Geography* 7: 399–431.

Reid, S. (1981), 'The decision-maker and export entry and expansion' *Journal of International Business Studies,* fall 101-111.

Reid, S. (1983), "Firm internalization, transaction costs and strategic choice", *International Marketing Review*, Vol. 7(4): 11-24.

Rindefleisch, A. and Heide, J.B. (1997), "Transaction cost Analysis: Past, Present, and Future Applications", *Journal of Marketing* Vol. 61:30-54.

Rinne, T; Steel, G.D; and Fairweather, J. (2010), 'Hofstede and Shane Revisited: The Role of Power Distance and Individualism in National-Level Innovation Success', *Cross-Cultural Research* XX(X) 1– 18.

Robson, C. (2002), Real world research: a resource for social scientists and practitioner-researchers 2nd ed. Blackwell Publishers Ltd.

Rodriquez, A. (2002), Determining the Entry Choice for International Expansion. The Case of the Spanish Hotel Industry. Tourism Management 23:597–607.

Roe, M.J. (2003), *Political Determinants of Corporate Governance: Political Context, Corporate Impact* Oxford University Press.

Root, F.R. (1987), Entry Strategies for International Markets, DC Heath, Lexington, MA.

Root, F.R. (1994), Entry Strategies for International Markets, Lexington Books, San Francisco, CA.

Priem, R.L., and Butler, J.E. (2001), Is the Resource-based view a useful perspective for Strategic Management research? *Academy of Management Review,* 26(1): 22-40.

Rugman, A.M. (1981), Inside the Multinationals: The Economics of Internal Markets, Columbia University Press, New York, NY.

Salavrakos I.D, and Stewart C. (2006) Partner selection criteria as determinants of firm performance in joint ventures: evidence from Greek joint ventures in Eastern Europe. East European Economics; 44(3):60–78.

Saunders, M., Lewis, P. and Thornhill, A. (2007), Research Methods for Business students 4th ed. Pearson Education Limited.

Salawu, B. and Hassan, A.O. (2011), Ethnic politics and its implications for the survival of democracy in Nigeria, *Journal of Public Administration and Policy Research* Vol. 3(2): 28-33

Salmon and Tordjman (1989), "Internationalisation of retailing", *International Journal of Retailing,* 4: (2): 3-16.

Sanders, W.G., and Boivie, S. (2004), 'Sorting things out: valuation of new firms in uncertain markets' Strategic *Management Journal*, 25: 167–186.

Sarkar, M. and Cavusgil, S.T. (1996), ``Trends in international business thought and literature: a review of international market entry mode research: integration and synthesis", *The International Executive,* Vol. 2: 825-47.

Sakarya,S., Eckman,M., and Hyllegard,H.K. (2007) "Market selection for international expansion: Assessing opportunities in emerging markets", *International Marketing Review,* Vol. 24(2): 208 – 238

Sato, Y. (2004), 'Some reasons why foreign retailers have difficulties in succeeding in Japan', *Journal of Global Marketing*, 18(1): 21-44.

Sauvant, K. (ed.) (2008): *The Rise of Transnational Corporations from Emerging Markets*, New York, Edward Elgar.

Schumann, J. H., von Wangenheim, F., Stringfellow, A., Yang, Z., Praxmarer, S., Jimenez, F. R., Blazevic, V., Shannon, R. M., Komar, G. S., & Komor, M. (2010), 'Drivers of trust in relational service exchange: Understanding the importance of cross-cultural differences' *Journal of Service Research*, 13(4): 453–468.

Scott, W. R. (2001). Institutions and organizations (2nd ed.). Thousand Oaks, CA: Sage.

Scott, W.R. (1987), The Adolescence of Institutional Theory, *Administrative Science Quarterly*, 32: 493-511

Scott, W. R., & Christensen, S. (Eds.). (1995), The institutional construction of organizations. Thousand Oaks, CA: Sage.

Scott, W. R., & Meyer, J. W. (1994), 'Institutional environments and organizations: Structural complexity and individualism' London: Sage Publications.

Sekaran, U. (1992). Research methods for Business, Chichester: John Wiley and Sons.

Segal-Horn, S., & Davison, H. (1992), 'Global markets, the global consumer and international retailing', *Journal of Global Marketing*, 5: 31–61.

Sekaran, U. (1992), Research Methods for Business. A Skill Building Approach, New York: John Wiley & Sons.

Sengupta, N. (2001), A new institutional theory of production. Thousand Oaks, CA: Sage.

Shannon, R. (2009), 'The transformation of food retailing in Thailand 1997-2007', *Asia Pacific Business Review*, vol. 15(1): 79-92.

Sharma, D. and Johanson, J. (1987), Technical Consultancy in Internationalisation, International Marketing Review, Vol. 4(4): 20-29.

Sharma, D. (1993), Introduction: Industrial Networks in Marketing, Cavusgil, S.T. and Sharma, D (eds.), Advances in International Marketing, Vol. 5: 1-9, Greenwich, JAI Press.

Sharma, D.D. and Blomstermo, A. (2003), "The internationalization process of born globals: a network view", International Business Review, Vol. 12(6): 739-53.

Shaw, E. (1999), 'A guide to the qualitative research process: Evidence from a small firm study', Qualitative Market Research: An International Journal, 2 (2): 59-70

Sheth, J.N. and Parvatiyar, A. (2001), Customer Relationship Management: Emerging Practice, Process, and Discipline, Journal of Economic and Social Research 3(2): 1-34.

Shrader, R.C, Oviatt, B.M and McDougall, P.P. (2000) 'How new ventures exploit trade-offs among international risk factors: lessons for the accelerated internationalization of the 21st century', Academy of Management Journal 43(6): 1227-1247.

Silverman, D. (2005), Doing Qualitative Research 2nd edition Sage Publications London.

Simon, H. A. (1959), Theories of decision-making in economics and behavioural science, The American Economic Review, 3: 253–282.

Slangen, A.H.L. and Rob J.M. van Tulder (2009), "Cultural distance, political risk, or governance quality? Towards a more accurate conceptualization and measurement of external uncertainty in foreign entry mode research", International Business Review, 18(3), 276-291.

Slater, S., & Narver, J. (1994), Does competitive environment moderate the market orientation—performance relationship? Journal of Marketing, 58(1): 46—55.

Smith, D. W., & Thomasson, A. L. (Eds.), (2005) Phenomenology and philosophy of mind. New York: Oxford University Press.

Somlev, I. P., & Hoshino, Y. (2005), Influence of location factors on establishment and ownership of foreign investments: The case of the Japanese manufacturing firms in Europe. International Business Review, 14: 577-598.

Stake, R.E. (1994), Case studies, In Denzin, N.K. and Lincoln, Y.S. (eds.), Handbook of qualitative research, Thousand Oaks, California: Sage

Sparks, L. (1995), Reciprocal Retail Internationalisation: The Southland Corporation Ito-Yokado and 7-Eleven Convenience Stores, in Akehurst, G. and Alexander, N. (eds.), The International Retailing, Frank Cass & Co., London, 57-96.

Stake, R. (1995), The Art of Case study research, Thousand Oaks CA: Sage.

Stake, R.E. (2000), Case studies, in the Handbook of Qualitative Research, Norman K. Denzin, and Yvonna, S. Lincoln (eds.), Sage Publications, Inc.

Steensma H.K, Tihanyi L, Lyles M, and Dhanaraj C. (2005), The evolving value of foreign partnerships in transitioning economies. *Academy of Management Journal* 48: 213–235.

Stenbacka, C. (2001), 'Qualitative research requires quality concepts of its own' *Management Decision, 39*(7):551-555

Sternquist, B. (1997), "International expansion of US retailers", *International Journal of Retail and Distribution Management,* 25(8): 262-8.

Sternquist, B. (1998), International Retailing, Fairchild Publications, New York, NY.

Sternquist, B. (2007). International Retailing (2nd ed.). New York: Fairchild.

Stottinger, B. and Schlegelmilch, B.B. (1998), 'Explaining export development through psychic distance: enlightening or elusive?', *International Marketing Review* 15(5): 357-372.

Suswam, G.T. (2011), 'An Appraisal of the role of Law in curbing the impediments to Foreign Direct Investment in Nigeria', PhD Thesis submitted to the Faculty of Law, University of Jos, Nigeria.

Swaan, W. (1997), Knowledge, Transaction Costs and the Creation of Markets in Post-socialist Economies, in: P.G. Hare and J. Davis, eds: Transition to the Market Economy, Vol. II, London and New York: Routledge, p. 53-76.

Tahir, R., Larimo, J. (2004), "Understanding the location strategies of the European firms in Asian countries", *Journal of American Academy of Business*, Vol. 5 (1/2): 102-9.

Tan, B, and Vertinsky, I. (1996), 'Foreign direct investment by Japanese electronics firms in the US and Canada: Modelling the timing of entry'. *Journal of International Business Studies,* 27, 655-681.

Tandon, S., Landes, M.R., and Woolverton, A. (2011), 'The Expansion of Modern Grocery Retailing and Trade in Developing Countries', Economic Research Report No. (ERR-122) 33 pp, July 2011. Available at http://www.ers.usda.gov/Publications/ERR122/ERR122_ReportSummary.html

Tatoglu E. (2000), Western joint ventures in Turkey: strategic motives and partner selection criteria. *European Business Review;* 12(3): 137–47.

Teece, D. J. (1981), The Multinational Enterprise: Market Failure and Market Power Considerations, *Sloan Management Review,* 22, Spring,: 3-17.

Teece, D. J, Pisano, G. & Shuen, A. (1997), 'Dynamic capabilities and strategic management', *Strategic management*, vol. 18(7): 509-533.

Teegan, H. (2000), Strategic and economic development implications of globalizing through franchising: Evidence from the case of Mexico. *International Business Review* 9 (4): 497-521.

Tesch, R. (1990), *Qualitative Research: Analysis Types and Software Tools*, Falmer Press, New York, NY.

The Guardian Newspaper (2011), 'Hundreds killed in Nigerian post-election violence', Sunday 24 April 2011. Available at http://www.guardian.co.uk/world/2011/apr/24/hundreds-killed-nigeria-post-election-violence. Accessed 2nd July, 2011.

Tihanyi, L., Griffith, D., and Russel, C. (2005), 'The effect of cultural distance on entry mode choice, international diversification, and MNE performance: a meta-analysis', *Journal of International Business Studies* 36, 270-283.

Timmermans, H., Borges, A. and Van Der Waerden, P. (1992), A Multinomial Logit Analysis of Substitution Effects in Consumer Shopping Destination Choice, Journal of Business Research, Vol. 24(March): 177-189.

Tong T, Reuer J.J, and Peng M.W. (2008), International joint ventures and the value of growth options. *Academy of Management Journal* 51(5): 1014–1029.

Tordjman, A. (1988), The French Hypermarket: Could it be Developed in the United States?, Retail and Distribution Management, July-August, 14-16.

Trading Economics report (2011), 'Nigeria Imports' available at http://www.tradingeconomics.com/nigeria/imports. Accessed 23rd July, 2011.

Treadgold, A. (1988), "Retailing without frontiers", *Retail & Distribution Management,* November/December: 8-12.

Treadgold, A. (1990), ``The developing internationalisation of retailing", International Journal of Retail & Distribution Management, Vol. 18(2): 4-11.

Tse, D. F., Pan, Y., & Au, K. Y. (1997), How MNCs choose entry mode and form alliances: The China experience, *Journal of International Business Studies,* 28: 779–805.

Tseng, C., and Lee, R.P. (2010), 'Host environmental uncertainty and equity-based entry mode dilemma: The role of market linking capability', *International Business Review* 19: 407–418

Tsoukas, H. (1989), 'The quality of idiographic explanations', *The Academy of Management Review*, 14, (4): 551-561

Turnbull, P.W. (1987), "A challenge to the stages theory of the internationalization process", in Rosson, P.J. and Reed, S.D. (Eds), Managing Export Entry and Expansion, Praeger, New York, NY.

Turnbull, P.W. and Ellwood, S. (1986), "Internationalisation in the information technology industry", in Turnbull, P.W. and Paliwoda, S.J. (Eds), *Research in International Marketing*, Croom Helm, London.

Teddlie, C; and Yu, F. (2007), 'Mixed Methods Sampling: A Typology with Examples', *Journal of Mixed Methods Research* Volume 1 Number (1) 77-100.

Udobong, S. (2007), 'Jumbo salary for officers at executive and judicial arms', *Economic   Confidential*,   April   2007,   available   at http://www.economicconfidential.com/coveraprilsalary.htm accessed 16th July, 2011.

Uhlenbruck, K., Rodriguez, P., Doh, J., & Eden, L. 2006. The impact of corruption on entry strategy: Evidence from telecommunication projects in emerging economies. *Organization Science*, 17(3): 402-414.

Ukpabi J. U. (2009), 'Potential of protected local institutional innovations in catalyzing Nigerian Agro-Industrial Development', *Journal of Agricultural Biotechnology and Sustainable Development* Vol. 1(3): 62 – 68.

Ulas D.(2005), 'Motives and partner selection criteria for formulation of IJVs in high-technology industries in Turkey', *Problems and Perspectives in Management*; (3):10– 21.

UN Report (2003), 'Strengthening Judicial Integrity and Capacity in Nigeria' Progress Report; Mar 03- July03 UN Office on drug and crime available at http://www.unodc.org/pdf/crime/corruption/nigeria/Progress_Report_2.pdf accessed 10 July, 2011.

UN   Report   (2009),   Human   Development   Report   available   at http://hdr.undp.org/en/media/HDR_2009_EN_Complete.pdf accessed 18th June 2010.

Usunier, J.C. (2000), Marketing Across Cultures, Prentice hall, UK.

Verbeke, A. & Greidanus, N. (2009), The end of the opportunism versus trust debate: Bounded reliability as a new envelope-concept in research on MNE governance. *Journal of International Business Studies*, 40(9), 1471–1495.

Vernon, R. (1983), "Organisational and institutional responses to international risk". In Herring, R.J (ed.) Managing International Risk, Cambridge University Press, New York, NY pp. 191-216.

Vernon, R. (1966), "International investment and international trade in the product cycle", *Quarterly Journal of Economics*, Vol. 80: 190-207.

Versi, A. (2007, September). Nigeria's Grand Plan. African Business, 13-22.

Vida, I. (2000), An empirical inquiry into international expansion of US retailers. *International Marketing Review,* 17(4–5): 454–475.

Vida, I. and Vodlan, M. (2003) A case study on retail internationalization in South-East Europe, in: M. Dupuis (E´ d.) Proceedings of the European Association in Education and Research in Commercial Distribution Conference, pp. 1–10 (Paris: ESCP-EAP).

Vida, I. and Fairhurst, A. (1998), "International expansion of retail firms: A theoretical approach for future investigations" *Journal of Retailing and Consumer Services,* Vol.5 (3):143-151.

Vida, I., Reardon, J., & Fairhurst, A. (2000), Determinants of international retail involvement: The case of large US retail chains, *Journal of International Marketing,* 8(4): 37–60.

Vision 2010 (1997), 'Nigeria's Vision 2010', Federal ministry of Information, Abuja.

Vodlan, M. and Vida, I. (2008); "Multinationals in Central and Eastern Europe: A Case Study of International Expansion by a Slovenian Retailer" European Retail Research, 22: 137-157

Walker, G., and Weber, D. (1984), "A transaction cost approach to make-or-buy decisions." Administrative Science Quarterly, 29: 373-391.

Walsham, G., (1995), "Interpretive Case Studies in IS Research: Nature and Method", European Journal of Information Systems, Vol. 4(2): 74-81.

Waren, C. (2002), Qualitative interviewing, In Gubrium J. F. and Holstein, J.A. (Eds), Handbook of interview research: Context & Method, Thousand Oaks, California: Sage 83-101.

Waziri, K.M. (2011), 'Intellectual Property Piracy and Counterfeiting in Nigeria: The Impending Economic and Social Conundrum', *Journal of Politics and Law* Vol. 4(2): 196-202

Weatherspoon, D. D., Reardon, T. (2003), 'The rise of supermarkets in Africa: implications for agrifood systems and the rural poor', *Development Policy Review,* 21: 333–355.

Weber, R. P. (1990). *Basic Content Analysis,* 2nd ed. Newbury Park, CA.

Welch, L.S. and Loustarinen, R.K. (1993) 'Inward-outward connections in internationalisation' *Journal of International Marketing* 1(1): 44-56.

Wernerfelt, B. (1984), 'A Resource-based View of the Firm', *Strategic Management Journal,* Vol. 5:171-180

White M.C. (2004), Inward investment, firm embeddedness and place- An assessment of Ireland's multinational software sector, *European Urban and Regional Studies* 11: 243-260.

Whitehead, M.B. (1992), "internationalisation of Retailing: Developing new perspectives" *European Journal of Marketing* 26 (8/9): 74-79.

Whitelock, J. (2002), "Theories of internalization and their impact on market entry", *International Marketing Review*, Vol. 19(4): 342-7.

Whitelock, J. (2004), "An evaluation of external factors in decision of UK industrial firms to enter a new non-domestic market: an exploratory study", European Journal of Marketing, Vol. 38(11/12): 1437-55.

Williamson. O.E. (1975), Markets and Hierarchies: Analysis and Antitrust Implications, New York, The Free Press.

Williamson, O.E. (1996) *The Mechanisms of Governance*. NY: Oxford U. Press.

Williamson. O.E. (1981), The Economics of Organisations: The Transaction Cost Approach, American *Journal of Sociology,* Vol. 87: 548-77.

Williamson. O.E. (1985), The Economic Institutions of capitalism: Firms, Markets, Relational Contracting. New York: The Free Press.

Williamson, O.E. (1991), 'Comparative economic organization: the analysis of discrete structural alternatives', *Administrative Science Quarterly,* 36: 269-296.

Williamson, O.E. (1991), The New Institutional Economics: Taking Stock, Looking Ahead, Journal of Economic Literature, 38(3): 595-613.

Williams, G. (1976), 'Nigeria: a political economy', in G. Williams (ed.) Nigeria: Economy and Society, London: Rex Collings, 11-54.

Williams, D. (1992), Retailer internationalisation: Am empirical inquiry. European *Journal of Marketing,* 26(8/9), 8-24.

Williams, D., McDonald, F., Tuselmann, H.J., and Turner, C. (2008), Domestic sourcing by foreign-owned subsidiaries, *Environment and Planning C: Government and Policy Vol. 26: 260-276.*

Wind, Y., Douglas, S.P., and Perlmutter, H.V. (1973), 'Guidelines for developing international marketing strategies', *Journal of Marketing* 37(April): 14-23.

Wind, Y., Perlmutter, H.V., (1977), On the identification of frontier issues in multinational marketing. Columbia *Journal of World Business*: 131–139.

Woodcock, G, Beamish, P and Makino, S (1994), 'Ownership-based entry mode strategies and international performance', *Journal of International Business Studies* 25: 253-273.

Wonacott, P. (2006), Wallets crack open in India: Foreign retailers salivate but struggle to find winning formula, *Wall Street Journal,* A14.

Wrigley, N (1992), Antitrust regulation and the restructuring of grocery retailing in Britain and the USA, *Environment and Planning A* 24: 727-49.

Wrigley, M. (2000a), "The globalization of retail capital: themes for economic geography", in Clark, G.L., Feldman, M.P., Gertler, M.S. (Eds), *The Oxford Handbook of Economic Geography*, Oxford University Press, Oxford: 292-313.

Wrigley, N. (2000b), "Strategic market behaviour in the internationalization of food retailing: interpreting the third wave of Sainsbury's US diversification", *European Journal of Marketing*, Vol. 34(8): 891-918.

Wrigley, N. (2002) 'Strategic market behaviour in the internationalization of food retailing: interpreting the third wave of Sainsbury's US diversification', *European Journal of Marketing,* 891–918.

Wrigley, N., & Currah, A. (2003), The stresses of retail internationalization: Lessons from royal Ahold's experience in Latin America. *International Review of Retail, Distribution and Consumer Research,* 13(3), 221–243.

Wright, M., Filatotchev, I., Hoskisson, R.E., and Peng, M.W. (2005), Strategy Research in Emerging Economies: Challenging the Conventional Wisdom, *Journal of Management Studies,* Vol. 42(1): 1-33

Wu, D., and Fang Zhao, F. (2007), 'Entry Modes for International Markets: Case Study of Huawei, A Chinese Technology Enterprise', *International Review of Business Research Papers,* Vol.3 (1):183 - 196

Yerokun, O. (1992), *The Changing Investment climate Through Law and Policy in Nigeria* in Ahunwan, B. (2002) 'Corporate governance in Nigeria' *Journal of Business Ethics,* 37: 269-287.

Young, S., Hamill, J., Wheeler, C., & Davies, J. R. (1989), *International market entry and development, Strategies and management*, Hertfordshire: Harvester Wheatsheaf.

Yin, R. K. (1989), *Case study research Design and methods*. London: Sage.

Yin, R. (2003), Case study research: Design and methods, Thousand oaks, California: Sage.

Yip, G.S., Biscarri, J.G., and Monti, J.A. (2000), "The role of the internationalisation process in the performance of newly internationalising firms", *Journal of International Marketing,* Vol. 8(3):10-35

Yiu, D., & Makino, S. (2002), 'The choice between joint venture and wholly owned subsidiary: An institutional perspective', *Organization Science*, 13(6): 667–683.

Zajac, E. J., & Bazerman, M. H. (1991), Blind spots in industry and competitor analysis: Implications of inter-firm (mis)perceptions for strategic decisions. *Academy of Management Review*, *16*(1): 37-56.

Zalan, T. & Lewis, G. (2004), 'Writing about methods in qualitative research: towards a more transparent approach', in R. Marschan-Piekkari and C. Welch (eds), Handbook of Qualitative Research Methods for International Business, Cheltenham UK and Northampton MA, USA: Edward Elgar: 507-28.

Zhang, Y. and B.M. Wildemuth, B.M. (2009), 'Qualitative analysis of content', In: B. Wildemuth, (Ed) Applications of Social Research Methods to Questions in Information and Library, Book News, Portland USA.

Zhang, X.D., Goeres, J., Zhang, H., Yen, T.J., Porter, A.C., and Matunis, M.J. (2008), SUMO-2/3 modification and binding regulate the association of CENP-E with kinetochores and progression through mitosis. Mol. Cell 29, 729–741.

Zhao, J. H., Kim, S. H., & Du, J. (2003), 'The impact of corruption and transparency on foreign direct investment: An empirical analysis', *Management International Review,* 43(1): 41–62.

Zhao, H., Luo, Y., and Suh, T. (2004), Transaction cost determinants and ownership-based entry mode choice: a meta-analytical review, *Journal of International Business Studies* 35, 524-544.

Zou, H. and Liu, X. and Ghauri, P. (2009), *International versus Domestic Orientation: New Venture Strategic Behaviour and Technology Leveraging.* In: Academy of International Business 2009 Annual Conference, San Diego, California, USA.

Zucker, L.G. (1987), Institutional Theories of Organisations, in Scott, W.R. and Short, J.F. Jr. (eds.), *Annual Review of Sociology*, Vol. 443-464, Palo Alto, CA Annual Reviews.

Glossary

Annotation	Text that can be linked to selected content in a source in Nvivo – like scribbled notes in a margin.
Case	A node with attributes such as gender or age used to gather content about a person, site, institution or other entity used in a research.
Case nodes	A section in Nvivo where data are stored; this may represent any unit of analysis in a study such as a person, institution, time period, or organisation. They represent a way of gathering the content that belongs to each entity together.
Coding	The process involved in translating responses into a form that is ready for analysis. In Nvivo, this is the process by which you gather data about a specific theme or idea at a node.
Detail View	The bottom-right pane in Nvivo where the researcher can explore documents, nodes, and models.
Developing	As used in this study, developing means having a relatively low level of industrial capability, technological sophistication, and economic productivity. Not having achieved a significant degree of industrialization relative to population with a medium to low standard of living.
Entry modes	Options available to the management of foreign retail firms to use for its operations in a host foreign market. A firm can use the independent mode or the collaborative mode.
Foreign	A thing pertaining to, or derived from another country or nation; not native. As used in this study, foreign retail firms mean – retail firms from other countries outside Nigeria.
Institutions	A custom, practice, relationship, or behavioural pattern of importance in the life of a community or society. Norms that for a long time have been an important feature of some group or society.
Internationalisation	Viewed as a process of increasing involvement of enterprises in international markets
Interview	A conversation between two people (the interviewer and the interviewee) where questions are asked by the interviewer to obtain information from the interviewee.
Interviewer bias	Bias and errors in research findings brought about by the actions of an interviewer. This may be influenced by who the

interviewer interviews, how the interview is undertaken and the manner in which responses are recorded.

List View	The top-right pane in Nvivo where a researcher can view the contents of the Nvivo folders.
Memos	Short and simple notes used to capture thoughts and insights a researcher has when working through the data.
Model	A visual representation of a project and its content in Nvivo
Observation	A data gathering approach where information is collected on the observation of people, objects and organisations without any questions being asked of the participants.
Pilot testing	The pre-testing of a research instrument like an interview guide prior to undertaking a full survey. Such tests involve administering the instrument to a limited number of potential respondents in order to identify and correct flaws in the design.
Qualitative research	An unstructured research approach with a small number of carefully selected individuals, objects or organisations used to produce non-quantifiable insights into behaviour, motivations and attitudes.
Queries	Queries are used in Nvivo to help the researcher discover and explore patterns in the data, test hunches and create and validate theories. They can be carried out at a broad level across all data, or on selected folders or items.
Sample	A subset of the population of interest
Secondary data	Information that has been previously gathered for some purpose other than the current research project. It may be data available within the organisation (internal data) or information available from published and electronic sources originating outside the organisation (external data).
Transaction cost	Costs incurred in making an economic exchange (i.e. the cost of participating in a market). They include such costs as: search and information costs ; bargaining costs; as well as costs of policing and enforcement of agreements.
Triangulation	Using a combination of different sources of data where the weaknesses in some sources are counterbalanced with the strength of others. The term triangulation is borrowed from the disciplines of navigation and surveying, where a minimum of three reference points are taken to check an object's location.
Validity	Whether the subject requiring to be measured was actually measured.

331

Appendices

Appendix 1:   INTERVIEW GUIDE

A. TYPE OF ARRANGEMENT

1. When was your subsidiary in Nigeria established?
2. In what form did the subsidiary originate?: e.g. Takeover of existing concern, Establishment of new company, a form of partnership, etc.
3. Is your decision to enter the Nigerian market a strategic one or an opportunistic development?
4. What factors did you consider in choosing your method of entry into the Nigerian market?
5. How much freedom of entrepreneurial activity do you allow your subsidiary? For example, would you allow it to diversify into related products beyond the product line of the parent firm?

B. COMPANY/MARKET CHARACTERISTICS

1. What factors are considered by your organisation in looking at foreign markets to enter especially in your decision to enter the Nigerian market?
2. To what extent has the level of competition in the Nigerian market affected your choice of entry mode?
3. How much do the customers understand the use of your products? Are your products customised to be users in any form?
4. How related are your product offerings to those already in existence in the Nigerian market?
5. To what extent does your company reputation/brand name affect your business relationships in your foreign markets and the Nigerian market particularly?
6. Has the size of your organisation affected your method of entry into the Nigerian market?
7. Are there any specialised processes/technological developments within your organisation that has influenced your entry mode choice into the Nigerian market?
8. Are there established steps/procedures in your organisation that are used in assessing your business relationships with other firms in your foreign markets?

C. TRANSFER OF TECHNOLOGY

1. Do you have any fears in the transfer of your company skills/technology that has influenced your choice of entry mode?
2. Did your company at any time consider the available networks in the Nigerian market in deciding your entry mode into the market?
3. Would you consider a local national to head your subsidiary in Nigeria?

4. Do you make any special effort to develop the adaptability of home-country employees to cultural/institutional differences when they are assigned to subsidiaries like Nigeria?

D. HOST/HOME -COUNTRY POLICIES

1. Has your organisation benefitted from any incentives provided by the Nigerian government in whatever form: Tariff or quota protection for your subsidiary's products in the market, tariff reductions on imports of products, corporate income tax reduction or holiday, or Investment credit?
2. If yes, have such incentives really been effective in increasing your investment in the Nigerian market?
3. Has the distance between your home country and the Nigerian market in addition to the method of entry used by other retail firms influenced your method of entry into the Nigerian market?
4. How has your company's method of entry into other markets influenced your entry strategy into the Nigerian market?
5. A number of host countries have extensive legislation and regulations on employment conditions and industrial relations, for example, requirements for training and upgrading of labour force, limitation on number of foreign nationals to be employed, etc. what requirements of this sort has your organisation faced in Nigeria and how has it reacted to it?
6. Has the fear of host-country nationalisation of foreign enterprises affected your investment in the Nigeria market?
7. Has your company been pressured to do things for reasons of internal politics in Nigeria? How did you react?
8. In order of importance, what do you regard as the most serious deterrents to your organisations investment in Nigeria?
9. Has the strength of the rule of law in Nigeria affected your decision about the mode of entry into the Nigerian market?
10. Do you have a general policy regarding the financing of operations in any foreign market like Nigeria, such as minimizing your equity participation?
11. Most developing countries usually prefer collaborations with local interests to wholly owned foreign subsidiaries:
a. Is this the case with Nigeria?
b. To what extent do such requirements deter the establishment by your company of foreign subsidiaries or reduce the flow of managerial and technical resources once the subsidiary has been established?

Appendix 2: Open coding of interview with Shoprite GM

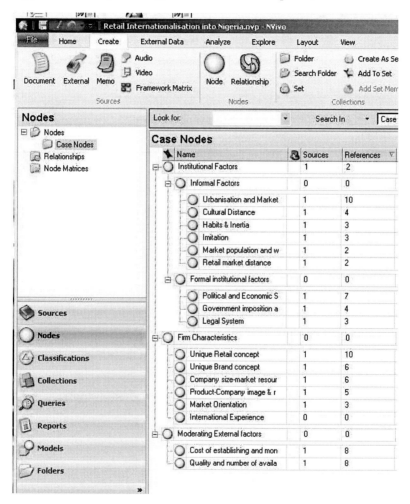

Appendix 3: Exported Nvivo node showing the coding for the Shoprite GM interview

Name: Internals\\Interviews\\SH-GM

Description: Interview transcripts from the interview with the GM Shoprite

Created On: 14/09/2009 15:17:16

Created By: A.M.

Modified On: 14/09/2009 16:46:33

Modified By: A.M.

Size: 10 KB

¶1: **Interview transcript from the interview conducted with the General Manager of Shoprite on the 8th September 2009 in his office at 'The Palm Complex' Victoria Island Lagos Nigeria.**

¶2:

A. ¶3: TYPE OF ARRANGEMENT

¶4: Q1. When was your subsidiary in Nigeria established?

¶5: GM: We came into Nigeria in 2004 but started operations in 2005.

¶6:

¶7: Q2.In what form did the subsidiary originate?: e.g. Takeover of existing concern, Establishment of new company, a form of partnership, etc.

¶8: GM: We started our operations as a wholly owned subsidiary. Our operation in Nigeria was taken as another outlet of our large conglomerate.

¶9:

¶10: Q3.   Is your decision to enter the Nigerian market a strategic one or an opportunistic development?

¶11: GM: It was a very strategic decision. We have always wanted to operate in Nigeria because of the huge potential of the market but we were restricted especially in the days of apartheid when South Africa faced major trade restrictions in foreign markets. This was why we waited till after the lifting of such bans to invest in markets like Nigeria.

¶12:

¶13:

¶14: Q4.   What factors did you consider in choosing your method of entry into the Nigerian market?

¶15: GM: Quite a number of factors were considered in our decision to invest in Nigeria. For example, apart from looking at the rate of return on our investment, other areas included: the level of involvement in the market we wanted, the cost of investing in the market, our knowledge of the market, protection of our company products and other resources, rate of inflation and other financial and political regulations, and many of such factors.

¶16:

¶17:

335

¶18: Q5.　　　How much freedom of entrepreneurial activity do you allow your subsidiary? For example, would you allow it to diversify into related products beyond the product line of the parent firm?

¶19: GM: Well we expect our subsidiaries to operate according to the dictates from the Head Office especially in the major areas relating to product assortment, pricing, promotion, and other related areas. Some local areas like supply chain networks are left to the subsidiary managers but minimum conditions as set by the Head Office must be met; for example we have over two hundred local suppliers in the Nigerian market we work with from time to time we assess their performances and decide whether to still have them on or stop doing business with them. So I'll say we all our subsidiaries some limited freedom of entrepreneurial activity; don't forget that individuals (like subsidiary managers) can wrongly use the company's resources if there are no limits placed on the usage.

¶20:

B. ¶21: COMPANY/MARKET CHARACTERISTICS
¶22:

¶23: Q1.　　　What factors are considered by your organisation in looking at foreign markets to enter especially in your decision to enter the Nigerian market?

¶24: GM: Like I mentioned earlier we consider so many factors both in the market and the environment in deciding which foreign markets to enter. "Shoprite has an aggressive expansion policy mainly because our growth has been hampered as a result of the trading ban imposed on South Africa in the days of apartheid. With its abolition, the company expanded into foreign markets. We have a very strong brand name and reputation, huge size and resources to commit to foreign operation, as well as advanced technologies and innovations to use in these markets.

¶25:

¶26: We waited for Nigeria to return to democratic governance before considering entry in order to reduce the risks involved in operating under a military government where there is no respect for the rule of law and no stability in the system both politically and economically. With a realisation of this in the 1990s, we were the first big retail firm to enter the market; we established our own store using our technologies and innovations in the Nigerian market.

¶27:

¶28: We couldn't find any partner of our size to work and developing a local relationship we felt would be too expensive and costly because it would mean transferring our assets and technologies to the local partner we know only so little about. This situation would need us to incur some additional cost just to be sure the local partner operates within our overall company policies and directions. All of these led to our use of the wholly owned subsidiary in the Nigerian market we wanted the control of our market".

¶29:

¶30:

¶31: Q2.　　　To what extent has the level of competition in the Nigerian market affected your choice of entry mode?

¶32: GM: As at the time of our entry into the Nigerian market in 2004/2005 there was no other organisation in the market like our own. Large retail establishments like Shoprite had divested from the market by the time we came in; we are the first major established chain to invest in the market this partly accounted for our decision to use our wholly owned subsidiary so as to be able to take advantage of this pioneering position. There was basically no competition at all by the time of our entry and the market seemed to be waiting to receive us because we had no major problems serving the market both in terms of the merchandise we offered, the service we provided, and the pricing for our products.

336

¶33: As at the time of our entry into the Nigerian market, the level of competition was quite low and competition was virtually non-existent such that there were no other firms giving our incoming operation a significant challenge which enabled us to introduce our retail structure conveniently into the Nigerian market. Our research had shown that the average Nigerian consumer has an idea of the supermarket/hypermarket format all we needed to do was to offer to the market a source of differentiation in the delivery of added values which involved the importation of our concept the consumers perceived as new. In doing this, we were very careful so as to be aware of the implications of introducing our store format and to see if there are possible oppositions that will be generated in the market.

¶34:

¶35:

¶36: Q3.　　How much do the customers understand the use of your products? Are your products customised to be users in any form?

¶37: GM: This is part of what I mentioned earlier. The consumers in the market were already used to the supermarket/hypermarket format and also had ideas about our range of products. I'll say we serve the market with more of our standardized products; there was no need for us to significantly modify our range of products to fit the local demand.

¶38:

¶39: Q4.　　How related are your product offerings to those already in existence in the Nigerian market?

¶40: GM: I will say 'very related' because we were providing the consumers just about the same products they are aware of but with added value and increased variety especially with the introduction of our own brand of some of the products. Most of the consumers saw this as different and embraced it positively.

¶41:

¶42: Q5.　　To what extent does your company reputation/brand name affect your business relationships in your foreign markets and the Nigerian market particularly?

¶43: GM: We are very particular about protecting our reputation and brand name. For our operations in the Nigerian market, just like we have it in all other international markets we serve, provision of high quality goods in a wide assortment, appropriately priced, having a nice store layout that is easy to access; in addition to our convenient locations and returns policy are all factors that have given us a very high store image". We are very careful in the choice of suppliers for some of our products especially local suppliers; that is why we ensure they meet some basic requirements before they can serve as our suppliers. So we ensure that any item that has our company name on it is of a high standard.

¶44:

¶45:

¶46: Q6.　　Has the size of your organisation affected your method of entry into the Nigerian market?

¶47: GM: Shoprite is a very large conglomerate with huge financial and human resources. In most markets in Africa we operate it we have moved into such markets through acquisitions like we did in Zambia and Tanzania. But with the absence of retail outlets in the Nigerian market to acquire, we decided to set up our wholly owned subsidiary since the firm has the required financial and human resource to commit to the Nigerian market. Our use of this entry method was made easier because we didn't need to build our outlet from the scratch. With the development of some mega shopping malls like 'The Palms' all we needed to do was to rent the required floor space to establish our outlet. This saved us a lot in terms of the financial commitment and the risk of investing in the market.

¶48:

¶49: Q7.   Are there any specialised processes/technological developments within your organisation that has influenced your entry mode choice into the Nigerian market?

¶50: GM: Our organisation has quite a lot of specialised processes we use in our every day operations; they range from inventory management, supply chain management, to packaging and pricing. We consider these processes very important especially in our operations in the Nigerian market where there are no large and established networks to work with. Protecting these processes was therefore all so important to us hence our decision to use the wholly owned outlet.

¶51:

¶52:

¶53: Q8.   Are there established steps/procedures in your organisation that are used in assessing your business relationships with other firms in your foreign markets?

¶54: GM: Our Head Office has set out some minimum conditions and characteristics that other firms willing to network with us must meet especially in the area of supplies. Amongst others, we look at the past history of the firms, their financial strength and profitability, composition of its management, areas of business- to see if this is related to our line of business, their human resource capabilities, knowledge of the local environment, as well as its other resources.

¶55:

¶56:

C. ¶57: **TRANSFER OF TECHNOLOGY**

¶58:

¶59: Q1.   Do you have any fears in the transfer of your company skills/technology that has influenced your choice of entry mode?

¶60: GM: Yes I mentioned this before. With the under-developed nature of the Nigerian market in terms of competition and quality of local partners in the market, we had problems in respect of trust. We didn't want to transfer our company assets and technology to local operators that will utilise these assets only to their own advantage at the expense of our organisation. Like earlier mentioned, we needed to protect these assets that we have from undue exploitation.

¶61:

¶62: Q2.   Did your company at any time consider the available networks in the Nigerian market in deciding your entry mode into the market?

¶63: GM: Yes we do. Our method of entry into foreign markets may change if there are huge and qualified networks in the market. You can see that the non-availability of qualified networks for example influenced our use of the wholly owned entry method in the Nigerian market.

¶64:

¶65: Q3.   Would you consider a local national to head your subsidiary in Nigeria?

¶66: GM: Why not if such locals have been well trained and understand our company procedures.

¶67:

¶68: Q4.   Do you make any special effort to develop the adaptability of home-country employees to cultural/institutional differences when they are assigned to subsidiaries like Nigeria?

¶69: GM: In most of our markets we ensure that our employees understand the cultural and institutional dynamics in the market this is the only way they can align company procedures to fit into the environment. Most time we ensure the employee understands the local language(s) in the host market as well as their basic cultures and believes. We have a wide range of employees and we offer regular training and exposure to allow them cope when posted into foreign markets.

¶70:
¶71:

D. ¶72: HOST/HOME -COUNTRY POLICIES
¶73:

¶74: Q1.　　　Has your organisation benefitted from any incentives provided by the Nigerian government in whatever form: Tariff or quota protection for your subsidiary's products in the market, tariff reductions on imports of products, corporate income tax reduction or holiday, or Investment credit?

¶75: GM: We have not benefitted from any of the above incentives since establishing our outlet in Nigeria especially in Lagos. Our research showed we can enjoy some of these incentives if we decide to establish our outlets in some designated locations like TINAPA free trade zone in Calabar; but we saw the huge potential and market size of Lagos and decided to exploit this first before thinking of expanding into other areas in the country. We're constantly monitoring the level of demand and market development in these other areas where there are government incentives to invest and may utilise it if we see the potential. But so far, we have not benefitted from any government incentives.

¶76:

¶77: Q2.　　　If yes, have such incentives really been effective in increasing your investment in the Nigerian market?

¶78: Q3.　　　Has the distance between your home country and the Nigerian market in addition to the method of entry used by other retail firms influenced your method of entry into the Nigerian market?

¶79: GM: We understand that no two markets are the same and despite the fact that we're coming in from another market in Africa (South Africa) with some similarities in cultures and believe, we have not assumed full knowledge of the Nigerian market. Though one would think that our use of the wholly owned subsidiary suggests knowledge and close proximity between both markets; other factors besides that of cultural and retail market distance account for this. We're still studying the Nigerian market to know how best to serve the consumers.

¶80:

¶81: Q4.　　　How has your company's method of entry into other markets influenced your entry strategy into the Nigerian market?

¶82: GM: Just like I earlier mentioned, we assess each market on its own merits; though we borrow from our experiences in other markets, our entry decisions into subsequent markets are not tailored to the methods we have used in our previous markets. Each market dictates the most appropriate strategy to used for its entry while borrowing from experiences in our operations in other markets.

¶83:

¶84: Q5.　　　A number of host countries have extensive legislation and regulations on employment conditions and industrial relations, for example, requirements for training and upgrading of labour force, limitation on number of foreign nationals to be employed, etc. what requirements of this sort has your organisation faced in Nigeria and how has it reacted to it?

¶85: GM: We have not really faced any of these restrictions in Nigeria because we have aimed at operating within the specified levels. In this Nigerian outlet for example, apart from me- The General Manager and the Marketing Manager, there are no other foreign nationals; all others are locals who have been trained and are experienced in their line of work. The Head Office has secured for us the necessary work permits and other requirements needed to work in Nigeria.

¶86: Also, to the best of my knowledge, there are no existing regulations compelling foreign firms to train and upgrade locals. It is however a major policy in our organisation to effectively train our employees to enable them perform efficiently. Upgrading locals will also be done in accordance with the set out company policies; so I will not be surprised if sometime soon a Nigerian assumes this position of GM here in Nigeria.

¶87:

¶88: Q6.   Has the fear of host-country nationalisation of foreign enterprises affected your investment in the Nigeria market?

¶89: GM: We looked into this in our decision to come into Nigeria; events of the past showed that the government in Nigeria has used this that was one of the reasons why we delayed in entering into the Nigerian market. We were better assured by the return of the country to democratic governance than the era of military rule. The nationalisation of foreign firms in Nigeria was done in the days of military rule where there was no regard for the rule of law. There was also the assurance that since the government was seriously trying to attract foreign direct investment into the country, it will not be thinking of nationalisation just yet. All of these affected our timing and method of entry into the Nigerian market.

¶90:

¶91:

¶92: Q7.   Has your company been pressured to do things for reasons of internal politics in Nigeria? How did you react?

¶93: GM: So far we have not; if we do experience any of such pressures am sure management would know how to deal with the situation.

¶94:

¶95: Q8.   In order of importance, what do you regard as the most serious deterrents to your organisations investment in Nigeria?

¶96: GM: I cannot really provide you an answer to this question in that order of importance. I will just mention the major areas I think serve as serious deterrents to our investment in the market. Firstly, the high level of insecurity in the country bothers us; also, the unpredictability in the political, economic and legal systems in the country, the high levels of inflation, the unregulated nature of the retail sub-sector, the long list of prohibited imports, and the rising unemployment levels all serve as threats to our investment in Nigeria.

¶97:

¶98:

¶99: Q9.   Has the strength of the rule of law in Nigeria affected your decision about the mode of entry into the Nigerian market?

¶100: GM: We have always had fears concerning the rule of law in Nigeria especially with respect to dispute resolutions. We're aware of the high rate of corruption in the judiciary and some measure of abuse of the court system. All of this accounted for our decision to operate our own outlet in Nigeria as such we're very cautious of all of our actions so as to avoid ant litigations that would warrant going to court. Recently however with the efforts of the government at sanitising the system, the credibility of the legal system is gradually returning.

¶101:

¶102: Q10.   Do you have a general policy regarding the financing of operations in any foreign market like Nigeria, such as minimizing your equity participation?

¶103: GM: No we don't have any policy on how much to invest in a foreign market. The situations in each of these markets determine how much of the company resources to invest in such markets. So our entry into different markets has different equity implications depending on our assessment of the host market conditions in line with established company policies.

¶104:

¶105:

¶106: Q11.   Most developing countries usually prefer collaborations with local interests to wholly owned foreign subsidiaries:

    a. ¶107: Is this the case with Nigeria?

¶108: GM: I know the Nigerian government try to encourage the growth of local firms but we have not been compelled in any way to collaborate with local networks in the market.

    ¶109:

    ¶110:

    b. ¶111: To what extent do such requirements deter the establishment by your company of foreign subsidiaries or reduce the flow of managerial and technical resources once the subsidiary has been established?

¶112: GM: If we assess the risk from such requirements to be very high the company may decide not to operate in such markets altogether.

Appendix 4. Shoprite GM Retail Model

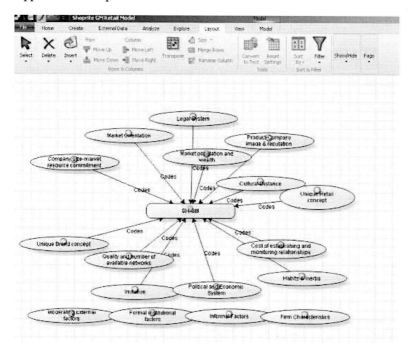

Appendix 5: Nigeria's Import Prohibition List

1. Live or Dead Birds including Frozen Poultry – H.S. Codes 0105.1100 – 0105.9900, 0106.3100 – 0106.3900, 0207.1100 – 0207.3600 and 0210.9900
2. Pork, Beef – H.S. Codes 0201.1000 – 0204.5000, 0206.1000 – 0206.9000, 0210.1000 – 0210.2000.
3. Birds Eggs – H.S. Code 0407.0000.
4. Refined Vegetable Oils and Fats – H.S. Code 1507.1000 – 1516.2000.29 [**but excluding Linseed, Castor and Olive oils. Crude vegetable oil are however NOT banned from importation**].
5. Cocoa Butter, Powder and Cakes – H.S. Codes 1802. – 1803.2000, 1805.0000, 1806.1000 – 1806.2000 and 1804.0000.
6. Spaghetti/Noodles – H.S. Codes 1902.1100 – 1902.3000.
7. Fruit Juice in Retail Packs – H.S. Codes 2009.110012 - 2009.110013 – 2009.9000.99
8. Waters, including Mineral Waters and Aerated Waters containing added Sugar or Sweetening Matter or Flavoured, ice snow – H.S. Codes 2202.1000 – 2202.9000, other non-alcoholic beverages H.S. Code 2202.1000 - 2202.9000.99 [**but excluding energy or Health Drinks {Liquid Dietary Supplements} e.g. Power Horse, Red Ginseng etc**] H.S. Code 2202.9000.91 and Beer and Stout (Bottled, Canned or Otherwise packed) H.S. Code 2203.0010.00 - 2203.0090.00
9. Bagged Cement – H.S. Code 2523.2900.22.
10. Medicaments falling under Headings 3003 and 3004 as indicated below:
    1. Paracetamol Tablets and Syrups
    2. Cotrimoxazole Tablets Syrups
    3. Metronidazole Tablets and Syrups
    4. Chloroquine Tablets and Syrups
    5. Haematinic Formulations; Ferrous Sulphate and Ferrous Gluconate Tablets, Folic Acid Tablets, Vitamine B Complex Tablet [except modified released formulations].
    6. Multivitamin Tablets, capsules and Syrups [except special formulations].
    7. Aspirin Tablets [except modified released formulation and soluble aspirin].
    8. Magnesium trisilicate tablets and suspensions.
    9. Piperazine tablets and Syrups
    10. Levamisole Tablets and Syrups
    11. Clotrimazole Cream
    12. Ointments – Penecilin/Gentamycin
    13. Pyrantel Pamoate tablets and Syrups
    14. Intravenous Fluids [Dextrose, Normal Saline, etc.]
11. Waste Pharmaceuticals - H.S. Code 3006.9200
12. Soaps and Detergents – H.S. Code 3401.1100 – 3402.9000 in retail packs
13. Mosquito Repellant Coils – H.S. Code 3808.9110.91.
14. Sanitary Wares of Plastics – H.S. Code 3922.1000 – 3922.9000 and Domestic Articles and Wares of Plastics H.S. Code 3924.1000 – 3924.9000.00 [**but excluding Baby Feeding bottles 3924.9020.00**] and flushing ceinstern and waterless toos toilets.
15. Rethreaded and used Pneumatic tyres but excluding used trucks tyres for rethreading of sized 11.00 x 20 and above 4012.2010.00.
16. Corrugated Paper and Paper Boards – H.S. Code 4808.1000, and cartons, boxes and cases

made from corrugated paper and paper boards H.S. Code 4819.1000, Toilet paper, Cleaning or facial tissue - H.S. Code 4818.1000 - 4818.9000 excluding baby diapers and incotinent pads for adult use 4818.4000.41 and Exercise Books - H.S. Code 4820.2000.

17. Telephone Re-charge Cards and Vouchers – H.S. Code 4911.9900.91
18. Textile Fabrics of all types and articles thereof and Yarn falling under the following H.S. Codes remain under import prohibition;
    1. African print [Printed Fabrics] e.g. Nigeria wax, Hollandaise, English Wax, Ankara and similar Fabrics under the following H.S. Codes – 5208.5110 – 5208.5900, 5209.5100 – 5209.5900, 5212.5100, 5212.5100, 5212.2500, 5407.4400, 5407.5400, 5407.7400, 5407.8400, 5407.9400, 5408.2400, 5408.3400, 5513.4100 – 5513.4900, 5514.4100 – 5514.4900, 5516.1400, 5516.2400, 5516.3400, and 5514.4900.00
    2. Carpets and Rugs of all types falling under H.S. Codes 5701.1000 – 5705.0000.

    But excluding the Following:

    3. Lace Fabrics, Georges and other embroided Fabrics falling under H.S. Codes 5801.2100 – 5801.9000, 5802.1100 - 5802.3000 and 5805.0000.00
    4. Made-up Garments and other Textile articles falling under H.S. Codes 6101.2000 – 6310.9000.99
19. All types of Foot Wears and Bags including Suitcases of leather and plastics H.S. Codes 6401.1000.11 – 6405.9000.99 and 4202.1100.10 – 4202.9900.99 [**but excluding Safety Shoes used in oil industries, Hospitals, Fire fighting and Factories, Sports Shoes, canvass shoes all completely Knocked Down parts.**
20. Hollow Glass Bottles of a capacity exceeding 150mls (0.15 litres) **of a kind used for packaging of beverages by breweries and other beverage and drink companies** – H.S. Code 7010.9021.29 and 7010.9031.00.
21. Used Compressors – H.S. Code 8414.3000, Used Air Conditioners – H.S. Codes 8415.1000.11 – 8415.9000.99 and Used Fridges/Freezers – H.S. Codes 8418.1000.11 – 8418.6900.
22. Used Motor Vehicles above **fifteen (15) years from the year of manufacture** – H.S. Codes 8703.1000 – 8703.9000
23. Furniture – H.S. Codes 9401.1000.00 – 9401.9000.99 and 9403.1000 – 9404.9000, **but excluding Baby walkers, laboratory cabinets such as microscope table, fume cupboards, laboratory benches (9403), Stadium Chairs, height adjustments device, base sledge, seat frames and control mechanism, arm guide and headguides. Also excluded are; skeletal parts of furniture such as blanks, unholstered or unfinished part of metal, plastics, veneer, chair shell etc. Also excluded are Motor Vehicle seats (9401.2000.00) and Seats other than garden seats or camping equipment, convertible into beds (9401.4000.00)**
24. Ball Point Pens – H.S. Code 9608.1000

Goods: Schedule 4 The Importation of which is Absolutely Prohibited

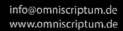

Printed by
Schaltungsdienst Lange o.H.G., Berlin